FAITH IN LIFE

AMERICAN PHILOSOPHY

Douglas R. Anderson and Jude Jones, series editors

FAITH IN LIFE

John Dewey's Early Philosophy

DONALD J. MORSE

FORDHAM UNIVERSITY PRESS   NEW YORK   2011

Library of Congress Cataloging-in-Publication Data

Morse, Donald J.
    Faith in life : John Dewey's early philosophy / Donald J. Morse.
        p.   cm.— (American philosophy)
    Includes bibliographical references and index.
    ISBN 978-0-8232-3470-7 (cloth : alk. paper)
    ISBN 978-0-8232-3472-1 (electronic)
    1. Dewey, John, 1859–1952.   I. Title.
B945.D44M68   2011
191—dc22   2011002495

Printed in the United States of America
13 12 11   5 4 3 2 1
First edition

For Don and Peggy Morse,
for their love of life

Contents

List of Abbreviations   ix
Acknowledgments   xi

	Introduction	1
1	Dewey's Project	12
2	Cultural and Intellectual Background	37
3	Rehabilitating Dewey's *Psychology*	62
4	The Nature of Knowledge	84
5	What We Know	113
6	Feeling, Will, and Self-Realization	145
7	Beyond Modernist Culture	190
8	A New Idealism	233

Notes   283
Bibliography   305
Index   311

Abbreviations

Unless otherwise indicated, all quotations from John Dewey are from *The Collected Works of John Dewey, 1882–1953*, edited by Jo Ann Boydston (Carbondale: Southern Illinois University Press, 1967–1991), published in three series as *The Early Works, 1882–1898*; *The Middle Works, 1899–1924*; and *The Later Works, 1925–1953*. Citations occur in text, in parentheses, according to the following abbreviations, where the abbreviations are followed by the volume number and page number of the citation in question:

EW   John Dewey, *The Early Works, 1882–1898*. 5 vols. Ed. Jo Ann Boydston (Carbondale: Southern Illinois University Press), 1967–1972.

MW   John Dewey, *The Middle Works, 1899–1924*. 15 vols. Ed. Jo Ann Boydston (Carbondale: Southern Illinois University Press), 1983–1988.

LW   John Dewey, *The Later Works, 1925–1953*. 17 vols. Ed. Jo Ann Boydston (Carbondale: Southern Illinois University Press), 1988–1991.

Acknowledgments

I would like to thank the editors of *Americana: The E-Journal of American Studies in Hungary* for their kind permission to revise and reprint my article "Situating Dewey," published in the fall 2007 issue of the journal, Volume III, Number 2 (http://americanaejournal .hu/vol3no2/morse, and Southern Illinois University Press for permission to quote copyrighted material from John Dewey, *The Collected Works of John Dewey 1882–1953*, ed. Jo Ann Boydston (Carbondale: Southern Illinois University Press, 1967–1991), especially from the *Psychology* (*Early Works, Volume 2,* 1967).

Many thanks go to Mark Johnson for his philosophical inspiration. While he may not agree with all of my findings in this book, I hope he will understand my motivation for writing it: I owed a debt to Dewey that I had to repay. In a future work, I intend to repay my other major intellectual debt and to investigate the merits of continuity. I owe special thanks to the two reviewers of the manuscript for their comments and suggestions. I have especially benefitted from the deep insights and kind encouragement of Scott Pratt, whom I would like to thank heartily, particularly for his suggestions regarding the relation between unity and disunity. I am grateful to Martin Coleman for making me aware of an important letter by Dewey, and to Webster University for making it possible for me to teach in Vienna and to research the history of the modernist tradition there. In addition, I am grateful to Ann Miller for her skillful editing throughout the text, to Eric Newman for his kindness and editorial expertise, and to the staff at Fordham University Press in general for making the publication of this work such a smooth process.

I am especially grateful to Kim Novak Morse, whose patience is remarkable; whose keen intellect is enviable; who encouraged me every step of the way, offered valuable suggestions, and, above all, showed me the meaning of courage.

In accord with this formal determination, spirit *can* abstract from all that is external and even from its own externality, its determinate being. It can endure the negation of its individual immediacy, the infinite pain, that is, in this negativity it can maintain itself affirmatively and be identical for itself.

—G. W. F. Hegel

INTRODUCTION

This book is the first full-length study of John Dewey's early philosophy. Most scholars entirely ignore Dewey's early efforts in favor of his later, more mature thinking. Those scholars who do explore Dewey's early work, most notably Jim Good and John Shook, who are pioneers in this area, consider the early efforts solely in terms of how they relate to Dewey's later thought.[1] There has been no single study devoted to understanding and interpreting Dewey's early philosophy as a whole, taken on its own terms as a sustained philosophical endeavor.[2]

The justification for such a project—a project that might help us better understand one of America's greatest thinkers—would hardly be required, were it not for the predominance of what I call the standard view of Dewey's early thinking, which holds that his early ideas are hopelessly naïve and not worth considering.[3] Until recently, the standard view has been so firmly in place that it has dissuaded most scholars from exploring Dewey's early efforts. Shook and Good have gone a long way toward challenging the standard view, however. They have shown in various ways how Dewey's early ideas are worth considering, particularly because these ideas seem to anticipate some of his best pragmatist insights.[4] By demonstrating that Dewey's early ideas are actually interesting and forward-looking, rather than hopelessly naïve, Good and Shook have done much to make us feel the need for a fuller and more detailed examination of Dewey's early philosophy. Building on their insights, I seek to fill this gap in the literature by presenting the first comprehensive examination of Dewey's early philosophy.

My main claim in this book is that by taking this comprehensive approach we gain surprising results. My examination will show that Dewey's early contribution to philosophy is significant in its own right, by which I mean that it is significant as a philosophy, independent of what it tells us about Dewey's later efforts or his overall philosophical development. Against the standard view, and going further than even Good and Shook have gone, I argue that the "young John Dewey," to borrow the phrase historian Neil Coughlan used to title his study,[5] was already a philosopher of real importance, someone who developed a new version of philosophical idealism that is still relevant.

In my reading, Dewey's primary concern at the beginning of his career is to overcome philosophical pessimism and to show that life is meaningful. The philosophical pessimism of Dewey's day, espoused by such thinkers as Schopenhauer and Nietzsche, held that the universe is inherently devoid of meaning, so that human beings (who crave meaning) can never be at home within it. Dewey's response is to argue that the universe is meaningful after all. He wants to show that we can have faith in life—that we can regard it as significant and worthwhile, harboring meanings and values conducive to human beings.

To develop this idea, and to instill faith in life, Dewey draws heavily on Hegel, as one might expect. But in my reading, he advances beyond traditional accounts of Hegelianism and creates his own unique version of idealism. For the early Dewey, *rupture*,[6] and not *harmony*, is the primary source of meaning; it is on this point that he differs from traditional Hegelianism. More specifically, for the early Dewey, it is the longing for the Absolute, and never its attainment, that creates ideal meanings for human beings. This longing for the Absolute creates ideal meanings by *disrupting* every actual event, compelling us to seek beyond the event for its higher significance, especially the higher significance (again, never to be attained) of belonging to a single unified whole that supports us. In short, it is our striving for the ideal—and our refusal of every partial instance of it—that gives life what ideal meanings it possesses. This position is what is new and compelling about Dewey's early philosophy, what takes him beyond any traditional account of Hegelian thought,[7] for which, typically, reconciliation or harmony is the primary concept. Moreover, as we shall see, how this position plays out at the social level, the level of creating a truly meaningful human culture, is what renders it most significant.

Dewey's view of meaning-formation is not only original, but it also anticipates the more radical readings of Hegelianism as a philosophy of rupture and transition that have become available only in comparatively recent decades, in the work of such philosophers as Theodor Adorno, Jean-Luc Nancy, and Slavoj Žižek.[8] In fact, Dewey's early position goes beyond these figures in that it presents what is perhaps the first systematic approach to philosophy resting on this basis. Dewey's early idealism therefore adds to the tradition of philosophical idealism a much-needed breadth of insight concerning the concept of rupture, beyond the merely suggestive offerings of recent Hegelians. For in *Psychology*, a major work of his early period, Dewey applies the concept of rupture to the whole gamut of philosophical problems, something these other figures never do. He applies the concept to questions ranging from the nature of sensation, perception, thinking, feeling, and willing, in all their various forms and shapes, up to the meaning of God, presenting us, in the end, with a thoroughgoing philosophy of rupture that amounts to a joyful affirmation of transition in all of its phases.

Moreover, and surprisingly, Dewey's early focus on rupture poses a challenge to his own later naturalism, which relies on the opposite concept of continuity. For one thing, this focus on rupture provides grounds for seeing Dewey's earlier and later philosophies as distinct positions.[9] And given some of the strengths of Dewey's early position that I will articulate, it cannot simply be assumed that Dewey's later philosophy is in every instance the more compelling one. The success of the challenge posed by Dewey's early philosophy is uncertain, but the challenge itself reinforces the idea that his early work deserves more consideration as a significant philosophical endeavor in its own right.

I will not venture to say in the present book whether Dewey's early position is correct or not. My approach is rather to offer a sympathetic reading of Dewey's early thought, so that we might first appreciate what it is trying to accomplish. Later commentators, if they like, can challenge Dewey's arguments. My task is one of recovery. I try to show what Dewey's arguments are and to present them, initially, in a favorable light. Above all, my aim is to build on the work of Shook and Good, to investigate Dewey's early philosophy at length, and to show that his early philosophy deserves fuller attention than it has received—fuller attention, especially, from scholars in American philosophy who have tended to ignore it, as well as from anyone interested in a new form of idealism appearing on the scene.

I want to stress that although my task is one of recovery, and I present Dewey's arguments as best I can, it does not follow that I agree with them. I do clearly believe that these arguments, whether or not they turn out to be correct, make an important contribution to philosophy. If my work helps anyone to understand Dewey's overall philosophical development, so much the better; but promoting this understanding is not my goal, which is merely to consider Dewey's early philosophy in its own right in a sustained fashion. Except in one important place in chapter 7, I have therefore confined my observations concerning any connections that may exist between the earlier and later philosophies to the last chapter of the present work. In that final chapter I emphasize the differences, in order to highlight what is distinctive about the early philosophy.

My examination of Dewey's early philosophy begins, in chapter 1, with a general description of Dewey's project. I examine some minor works surrounding the *Psychology*, on the grounds that in the build-up (and aftermath) to something momentous, one can often detect significant motives. I focus, in particular, on a little-read piece about nihilism that Dewey wrote with uncharacteristic force and passion. In "The Lesson of Contemporary French Literature,"[10] Dewey bemoans the deeply rooted pessimism of his times and is at some pains to characterize its precise contours, in order to know best how to combat it. I also focus on "The Present Position of Logical Theory" (EW 3: 125–41), an article in which Dewey settles on one main cause of pessimism, namely, the confrontation with scientific materialism that seems to render the universe (and human beings within it) barren of meaning, merely "the playground" of indifferent "natural forces" (EW 3: 42). Dewey is vitally concerned here, as I try to show, with how human meaning is possible in the world.

More specifically, I show in chapter 2 that Dewey is concerned to address and overcome what we would now call *modernism*, the cultural condition or malaise in which we believe there is an unbridgeable separation between human meaning on the one side and brute, indifferent nature on the other. In a neglected article titled "Poetry and Philosophy" (EW 3: 110–24), Dewey holds that pessimism is a cultural condition that leads to the belief in the utter meaninglessness of the universe, and it must be overcome.

In chapter 3 I turn to the *Psychology* (EW 2: 1–366) and show that it consists in an attempt to overcome the main philosophical presuppositions of modernism. I argue that the book's main concern is not, as many scholars suppose, to develop a science, but rather to show how meaning occurs in the world. This is a point that Dewey stresses repeatedly in the *Psychology*: that he is showing us how meaning is made, and is actual and present in the course of things. The book therefore fits nicely into Dewey's project of combating pessimism. I also describe Dewey's method in the *Psychology*, and provide a brief outline of the book.

In chapters 4, 5, and 6 I examine in some detail Dewey's account of the process of meaning-making in the *Psychology*. Chapter 4 considers the conditions of knowledge that Dewey insists upon: "apperception" and "retention" (EW 2: 78). I show that Dewey gives a convincing argument for the existence of these powers of the human mind, powers that allow us to negate external facts and to transform them into sensations, which already begin to have an ideal content and out of which we construct the world, considered as an organized and meaningful whole.

In chapter 5 I discuss the nature of knowing proper, in which the conditions of knowledge examined above are activated and begin to produce a world of known and meaningful objects. Here we see how the mind builds up an entire universe of known objects out of its sensations. The key to Dewey's account of both knowledge and meaning is the notion of relational terms. The idea is that "*meaning always takes us beyond the bare presentation, to its connections and relations to the rest of experience*" (EW 2: 121). Dewey argues that knowledge and meaning occur only when the self (which he defines as an activity, not a substance) negates the given and takes it up into its own pre-existing system of interrelated meanings. The self does this in various ways, not only through reference of the given object to previously known objects, but also through how the object makes us feel and relative to what we will or intend with respect to it. In knowledge, feeling, and will, the self creates in the process of its apprehension of objects an ideal arrangement of things that is conducive to its own needs. Going beyond bare, isolated particulars, the self creates a meaningful whole of interrelated moments in which it can find a definite place for itself. It satisfies its deepest need to belong by constructing a world in which it does belong.

Dewey, in effect, rejects all forms of foundationalism and presents us with a new coherence theory of truth. It is a theory whereby we come to know objects (and to find our place among them) by detachment from the given and by organized growth away from it—a theory of truth that, uniquely, makes room for feeling and will, as well as knowledge, in its conception of things (a point I will emphasize in chapter 6). In Dewey's view, we never simply accept the world as given. Instead, we always create a world in which we can feel at home.

Negation,[11] or detachment from the given, is thus the key to knowledge and the ideal formation of meanings, and it is an endless process. The self always displaces one term in favor of another as we build up and enlarge our experience based on our ideals. Dewey calls for us to embrace this never-completed, ever-growing process of meaningfulness as the very basis of life itself. He shows us how meaning occurs by enlarging us, shattering our former selves, to be sure, but at the same time installing in our experience of the world meanings that are conducive to our knowledge, feeling, and will.

Pessimism, therefore, can be overcome because at the heart of our experience of the world exist ideal meanings, which we ourselves have put there, and which therefore guarantee that we experience the world with our own meanings and values within it. Said another way, there is no "world" for us in which our meanings and values do not exist. Any world we experience has already been shaped and formed by our ideals. True, this does not mean that the world in the end will ultimately harbor our meanings and values. But this is where Dewey's concept of faith comes in. Seeking an ideal version of things,[12] and not resting content with any finite determination, we are driven on to create ideal meanings and to keep the process of meaning-making going. Because there *could be* an Absolute meaning at the conclusion of all things, we are always compelled to keep going on to create further meanings in the hope of reaching the Absolute. We are thereby creating ideal meanings precisely in our failure to produce the Absolute ideal meaning, which escapes beyond us. Faith, for Dewey, means driving toward the ideal, toward making it actual, a process that actually does allow us to produce meanings in the world.

One of the most important ideals we possess is the ideal of a genuine community—an ideal that Dewey believes we should strive to realize above all others. In chapter 7, drawing on his *Outlines for a Critical Theory of Ethics* (EW 3: 237–388), I show how the early Dewey conceives of this community ideal, and how he uses it in particular to combat modernism considered as a problematic form of cultural life.

Modernist thought insists on the socially detached individual, one who must draw on his or her own inner resources alone to determine how to live. Society can be no guide, for it is ultimately indifferent to the individual's concerns. The heroic, isolated self must give itself its own law in opposition to society. Armed with his new idealism, in which the negation of one term leads to another, or in which the movement between the two terms gives them their meaning, Dewey argues for a new form of social life that relies on the interplay and continual movement between individual and society. On the one hand, the society requires that individuals perform certain "functions." On the other hand, individuals who perform these functions develop capacities as individuals, who in turn contribute something unique to the society. In the ideal community life, individual and society mutually enrich and enlarge one another rather than work antagonistically against one another. Each person will have found a definite place for himself or herself in the society, and the society will benefit as a result. A meaningful whole will exist to which each person belongs, and to which each contributes, rather than a society that exists as an alien and indifferent force opposing each person in his or her individual life and development (EW 3:303–4; 320).

This is an ideal, for Dewey, that is worth fighting for. In fact, the key to overcoming pessimism is to find joy in life in the struggle to create this meaningful world—a single, interconnected world in which each unique individual has his part to play in the whole and is not merely cast out and ignored by indifferent forces. This is the ultimate message of Dewey's early philosophy: life is worth living in the pursuit of this ideal of community life.

After presenting this comprehensive reconstruction of the early ideas, I then turn in chapter 8 to discussing their significance. I seek to show, in particular, that Dewey's view comprises an original version of idealism that contributes to both nineteenth- and twentieth-century thinking. I first show that Dewey's idealism differs from that of his teacher, George Sylvester Morris, with whom he studied Hegel and who scholars often think is responsible for Dewey's Hegelianism. Morris, according to Dewey's own citation of his words, holds that " 'the very sense of philosophical idealism . . . is to put and represent man in direct relation with the Absolute mind'" (EW 3: 9).[13] Yet Dewey's idealism argues for an indirect connection to the Absolute, with disruption or rupture serving as the fundamental trait of our experience of it. Dewey thus advances beyond Morris' quaint nineteenth-century idealism toward a more relevant twentieth-century Hegelianism, where discord and disruption seem to be more appropriate categories of description.

I next show how Dewey's idealism differs from that of Hegel himself, making it clear that the early Dewey is not simply a blind follower of Hegel, as many scholars suppose, but in fact advances a novel version of idealism—an idealism with Hegelian inspiration, to be sure, but not one reducible to Hegel's philosophy as such. Hegel holds in the lesser *Logic* (section 23) that thought immerses itself in the object and in this way thinks the true nature of things.[14] But, as we shall see, Dewey holds that we never obtain a grasp of the given object, but instead from the beginning always move off away from the object in the development of its ideal formation. In this way, he goes beyond Hegel's philosophy of circles, in which the direction of thought merely returns to its starting point in the object. The early Dewey moves beyond a traditional reading of Hegel's philosophy towards a more open-ended philosophy of uncertain progression.

In this study, I also contrast Dewey's idealism with other nineteenth-century philosophies that also make pessimism a central focus and concern. I have in mind here both Schopenhauer and Nietzsche, who both advocate for their own versions of pessimism. Against the embrace of pessimism by these figures, I show how Dewey's early view creates a space for the affirmation of rupture (and its movement) as an affirmation of life itself. Unlike Nietzsche's pessimism, which finds life to be indifferent yet says that we should embrace it nonetheless, Deweyan idealism renders life no longer indifferent, but filled with meanings and values, especially for individuals in genuine communities, and *on this basis* says life is worth embracing. Deweyan idealism challenges the Schopenahuerian-Nietzschean presumption that at its base life is without significance, and his idealism does so without nostalgia, because it embraces rupture.

Lastly, I consider Dewey's idealism in relation to contemporary philosophies, showing that here, too, his position has something to offer. As I mentioned above, the systematic nature of Dewey's philosophy of rupture offers breadth to the otherwise merely suggestive implications of such thinkers as Adorno, Nancy, and Žižek, who do not show how rupture functions systematically in all areas of meaning-making experience. Dewey thus lines up with many cutting-edge thinkers today, but he also adds to their explorations insights relative to the nature of sensation, feeling, thought, will, and more. Moreover, I also pause to consider how Dewey's early idealism compares to his own later pragmatism. Could it be that, contrary to received wisdom, the earlier idealistic philosophy actually offers an advance over Dewey's later philosophy in some way? While not arriving at a conclusive answer to this question, I do offer the suggestion that the early Dewey's emphasis on rupture could possibly have greater explanatory value than the later Dewey's emphasis on *continuity*. The later Dewey insists upon a continuous development from the biological to the cultural, a concept central to his whole effort to rethink philosophy as a form of cultural interaction and criticism (LW 12:30ff). However, the early Dewey's emphasis on rupture rather than continuity may better account for the shift from the biological to the cultural. According to Žižek, for example, we must first negate our natural impulses, and repress their manifestation within us, in order to create culture; culture requires repression, discontinuity, the break with nature.[15] If that is correct, then rupture, and not continuity, would seem to better account for the emergence of culture. The issue cannot be decided in the present text, to be sure, but that Dewey's early philosophy can offer a compelling alternative to the later Dewey's account of culture, and even pose a challenge to the later Dewey on this score, suggests that there is more to Dewey's early philosophy than is typically recognized.

Having argued for these ideas, I draw the conclusion that Dewey's early work amounts to a significant new form of idealism, one that makes important contributions to philosophy in its own right. Taken solely on its own terms, Dewey's idealism goes beyond traditional readings of Hegel; it lines up with, and even advances beyond, some important contemporary insights concerning the nature of human meaning; and it even challenges Dewey's own later naturalism. Lastly, and perhaps most importantly of all, Dewey's idealism gives us grounds for embracing life. For it argues compellingly—and contrary to the modernist presumption, still very much in force, that the world is indifferent to human concerns—that there is meaning in the world, after all.

ONE

DEWEY'S PROJECT

Beyond the Standard View

Any extended study of John Dewey's early philosophy must grapple with the fact that this body of work has not been well received. Given the kinds of naïve claims it is making, the critics have said, this philosophy is not worth lingering over, except perhaps if one is interested in tracing Dewey's philosophical development as a whole. Dewey's project at this time was to defend Hegel in some rather bizarre ways, so the argument goes, and there does not seem to be anything in the philosophy of this period that is still worth considering today.

This assessment is what I call the standard view of Dewey's early philosophy. The standard view tells us that Dewey's early philosophy is, at best, uninteresting, and, at worst, an embarrassment to its author.[1] As a Hegelian, Dewey is supposedly committed to defending an absurdly naïve position in which the universe is believed to be some kind of gigantic thinking mind. Moreover, his Hegelianism is

{ 12 }

considered particularly unlikely, holding that the best science of the day, especially the psychology, can be interpreted in Hegelian terms; and he makes all sorts of contortions of the intellect to force scientific conclusions into a Hegelian mold. To be sure, this view grants the importance of understanding that Dewey was a Hegelian if we want to better understand his later philosophy with its emphasis on organic unity. But his early thought is held to be uninteresting, even absurd, apart from its relation to his later philosophy.[2]

The standard view seems like a solid position; it is certainly venerable. But this view is not without its difficulties. It mischaracterizes Hegel's philosophy, for one thing. But the main problem with the standard view is that it fails to grasp the actual aim of Dewey's effort, which is not simply to defend Hegelianism at all costs.

To begin to appreciate what Dewey is really up to we must first develop a better understanding of the nature of his most central endeavor, which is to see to what extent we can have faith in life. What goes largely unrecognized, eclipsed by the seeming optimism of Dewey's later work, is the extent to which Dewey's early thought is a direct response to pessimism. His early work is a response that feels keenly the crisis of the possible meaninglessness of the universe, yet resolves itself in favor of faith—not in God, Transcendental Ego, or Absolute Spirit—but in life itself and the significance of living.

In this respect, Dewey's work in the nineteenth century forms an important link (and counterweight) to that of other writers dealing with similar ideas, particularly Schopenhauer and Nietzsche.[3] It also compares favorably to new interpretations of Hegelianism coming from the Continent, interpretations of Hegel not as the totalitarian philosopher of enforced harmony in the Absolute but a philosopher of actual life and its ruptures, its agonies and tensions. For *rupture* is an important part of Dewey's early philosophy. It is primarily through rupture and disruption, the early Dewey believes, that meaning is made, so that to embrace the process of rupture is to embrace a meaningful life as such. Dewey's Absolute is not a pre-given substance, but rather the ideal point of thinking that forever unsettles our given world; and it is, for him, through this very unsettlement, this negation of the given, that ideal meanings are created and life can be affirmed (as he shows in some detail in his *Psychology*). Life's very tensions and agonies, therefore, are for Dewey the basis of its meaningfulness, so that it is false to say, with the pessimists, that life is devoid of meaning. The very fact of life's divisions and separations, which pessimists take as proof of life's utter meaninglessness, Dewey shows to be the basis of life's meaning and the reason to embrace it.

In my interpretation, then, two of the most significant aspects of Dewey's early philosophy are 1) that it employs a concept of rupture, and 2) that through its concept of rupture it gives us a new way to combat philosophical pessimism and to find meaning in the world. It poses a serious challenge to pessimists and teaches us how to have faith in life. But Dewey also goes further than this, using his new concept of life affirmation as the basis of a critique of culture. He finds that modern times have been caught in the grips of an unhealthy despair, which his thought endeavors to overcome through a serious reworking of the modern (that is to say, alienating) relationship between the individual and society. In this respect, his early philosophy is also significant because it offer us a new critique of modern culture.

Three core concepts, then, define Dewey's early work as I interpret it. These concepts are rupture, meaningfulness (or faith in life), and critique. These three concepts had never before been brought together in the exact combination in which they are arranged in Dewey's early thought—neither in Hegel's idealism, in the idealism of Dewey's teacher George Sylvester Morris, nor anywhere else. His is a new and original philosophy, one dealing with issues of genuine interest, and therefore a philosophy that is worth investigating fully and carefully.

Dewey's idealism is open to criticism, to be sure, but it deserves the serious criticism appropriate to a significant and well-worked-out position, not the dismissive criticism appropriate to an unoriginal and youthful indiscretion, nor to an undeveloped pragmatism-in-waiting. Like all idealisms, early Deweyanism is open to the challenge that it is too spiritualistic and mystical, as well as too humanist, privileging human beings over animals and nature. But Deweyan idealism—the early work—marks an interesting new development of the idealistic school that should be studied (and criticized) alongside other idealisms such as those of Fichte, Hegel, Royce, and Bradley, and alongside the work of other important nineteenth-century figures such as Nietzsche and Schopenhauer. Our understanding of nineteenth-century thought, and its continuing relevance for us, is incomplete as long as we lack a fuller reckoning with Dewey's early philosophy. And any serious effort to overcome pessimism and despair must certainly retain its relevance for our own time, which is not lacking in reasons for despair.

Dewey's Main Concepts

To clarify the main aspects of this new philosophy, I will define in more detail its three central concepts, but it should be stressed that the evidence that these concepts are at work in the philosophy can only be laid out during the course of the whole of the present study. For to a certain extent Dewey himself does not always appreciate his best insights. He does not give all these concepts names as I do here. Nonetheless they are at work throughout his early philosophy and are one with his intentions. To see this one must grasp the whole narrative of Dewey's early thought, but to assist the reader in seeing up front what is new in Dewey's early work, I provide the following shorthand summary. Dewey's three central concepts are:

Rupture. In general, meaning, for a Hegelian, is a dynamic process. The meaning of an event is never given to us all at once, but rather develops through time. The way it develops is through the working interaction of disruption and harmony. The play between these two forces gives the meaning, in the sense that a static state by itself is never a complete meaning, but requires development to unfold its full potential and significance. Harmonious states require disruption and movement to fulfill them and attain their true meaning. On the other hand, disruption by itself is insufficient for meaning to occur, because there must be some settled, well-arranged, or harmonious state that we achieve in order for there to be a space for us to apprehend and enjoy meanings and for meaning to exist. Thus, harmony and disruption are each needed for meaning-making.

However, they are not necessarily needed in equal degrees. Hegelians might differ on where to put the emphasis. To say that Dewey's early philosophy emphasizes rupture is to say that his position entails, to be sure, the working interaction of disruption and harmony, but that disruption is the primary concept. The early Dewey's innovation is to assert that meaning occurs primarily through rupture. In Adorno's words, the idea is that "connection is not a matter of unbroken transition but a matter of sudden change."[4] Meaningful events occur "not through the moments approaching one another but through rupture," through the moments suddenly breaking apart from one another and becoming differentiated.[5] The term *rupture* derives from Adorno's reading of Hegel, and is never explicitly used by Dewey. However, I hold that the concept is nonetheless the overriding concept at work in Dewey's early thought. The *logic* of Dewey's position fully accords with the logic of rupture, as we will see.

This means, more specifically, that settled states are "undone," and that this "undoing" is the primary force in the meaning-making process. Rupture, for Dewey, is primary in the sense that it is the *source* of the meaning that occurs in the harmonious state in which we possess meaning. For Dewey in these early years, any actual, harmonious state that is attained derives its meaning from an absent ideal, from something outside of the state, against which the state must be measured in order to receive its significance. The emphasis is on the disruptive quality of this absence. A lack is felt, and this drives us beyond our current condition. The emphasis is on the lack as the creative source of idealization and meaning. To be sure, there must be harmonious states, namely states of temporary rest in which we can enjoy the partial realization of our ideals. And our attainment of these harmonious states counts as some evidence that we are partially realizing the ideal. But rupture is primary, in the sense that these harmonious states get their meaning from rupture, from the absent ideal. Rupture drives the process, the search for ideals, which leads us to partially find and obtain some idealized meanings (which we recognize by the harmony they impart), but these ideals are attained and enjoyed only partially, only relative to some ultimate harmony that is missing, that is always missing, always lacking in our lives, and yet, precisely in this lack, leading us on to obtain partial instances of it (EW 2:273; 358).

Meaning. As defined by the early Dewey, this is the belief that the sense and importance of things consist in the establishment of ideal relationships between them, rather than in their actual relationships. Bare, given particulars have no meaning for Dewey. They become meaningful only through the process of rupture, by which they are negated in their actuality and taken up by the self into a coordinated set of practices and previous understandings of things that alone confer significance upon them. Because there are no bare facts that ever reach the self without having already been rendered meaningful, Dewey holds, there is meaning in the world, in events, that we can embrace, and we can affirm life as being a place of significance for human beings, a place, moreover, that always has the potential to grow in ideal significance through rupture (EW 2:121).

Critique. On the basis of his view that life can be embraced, Dewey turns toward the culture of his own times (which is perhaps still that of our own times) and criticizes it for its pessimism and despair. What this means, more specifically, is that he criticizes it on the grounds that it encourages the withdrawal of the individual in the face of life. "Cynicism," egoism, hyper-self-consciousness, "*aestheticism*," the despair of the isolated individual—these have become common features of modern culture, as Dewey sees it, and he critiques the culture for continually producing these features.[6] He also formulates a new vision of culture and society that he thinks will help create more healthy and outgoing individuals in the world.

The "Logic of Rupture"

To gain an initial sense of what is unique and important about Dewey's version of idealism, consider, by way of contrast, some of the prominent idealisms of Dewey's own day.[7] Nearly all of them can be seen as responding to pessimism, in that they each try to render external nature conducive to mind and its meanings—to find a place for human meaning in the universe. But they also nearly all achieve this position by resolving external nature and mind into an overarching harmony or unity, whereas Dewey will insist instead on disruption or disharmony as the basis of meaning in life.

T. H. Green, for example, who was one of the most prominent idealists when Dewey was writing his early works, shares with him the argument that, in the words of Anthony Quinton, "Nature is a system or tissue of relations" and that "relations . . . are the work of the mind. Therefore, nature, at least as regards an essential aspect of it, is the work of the mind."[8] But Green goes further and also asserts, according to Quinton, that "the nature that the individual mind constructs in experience is not wholly that mind's construction. It intimates the existence of an eternal consciousness adequate to support the system of nature as a whole."[9] This eternal consciousness is Green's Absolute, which involves the belief in an ultimate Mind that grasps all things within it, an ultimate unity bringing all things together. As Quinton explains, for Green, "this all-inclusive system of relations that constitutes nature . . . presupposes an all-sustaining mind. It is a unity and, therefore, must be held together by a single mind, the eternal consciousness. We are all, Green contends, parts or participators in this eternal consciousness."[10]

A similar claim for the primacy of the finished and accomplished Absolute, for the definite existence of a harmonious, "eternal consciousness," is made by other important idealists in Dewey's day. Bradley, for example, who was, as W. J. Mander points out, "the greatest thinker of the idealist movement," likewise believed in one unified reality in which all particular things are submerged and in which, in fact, they lose their own individual reality.[11] Bradley admitted that the world appears to exist as a series of related things; he accepted, in appearances, anyway, "the thoroughly relational nature of all things," but "he argued that all relational thought . . . leads to contradiction and thus that reality is wholly nonrelational or monistic."[12] He argued for the existence of a "nonrelational, monistic whole. . . . Bradley's attack on relations was uncompromising. It even extended to the self; that, too, he argued, is relational and thus unreal."[13] The only reality, for Bradley, was the single, unified reality of the Absolute. Or, as Bradley himself puts it, "We have seen that Reality is one, and is a single experience."[14]

Even an idealist such as Caird, another prominent figure in Dewey's time, a figure who, as W. J. Mander explains, "stood out as a champion of the dynamic side of things" and argued for "the notion of universal and ceaseless evolution"—even he still believed that ultimately the Absolute Mind was eternal, fully present to itself, a harmonious and timeless whole.[15] As Mander makes clear, Caird believed that things developed within the Absolute, but he did not believe that the Absolute developed. "Caird freely admits that the Absolute *itself* does not evolve. Time and change hold only *within* it. It may contain nothing but change, yet it itself does not change."[16]

Each of these idealists shares the belief that the Absolute is fully present; it is present to itself in eternity. In this sense, they each privilege harmony as the superior or ultimate member of the working pair of harmony and disruption. Bradley will, in effect, deny all relations, all movement and disruption, while Caird will allow for these things, but in the end the Absolute for both thinkers is conceived as the final container and unifier of any dynamic processes of development. The Absolute exists as a real entity standing above all events and encompassing all time states, with every discrete moment united within its infinitely larger perspective. All moments are brought together into a unified whole. In this way, by believing these things, the other idealists privilege harmony over rupture.[17]

The early Dewey, by contrast, privileges rupture over harmony. In other words, he holds that the Absolute is missing. It is absent. And because of this absence, we are compelled to seek for its presence, its higher unity. We are compelled to try to create ever more harmonious states, in other words, precisely because of something that is lacking, some antagonism or tension that continues to develop in our lives, no matter how harmonious they become. The absence of any absolute harmony makes us seek it. What we feel is the absence and the longing for its presence; and this makes us try to create it, to bring it into existence over and over again.

Dewey explains his position in this way in the *Psychology*: There is an "ideal will," he says, which "serves as a spur to the actual self to realize itself. It leads to discontent with every accomplished result, and urges on to new and more complete action" (EW 2: 358). He explains further: "the self has always presented to its actual condition the vague ideal of a completely universal self, by which it measures itself and feels its own limitations. . . . The self always confronts itself . . . with the conception of a universal or completed will towards which it must strive." However, "what this will or self as complete is, it does not know. It only feels that there is such a goal" (EW 2: 358). There is an ideal whose precise meaning and complete presence eludes us in our experience, and whose vagueness and lack of full existence in the present moment we feel. It is this absent, unrealized ideal that serves as "a constant motive power," compelling us to seek it (EW 2: 359). And we do, at times, attain partial instances of the ideal because of this search. When we experience truth, beauty, and morality, we have realized the ideal to some extent. "The feeling of harmony, which is the mind's ultimate test of intellectual truth, aesthetic beauty, and moral rightness, is simply the feeling of the accord between the accomplished act and the . . . ideal" (EW 2: 358). All of these accomplishments are the result of our search for a missing ideal. They are the harmonious states we do obtain and in which we possess meanings. But the absent ideal defines them and is the source of their meaning. The absent ideal is "a constant motive power, which has energized in bringing forth the concrete attainments in knowledge, beauty, and rightness" (EW 2: 359).

Far from postulating a completed Absolute, therefore, the early Dewey stresses its absence and incompletion. What he insists upon is the "progressive appropriation of that self in which real and ideal are one," that is, not a fusion somewhere (e.g., in eternal consciousness) of real and ideal self, but the break between them as the vital source of life's ongoing, "progressive" development (EW 2: 363). Harmonious states of meaning are achieved, in which the self's actual state is closer to an ideal one, but then these harmonious states break apart, and then lead to new harmonious states, which then break apart again, and so on. And the breaking apart is the decisive and primary phase of this progression because the ideal will is "the source, the origin of ideals," the source of the meaning in the harmonious states, which then gets partially realized in the life of the actual self and its experience (EW 2: 358). The meaning of the unified experience derives from outside of it, measured by what is missing from it, although the unities that are achieved are the place or space in which the meanings can occur as we progressively realize them and draw closer to the ideal (EW 2:363). But Dewey stresses that, though we feel we are closer to the ideal in these harmonious instances of life, closer to our true selves, as in the experience of beauty, for example, still "this does not mean that we have a prior conception of our nature" (EW 2: 273). We are struggling for the Absolute meaning that is missing from us, whose nature we do not know or understand, and it is this struggle that produces meaning.

In a fascinating letter to his wife written in 1894, Dewey sums up his philosophy up to that point, the philosophy of his early work.[18] In the letter, we can see especially well the role that Dewey believed struggle and disruption played in his early thought. The letter describes an encounter he had with Jane Addams, a pivotal encounter judged by the contents of the letter, for it seems that this encounter may have encouraged him to change his early philosophy and to shift it in new directions. Addams, according to Dewey in the letter, explains that "she had always believed & still believed that antagonism was not only . . . useless and harmful, but entirely unnecessary; that it lay never in the objective differences, which would always grow into unity if left alone."[19] Dewey, who was already starting to lose his Hegelianism at this point, first agrees with Addams. But then he objects and asks her whether she did not think "personal antagonisms" as well as "that of ideas & institutions" existed and "that a realization of that antagonism was necessary to an appreciation of the truth, & to a consciousness of growth." Addams disagreed, "& she said no."[20] Dewey confides to his wife that he was not persuaded. "At least I can't saee [sic] what all this conflict & warring of history means if it's perfecterly [sic] meaningless; my pride of intellect, I suppose it is, revolts at thinking its all *merely* negatively, & has no functional value."[21]

Here we have the heart of Dewey's early philosophy. The letter states in an informal way what Dewey's philosophy also struggles to articulate, namely that antagonism has a functional value; that it is "necessary to an appreciation of the truth, & to a consciousness of growth." Indeed, judging by the account provided in this letter, it was Addams, and not Dewey, who maintained something like the traditional Hegelian approach, holding that antagonism, disruption, and rupture are all "a mere illusion because we put ourselves in a wrong position & thus introduce antagonism where its all one."[22] Dewey balks at this idea and says to his wife: "When you think that Miss Addams . . . believes it in all her senses & muscles—great God."[23] Dewey himself does not believe it. "She converted me internally," he says, "but not really, I fear."[24] He believes the opposite, in fact, namely that antagonism is "functional" and has a creative role to play; and so here we can see Dewey's philosophy of rupture confirmed and assented to in his own personal estimation of his work. For, as becomes crystal clear in the letter, Dewey, oddly enough, eventually is converted to Addams's way of thinking, but, at the moment of conversion, looks back on his previous philosophy and describes it as I have described it: "I can sene [sic] that I have always been interpreting the Hegelian dialectic wrong end up—the unity as the reconciliation of opposites, instead of the opposites as the unity in its growth, and thus translated physical tension into a moral thing."[25] Here Dewey likens the central concept of his previous philosophy, his early philosophy, to physical tension, an active struggle, an antagonism, or what I have called disruption and rupture. And he describes that previous philosophy as he has understood it in his work, as achieving unity through opposites, *through* tension and disruption, rather than saying, as he now wants to say, with Addams, that the opposites *already constitute* a "unity in its growth." In the end, he is converted to Addams's way of thinking; he changes his previous view, and he says: "I guess I'll have to give it uall [sic] up & start over again."[26]

Further examination of this fascinating letter would take me too far from my present purpose of giving a first, initial look at Dewey's concept of rupture and the primacy he gives to it. The letter offers a keen insight into why Dewey may have left his early philosophy behind; namely, he was converted by Addams into believing that unity was more fundamental than antagonism. Such an insight has far-reaching implications for interpreting Dewey's later philosophy, but this is not my goal. What the letter reveals for our present purposes is that Dewey, in his own estimation of his early work, had indeed taken rupture (or "antagonism") to be primary. He believed that antagonism should not be seen "merely negatively" but had real "functional value" instead. It could lead to something valuable.

It will take the full length of the present book to articulate sufficiently just what Dewey means by ascribing a functional value to antagonism and to explain how this idea plays out in a systematic way in his early philosophy. The point to emphasize for now, however, is that tension is creative for the early Dewey. Unity of meanings can be achieved, but the source of meanings, the value they come to embody, derives from the clash of energies at work within them, from the disruptive quality that leads them to be unities no longer and to press forward in search of higher unities that they might become, but that are nowhere present within them.

The next point to notice is that Dewey employs the concept of the primacy of rupture in the service of a larger goal. Ultimately, he is concerned to overcome pessimism. He wants to show that there is meaning to life. His innovation is to show that this meaning is achieved in and through antagonism and disruption. The key idea to be developed throughout the present work is the idea that in Dewey's early work, the antagonisms that may exist between the self and the world are not such as must lead to pessimism, but are rather the very means by which pessimism can be defeated. It is a striking idea: the forces of pessimism are turned against themselves. Division and alienation are seen as creative and productive forces, giving rise to unified meanings in life, rather than as the occasion for total separation, antagonism, and inevitable despair.

A Response to Pessimism

Many people will be surprised to think of Dewey's philosophy, whether earlier or later, as somehow responding to pessimism, for Dewey is heavily associated with a kind of stubborn, blind optimism. Scholars often claim, for instance, that Dewey has no tragic sense, or that he is far too optimistic about life and its progress.[27] That Dewey is at all concerned with pessimism and other dark matters will therefore strike many as unlikely.

In the remainder of this chapter I will demonstrate not only that the early Dewey is concerned with pessimism, but that it is indeed his central concern. Many scholars miss this about the early Dewey, first because they are held captive by the standard view that there is nothing very interesting to find in the early work, and therefore they rarely read it; second, because Dewey's real effort is often couched in technical terms that may prevent readers from grasping his actual message. People often miss the concern with pessimism, too, because philosophical pessimism is often seen as a topic of concern in Continental philosophy but not in American philosophy, and disciplinary boundaries get in the way of understanding. We must remember, however, that the early Dewey was a Hegelian, and insofar as Hegel himself was concerned with pessimism, so would Dewey have been.

On what grounds, then, can we say that John Dewey's early philosophy was a response to philosophical pessimism? Sometimes an author's real focus—his main, driving idea—comes out only in the margins of his work. Writing can be an act of wandering, the mental equivalent of an aimless stroll, in which the main ideas, like the interesting stops on a walk, are hit upon rather than explicitly planned for or foreseen. This is especially true of Dewey's thought, which, as one glance at his collected writings shows, contains this wandering element to a great degree. Especially in the early work, there seems to be no core, central text that spells out Dewey's entire effort and exhausts his interests. There is no single, privileged text, although the *Psychology* comes close and constitutes his major early work. Instead, young

Dewey's mind ranges widely, exploring this idea and that, from the nature of logical theory to tips for educational practice to the latest interpretation of French literature. Given that Dewey was considering so much diverse material at once, one might almost expect that when his own coherent philosophy actually begins to form, his real interests will be happened upon in the process of inquiry, rather than explicitly anticipated, carefully developed, and put into a single text.

And this is what occurs. Dewey's main concern emerges in the smaller, occasional pieces that, despite their lack of professional philosophical intent, still detain him. This reading can be corroborated by the way in which, despite the wandering nature of Dewey's early work, his core ideas begin to shape and inform the other matters he is concerned with in his philosophical strolls. The marginal ideas, as we will see, begin to crystallize into an entire philosophy.

A key marginal text in this regard is a seemingly casual review of a book on French literature that Dewey nonetheless addresses with a peculiar passion and energy. The topic of the book is pessimism.

In "The Lessons of Contemporary French Literature," Dewey offers a review of Paul Bourget's *Essais de Psychologie Contemporaire*, a work that appeared in 1889 (EW 3: 36–42). What Dewey finds fascinating in this book is its "criticism of the souls of the writers passed in review," namely Baudelaire, Renan, Flaubert, Stendhal, and Taine. "Its aim is not external description," Dewey goes on, "but internal penetration. It is psychological analysis of the French spirit as revealed in its representative authors; it is the dissection of their thoughts, their emotions, their attitude toward the problems of life" (EW 3: 36–37). The attitude Bourget reveals in the five French authors is, as Dewey quotes him, " 'the same creed of the thoroughgoing emptiness of the universe. These magnificent minds are completely nauseated with the vain strivings of life' " (EW 3: 37). The French wisdom of the day seems to exude above all, as Bourget tries to show, a great exhaustion with existence itself. In Dewey's words, which should be noted for their sensitive appreciation of the position, "Everywhere . . . is there to be found the gradual enfeebling and paralysis of the will;

the decay of hope, courage and endeavor; the growing belief that the world is bankrupt" (EW 3: 37).

As so often in his early work, Dewey uses a review or occasional piece to help explore and shape his own viewpoint. In the case of the Bourget review, Dewey uses the piece to come to terms with his own view of pessimism. As he delves deeper into what interests him in the book by Bourget, he finds it to be its precise analysis of the causes of pessimism (and, by the end, the search for a way to circumvent these causes). "The interest [in the work]," Dewey explains, "does not center in this general conclusion [of the emptiness of the universe]. It gathers about the analysis of the various influences which have shaped this pessimism, and the various forms which it takes" (EW 3: 37).

Dewey goes carefully through Bourget's account of what causes pessimism. He identifies three crucial causes: "dilettanteism, the influence of physical sciences, and . . . romanticism" (EW 3: 38). By *dilettanteism*, Dewey means what Michael Principe has called, after Arthur Danto, "directionless pluralism,"[28] or simply relativism: "the feeling that so many things in general are true that nothing in particular is very true. It is . . . a disposition which induces a thinker to lend himself to all points of view without giving himself to any" (EW 3: 38). The dilettante refuses to hold on to any one belief firmly; he is always ready to see, with equal justification, the other side of things. All beliefs in this way are leveled out, none truer or more worth fighting for than any other. "Thus dilletanteism leads to pessimism," Dewey thinks.

> It is not the wild pessimism of the nihilist; it is not the soured pessimism of Schopenhauer; it is the mild and tender consciousness that the doom of transitoriness is upon all aspects of life, upon all forms of what we call truth. The sentiment that all shades of belief have their own relative justification, that from its own standpoint each is as true as any other, is, in reality, the sentiment that no belief has justification. Such a feeling is pessimistic, for it finds that the universe takes no sides; it is more than impartial—it is indifferent. The world of the lover of culture has no bias in

favor of anything—not even of truth and goodness. It teaches but one thing—the hopelessness of action which is more than playing with various forms of experience in order to obtain from them some self-development. (EW 3: 39)

The dilettante embraces inaction. His pessimism stems from his extreme subjectivism. If no beliefs are truer than any others, none are worth acting on. "The part of the wise man is to take no part" (EW 3: 38). Aside from an egoistic self-creation and inverted withdrawal into personal fantasy, there is no cause for doing anything. One might as well resign from life's noisier, external happenings. One might as well resign from life—especially since, as Dewey notes, no one can really convince himself for long that his own private interests are more important than the universe (EW 3: 39). When such a person realizes the universe is, in fact, vastly more important than him and his private self-development, but that it is also, as he still thinks, utterly indifferent, this leads to pessimism. One concludes in horror that the universe does not care about anything whatsoever, least of all one's individual projects.

The second cause of pessimism is the effect of science on our feeling. Science shows that "human nature is simply one part of physical nature" (EW 3: 39). But physical nature is ultimately indifferent to the needs and aspirations of human beings. If good things happen, it is pure happenstance and on equal par with bad things. "Reason and health are, in Taine's words, happy accidents" (EW 3: 39). Physical nature is nothing but a material process of endless changes, each with its own cause, life and death, health and insanity, each occurring with equal causal justification. Reduced to physical beings, human beings reduce away. The main ideas of science "resolve all human aspirations, loves, and ideals into the insignificant outcome of petty changes. All hope is vain, all effort is fruitless, all aspiration unavailing. Thus there arises . . . the swelling tone of the worthlessness of life—the tone of saddened pessimism" (EW 3: 40).

Human personality in truth has no effect on events. Events occur, rather, in mindless, blind ways, without purpose or intention, and human personality follows suit. As a result, we have only "the simulacrum of personality" (EW 3: 40). We have no free, independent will. Like rocks, trees, and other animals, like all natural forces, we can only submit to blind forces, and in submitting "give up the possibility of moral action and of religious faith" (EW 3: 40). As a result, without these very human meanings that give significance to our efforts, "life is shorn and empty" (EW 3: 40).

The third cause of pessimism that Dewey, using Bourget, identifies and explains carefully in his own terms, is romanticism. By *romanticism* Dewey means sensualism, the view of life that finds meaning to reside solely in ever-greater stimulation of the affects. "In all ways and at hazards, fresh, vivid, and continual emotion!" (EW 3: 40). This view leads to pessimism because it is so much at odds with actual, everyday life. "The school staked its belief in the worth of life upon the one point whether life affords the desired abundance and intensity of passions; and it found every passion a pathway to a grave" (EW 3: 41). Reality sets in. The world does not provide endless stimulation. In addition to stimulation, it offers boredom; it offers the mundane and humdrum. It offers, too, the pains and ills of excessive living; it offers fatigue, illness, and death. Having pinned all hopes in life on intense, vital passion—a passion that cannot be sustained— the romantic ends up losing all hope in life whatsoever. He had given too much allegiance to one view of life, an unsustainable one, and in the end stands bereft of any positive consideration for the life that has failed to meet his expectations and has let him down.

Having thus identified the causes of pessimism in his age, through the work of Bourget, Dewey then turns to refuting this pessimism. His efforts are instructive for the whole of his early philosophy.

Each form of pessimism, Dewey says in agreement with Bourget, amounts to "a nausea . . . at the emptiness of life" (EW 3: 41). Such is the collective meaning of these forms. Yet each form, with its own distinct cause, nonetheless forgets the crucial role of *faith*. The faith Dewey has in mind here is the faith in the reality of "spiritual things," "unseen ideals," "moral choice," "personality" (EW 3: 41–2). He means that there must be some ideal quality to things beyond how they appear in their brute givenness. There must be "a criterion which, though unseen, shall serve to measure all that is seen and felt" (EW 3: 42). We can see here that Dewey's impulse is very strongly to combat pessimism with faith. Indeed, he goes so far as to say that "the problem of the nineteenth century reduces itself to a choice between faith and pessimism" (EW 3: 42)—a quote that should serve to demonstrate that pessimism, or coming to terms with the terror of the possible emptiness of life, does indeed form the core problem of Dewey's philosophy at this time.

Dewey seems to perceive keenly the agonies of his age. He seems to be very much aware of the deep dread that life is capable of evoking, especially, it seems, in the nineteenth century, with something like the death of God very much occupying people's minds. Indeed, Dewey captures this dread in accurate, and even chilling, language. He speaks of the "nausea" of the age, "the emptiness of life," and so on. Even so, that Dewey felt the force of pessimism has been denied in a major study of his early years. In *Young John Dewey: An Essay in American Intellectual History*, Neil Coughlan states that Dewey definitely was not dealing with any kind of spiritual crisis, as other thinkers of the age were doing. After providing a splendid account of the bone-chilling despair that gripped Dewey's good friend and philosophical collaborator, G. H. Mead, for countless years of his life, a despair very similar to the one that haunted William James, Coughlan makes this observation:

> All of the intellectual and productive giants with whom Dewey's career is closely associated were afflicted with one or another trouble of the spirit: Mead, James, Veblen, Santayana, Bertrand Russell, even G. Stanley Hall. Dewey alone was exempt. No crabbiness, no *idées fixes*, no discernible fatigue, no alienation.[29]

Dewey alone among his peers, Coughlan states, existed without the spiritual troubles that others shared.

The problem with Coughlan's view of Dewey, however, is that it ignores essays like "The Lesson of Contemporary French Literature," where Dewey is clearly concerned with pessimism. Moreover, even

assuming that Dewey showed no discernible fatigue and that he had
something of the heroic temperament about him, working with immense industry throughout his long life and rarely if ever expressing
despair, it does not follow from this that he had no trouble of the
spirit. Such trouble can manifest itself in many ways, even in produc-
tivity, especially if, as is the case with Dewey, what is produced
amounts to a major effort to come to terms with despair and to teach
us how to live in the face of it. Indeed, as William James biographer
Richard Robertson observes, James maintained that "even for the heroic mind, 'the objects [of despair] are sinister and dreadful, unwel-
come, incompatible with wished-for things.'"[30] What appears to be
Dewey's divine composure in the face of what caused so many others
despair may well be the manner in which he confronts, and philosophically overcomes, his despair, as I hope to show in what follows.

It is worth keeping in mind that Dewey's first published essay was
an attempt to combat materialism, a position closely associated in
Dewey's early days with philosophical despair and pessimism (EW 1:
3–8). In addition, it should be noted that not all biographers agree
with Coughlan about Dewey's untroubled spirit. Robert Westbrook,
for one, emphasizes that in his youth Dewey experienced a profound
sense of "alienation" that he subsequently sought to overcome.[31] Indeed, Dewey even seems to have had a mystical experience in his life,
the nature of which argues strongly in favor of his having confronted
pessimism and won. Westbrook reports that Dewey told Max East-
man he once had an intense moment where he suddenly felt a kind
of absolute security and confidence in life descend upon him, "an
experience of quiet reconciliation with the world, a feeling that
'everything that's here is here, and you can just lie back on it.' He
compared it to the poetic pantheism of Wordsworth or Whitman as
an undramatic yet blissful moment of 'oneness with the universe.' He
would never lose touch with this feeling."[32] That Dewey would experience sudden and profound security in this way suggests a prior state
in which he felt insecure, that is, a state in which he may have felt the
need for security, and which his moment of faith seems to have attained for him.

In any case, Dewey's solution to pessimism at this time, as presented in "The Lessons of Contemporary French Literature," is also faith, faith that human personality—or our distinctly human meanings and values—belongs to the universe after all, and is not wholly alien to nature and the world. It is a faith that human beings fit in; that they are at home in the course of things. "Faith," Dewey explains, "involves the determination that personality shall not be the playground of natural forces, but shall itself be a moving force counting for something in the universe" (EW 3: 42).

What the early Dewey wants to show, above all, is that pessimism can be overcome. Recall that, for him, "the problem of the nineteenth century reduces itself to a choice between faith and pessimism" (EW 3: 42). We must choose one or the other. The gloom of life is too thick to avoid; we must either succumb to it or find the resources to pierce through its darkness. We can find the resources, Dewey thinks, for overcoming this despair, the acute feeling of the emptiness of life. We can legitimately believe that human life is "a moving force counting for something in the universe" (EW 3: 42). We can have faith in life.

It is interesting to note that when Dewey moves away from Bourget's analysis and provides his own account of the problem of pessimism in another early article, he settles on one single and most important cause of the pessimistic temper—the problem of how the scientific understanding of the world affects human life. In "The Present Position of Logical Theory," Dewey notes "the remarkable fact" that the contemporary age is defined by a major "contradiction" (EW 3: 125). The contradiction consists in our simultaneously embracing the scientific account of things (i.e., naturalism) and resisting it. Science has given us an amazing amount of knowledge and the opportunity to understand reality better. We accept it in terms of what it teaches us about the nature of the world. Yet, at the same time, we reject science when it encroaches upon more humane and human areas, such as morality or religion. When it comes to everyday life and its direction, there is no trust in scientific intelligence.

Dewey accounts for this contradiction in our cultural life by saying that "science has got far enough along to make its negative attitude towards previous codes of life evident, while its own positive principle of reconstruction is not yet evident" (EW 3: 125). Science, in other words, has destroyed our previous, inherited beliefs about values and the meaning of life, but it has not replaced them yet with anything else. Science destroys, for example, our previous belief in human personality counting for something in the universe, a belief inherited from Christianity. Instead of the idea of our having a soul, around which the entire drama of the universe revolves, science reduces us to mere physical elements, no different in quality than any other. It displaces man from the center of things and makes him an animal like others, different only in degree of physical organization, not in terms of any higher meaning or significance. Reduced to nature, we can only accept its merciless destiny. "So . . . the methods of physical science, pure naturalism, lead to pessimism simply because they do not allow that free movement of personality called choice" (EW 3: 42). Previously we might have appealed to supernatural aid for the guidance of life; thanks to physical science, we can only appeal to the mindless push and pull of brute physical events.

Science has thus destroyed our previous codes of life, but it has not yet constructed alternatives. It has not yet shown how physical nature could make room for value and the possibility of better and worse directions for living. Science is still only in its destructive stage as regards traditional beliefs and concerns. It merely spells out the facts, facts that vitiate traditional conceptions. We are therefore left with the disintegration of our previous beliefs and nothing in their place. This existential vacuum brought on by science forms for Dewey the crucial, definite form of pessimism. Thanks to science, we are now exposed without assistance to the brute facts of physical nature—to a cruel, indifferent universe of which we are mere playthings. Life now seems completely cold and hopeless by human standards—standards of human warmth, feeling, love, and consideration. "Life," it seems, "is shorn and empty" (EW 3: 40).

It is important to realize that the problem of pessimism thus formulated by Dewey corresponds point for point to the main problematic of Hegelian philosophy. Dewey is saying that where once we thought we were at home within the universe, due to science we have become alienated from it. The experience of such alienation in fact defines the fundamental impulse of Hegel's philosophical efforts as well. "The aim of knowledge," Hegel says, "is to divest the objective world . . . of its strangeness, and, as the phrase is, to find ourselves at home in it."[33] The objective world is strange, for Hegel, because we experience it as other than us—as a series of merely brute, indifferent, physical events, while we experience ourselves warmly and intimately as spirit or mind (or personality). Hegel states explicitly in the preface to the *Phenomenology of Spirit* that the age has lost its old traditions and that his philosophy seeks to rectify this.[34] And he explains how the act of the intellect itself, as soon as it arises, separates off from the universe by distinguishing itself from the objects that it comes to know, an act that, as Robert Stern reminds us, is equivalent to the Fall itself.[35] There is even a story told that Hegel, when asked by Heine to notice how beautiful the stars looked at night, replied, "The stars, hum! hum! The stars are only a gleaming leprosy in the sky."[36] For Hegel, human experience is alienated from the natural world, and the goal of philosophy is to overcome this alienation. Hegelian philosophy seeks to reunite man with nature by showing how nature, after all, contains room for the growth of human spirit.

We can see now, I hope, just how gross a misinterpretation it is of Hegel to say that he naively believed the universe to be some kind of gigantic thinking mind. The impulse of Hegel's philosophy is not to show that "the world is mind," as some critics maintain.[37] The impulse rather is to show that nature is not alien to the human mind, that nature makes room for the human mind. True, Hegel will argue that nature makes room for mind because nature turns out to have been mindlike from the beginning. But, as Richard Schacht has shown, for Hegel the world in the beginning is only *incipient* mind; it is, as it were, merely capable of becoming mind, which it then becomes, in part, when it evolves into thinking, feeling human beings.[38] There is an incipient possibility for mind in nature itself; mind is therefore not an alien addition to the universe, not a foreign element, but rather something happening *inside* the universe as a continuous outgrowth and part of it. Nature is not entirely antithetical to mind, in other words. Nature has room and place for mind in its ongoing development. Such is the major claim of Hegel's philosophy.

We can see, then, that Dewey's own concern with pessimism—with the consequences of human alienation, of personality not counting in the course of things—very much parallels that of Hegel. Like Hegel, Dewey, too, is concerned that our exposure to nature will strike us as a naked exposure to an alien force. The great fear (a fear capable of driving us to despair) is that we simply do not and never will belong to the universe, that we and our values and interests are hopelessly other than the universe, which is indifferent to us from beginning to end. This fear Dewey and Hegel share.

Hegel's influence, in fact, provides the very problematic of Dewey's philosophy. Overcoming pessimism—overcoming the possibility of succumbing to the idea of an indifferent universe—is the primary and sustained motive behind Dewey's early intellectual efforts, just as it was for Hegel, his great teacher. This is not to say that Dewey's early philosophy reduces itself to Hegelianism pure and simple. One can be a disciple in a nonpejorative sense, accepting the general framework and problematic of a given philosopher because these seem to be true to life's needs, and, working within these, offering something new and helpful. One can in this way make an important contribution to the larger effort. It is in this sense that the early Dewey is Hegelian. He accepts the master's problematic, but makes his own original contribution in how he seeks to resolve it.

The general direction of Dewey's original effort to alleviate the problem of pessimism stands out in a single sentence from "The Present Position of Logical Theory." Dewey writes: "It seems to me obvious enough that the contradiction [in our culture] is due to the fact that science has got far enough along to make its negative attitude towards previous codes of life evident, while its own positive principle of reconstruction is not yet evident" (EW 3: 125). Science does have, in other words, a positive direction to offer in the way of reconstructing our destroyed moral and religious beliefs. The problem is that this positive principle is not yet evident. The solution is to make the principle evident.

At this point, again, Dewey draws on Hegel, in terms of a possible solution. Both thinkers want to show how nature *can* produce meaning. But Dewey offers a renewed effort to show it, with special focus on taking science further than it has so far developed and showing how its naturalism is compatible with human meanings. The idea is to show that "science" in the narrow sense of the term, as an intellectual commitment to the facts, is consistent with a philosophical (or Scientific) grasp of the real, in which human meaning is possible. Deweyan idealism forms the scientific wing, as it were, of the Hegelian mansion. His *Psychology*, in particular—an important early work that I will analyze in more detail in chapters 3, 4, 5, and 6—aims to show how facts are consistent with a world of human concern. In particular, in the *Psychology* Dewey will attempt to demonstrate that the creative power of rupture, of breaking away from facts towards their ideal rendering, is actually the means by which facts come to be ideal. The faith in life that Dewey embraces is the faith that in moving away from life (as it is without ideals) we move towards it (as the place where ideals can be realized). We help ideals take shape in facts by negating them as mere facts and reshaping them into something closer to an ideal. We help to make the world more meaningful through our efforts and the world allows us to do so.

Before we consider Dewey's unique solution to the problem of pessimism, however, we will benefit by first lingering a while longer on the nature of the problem. As the later Dewey said, "a problem well put is half-solved" (LW 12: 112). To grasp in full Dewey's solution, we must first understand the true extent and nature of the problem itself. More specifically, we must come to see how deeply engrained the idea has become that facts are *inherently* devoid of all meaning and incapable of being made better by us. We must come to see just how far-ranging in cultural terms—in terms of the overt creations and productions of social life—the problem of pessimism has come to be. We must also appreciate the true philosophical basis of the cultural problem and gain a more thoroughgoing account of its elements and arguments. Only when we appreciate the extent to which Kantianism, in particular, forms the very root of the problem of pessimism as Dewey sees it, can we fully appreciate the way in which Dewey, in drawing on Hegel to go beyond Kant, seeks to go beyond our cultural malaise of pessimism as well.

TWO

CULTURAL AND INTELLECTUAL BACKGROUND

Pessimism as Modernism

A culture of pessimism—what would it look like? What kind of mood or atmosphere would it express? What types of art works would it produce? What creeds would it espouse? Just such a culture existed in Dewey's day, and it went by the name *modernism*. I will first define modernism and then consider Dewey's objections to it. As we will see, defined in philosophical terms, modernism means Kantianism, and it is this philosophy, above all, that the early Dewey opposes.

To define modernism, I will make special reference to Vienna at the turn of the twentieth century, for it is here that, to my mind, the movement finds its most characteristic expression, although we must remember that modernism was a major cultural movement affecting the entire Western world, and not just Vienna. Allan Janik and Stephen Toulmin explain modernism in their book *Wittgenstein's Vienna* in relation to the great cultural critic Karl Kraus.[1] Kraus, they say, who was influenced by Schopenhauer and Kierkegaard, developed a worldview according to which there existed something deeper and more mysterious than the everyday, apparent world.[2] Kraus thought of this distinction explicitly in terms of gender. As Janik and Toulmin make clear, Kraus thought of the feminine in terms of emotions and the masculine in terms of instrumental reason.

> The emotional essence of woman is not wanton or nihilistic, but is rather a tender *fantasy*, which serves as the unconscious origin of all that has any worth in human experience. Herein lies the source of all inspiration and creativity. Reason itself is merely a technique, a means by which men obtain what they desire. In itself it is neither good nor evil, it is merely effective or ineffective. Reason must be supplied with proper goals from outside; it must be given direction of a moral or aesthetic type. The feminine fantasy fecundates the masculine reason and gives it this direction.[3]

On the one side, we have instrumental reason, which aims to get things done. On the other, we have creative fantasy, which is deeper and more mysterious, and which gives direction to what we do. Emotion provides the ends of action, reason the means.

Janik and Toulmin make clear too that, as Kraus sees it, "fantasy . . . is under attack on all sides in the modern world."[4] Kraus felt that instrumental reason was dominating the world, leaving little room for fantasy in our lives. He thought that the modern, bureaucratic world, which privileged functional reason, provided almost no space for the deeper, more difficult-to-define aspects of our existence, so that we were everywhere compelled to act but without any real feeling. We obeyed reason's command to achieve things, to be effective, but we lost any sense of what we ought to achieve. The modern world was dominated by a cold business culture devoid of the "tender fantasy" or feeling that alone gives meaningful direction to our lives.[5] The proper response to this situation, many Krausians believed, was to withdraw from the world into one's own inner private life.

The movement known as modernism was born, in Vienna at least, from these Krausian reflections. An eruption of intense cultural activity occurred in their wake. Janik and Toulmin explain how in various arts, and in philosophy as well, Kraus's fundamental ideas find expression. In architecture, Adolf Loos, the master functionalist, strove to put reason in its place by stripping his buildings of all ornament: the rational purpose of a building was to stand on its own; any aspects of beauty or feeling were to be found outside of reason and rational function. Fantasy was to be preserved by keeping it out of the picture—its mysterious sources to be untouched and unmolested by reason.[6]

In painting, Gustav Klimt and Oskar Kokoschka affected a similar aim by trying to allow the deeper, expressive meaning of their subjects to shine forth from their paintings.[7] As Carl Schorske has discussed in *Fin-de-Siècle Vienna: Politics and Culture*, Klimt broke with tradition and gave wild, uninhibited expression to his sexual fantasies.[8] Thus he painted naked young women in postures of writhing ecstasy, in, for example, *Watersnakes II* and *Fishblood*.[9] His works bordered on the pornographic, and as Schorske points out, for Klimt this liberation of inner life actually "was turning into a nightmare of anxiety."[10] With his instinctive life freed from all constraint, Klimt in some sense became horrified by what he saw.

Kokoschka, for his part, "sought the spiritual within the intensely individual faces he painted." He tried to "bring out the reflection of a man's character dynamically in his face, especially his eyes, and in his hands."[11] Here again a deeper, hidden meaning was revealed beneath the merely surface phenomena. It should be noted, however, that for Kokoschka, as for Klimt, the freedom of inner expression led to fearful results. In his depiction of male-female relationships, Kokoschka broke out into openly sadistic work, for example depicting a man strangling a woman and trying to stab her.[12] Thus, modernism clearly had a darker side that must be noted to fully understand the movement. There was no guarantee that the deeper meanings underneath human reason were benign or even healthy.

Indeed, as Käthe Springer has observed, dark and disturbing results grew out of modernism in Vienna. "The Viennese decadent movement," as Springer calls it, "looked for the inner person, sought out his moods, and distanced themselves from nature and the external world."[13] The result was "the glorification of the irrational and the artificial, an attraction to illness and decay. . . . The prevailing mood involved a sense of the fleeting nature of all things . . . and the constant presence of death—expressing the individual and collective insecurity of the times and their pessimistic presentiments."[14] Ungrounded, separated entirely from the external world, the inner psyche of the modernist risked becoming unhinged. In music a similar Krausian separation of creative fantasy and reason was achieved by the great modernist musician Arnold Schoenberg, whose creations could also be very dark. Schoenberg "wished to teach them [composers] *how to express themselves.*"[15] To achieve greater expressive power, he developed atonal music, music that freed composers from reliance on the traditional systems of a music organized around a single, most important tone. He also created the twelve-tone system, whose aim was to help the composer express his or her own inner artistic integrity.[16] What mattered to Schoenberg was not the sound of the composition, but its genuineness.[17] To achieve this "authenticity of the musical idea," the composer must engage in "a 'creative separation' of all dramatic or poetical ornament from the musical idea itself and its presentation according to the laws of musical logic."[18] Only by breaking away from all things save the musical idea itself, and its logic, could the composer truly and freely express the rich range of feelings he had within himself.

Janik and Toulmin explain, lastly, how in philosophy, through Ludwig Wittgenstein's *Tractatus Logico-Philosophicus*, Krausian ideas manifest themselves as well.[19] This is a long story, but in essence the early Wittgenstein tried to achieve a total separation of the reasoned, instrumentalized world and the mysterious worlds of fantasy, feeling, and imagination.[20] In the first, larger part of the *Tractatus*, Wittgenstein shows what we can speak about, that is, the everyday, matter-of-fact worlds of empirical life and scientific knowledge, which are imbued with rational (that is, instrumental) purpose. But by culminating his work with, in the words of Newton Garver, a "remark . . . commending silence for everything other than scientific statements,"[21] Wittgenstein opens up a space for all the rest—for what lies beyond scientific and instrumental reasoning, namely ethics and aesthetics, which remain untouched by reason. These cannot be spoken about, cannot be rationalized or reduced to mere calculation. They remain powerful, determining motives in a person's character despite the rationally overdetermined world.[22]

In each of these cases, we have an immense cultural achievement—an achievement in architecture, painting, music, and philosophy. Each case rests on the idea that a deeper, more expressive side to life lies beneath reason. Beneath our intelligible, communicable, matter-of-fact existence, an abyss of unmasterable emotions resides, a profound source of all imagination, and of deeper, richer nuances of meaning. Drawing on Schorske's claim that Nietzsche was a major figure in the modernist tradition and that Nietzsche's concept of the Dionysian was vital to that tradition, we can say that in the modernist view of existence there exists something like Nietzsche's Dionysian revelry beneath the Socratic picture of the intelligible world.[23]

In his book *Fin-de-Siècle Vienna*, Carl Schorske explains the meaning of modernism most precisely in political terms:

> Traditional liberal culture had centered upon rational man, whose scientific domination of nature and whose moral control of himself were expected to create the good society. In our century, rational man has had to give place to that richer but more dangerous and mercurial creature, psychological man. This new man is not merely a rational animal, but a creature of feeling and instinct. We tend to make him the measure of all things in our culture. Our intrasubjectivist artists paint him. Our existential philosophers try to make him meaningful. Our social scientists, politicians, and advertising men manipulate him.[24]

The essence of modernism is the discovery of psychological man—the discovery of a hidden version of ourselves, existing at a level deeper than that of the everyday, transparent self. In effect, it turns out that we are not fully rational beings, after all, as the liberal tradition maintains. The name alone of Sigmund Freud (another denizen of late nineteenth-century Vienna) helps capture the true meaning of the modernist reaction against the totally rational man of liberal culture. A new, precarious view of ourselves has appeared on the scene, and henceforth we would be unable to escape the view that we have a darker, less intelligible side that determines who and what we are. Unconscious drives, not rational and intelligible motives, guide our behavior. The assumptions of traditional liberalism are incorrect. We are not sturdy ships captained by our rational minds. We are more like ships gliding through the sea without a captain. The captain we had counted on, human reason, turns out to have been a phantom all along.

Dewey's Response to Modernism

It turns out that Dewey was well aware of modernism thus defined—namely, as a widespread cultural phenomenon that maintained a rigid separation between the transparent, everyday world of conscious thought and our deeper and richer emotional contacts with the world. Dewey could not, after all, have been unaware of this massive cultural phenomenon, and as a thoughtful and even brilliant young man, he must have had an opinion regarding what was happening around him.

Dewey's response to modernism can best be captured, perhaps, in an early essay of 1890 entitled "Poetry and Philosophy." While generally sympathetic to the nature of the problem modernists confronted—how to find meaning in the world—Dewey's response emphatically rejects the modernist solution of withdrawing into the deeper and more hidden resources of the self in order to find that meaning. Dewey begins this essay with a quote from Matthew Arnold: " 'The future of poetry is immense, because in poetry our race . . . will find an ever surer and surer stay' " (EW 3: 110).[25] In the quoted statement, Arnold makes a quintessentially modernist claim that poetry will replace religion, science, and philosophy as guides to life, because modern life demands ever-greater access to human feeling (and poetry, presumably, is more about feeling).

Explaining Arnold's position, Dewey writes:

> In a world of disintegrated intelligence and a broken authority, Arnold sees men more and more turning to poetry for consolation. . . . We may say science is verifiable, but it lacks sympathy, consolation, humanity; it does not afford instruction where instruction is most wanted,—in the ordering of life. (EW 3: 110)

Science seems to destroy our traditional beliefs and challenges the deeper needs of our feelings. Poetry, on the other hand, provides "a kind sympathy with all of its [life's] colored moods." Therefore, as Dewey puts it, "What more do we want? What more natural than, in the difficulty of our times, men turning to poetry for guidance?" (EW 3: 111). Here, indeed, is the essence of modernism; Dewey has put his finger precisely upon it. The liberal tradition, with its emphasis on reason and science, has lost its hold; it has become too abstract, indifferent, and remote. Belief in a promising rational order has disintegrated, leaving men with their feelings and instincts (expressed by poetry) as the true guides to life.

Arnold's poetry is instructive in this regard, as Dewey sees it. For it speaks openly of the loss of order and meaning that besets the age. "Arnold's distinguishing sign . . . is the melancholy beauty with which he has voiced the sense of loss; his sad backward glance at the departure of old faiths and ideals . . . the shapeless, hopeless hope for the dawn of a new joy, new faith" (EW 3: 114–15). Here again we have the central problem of the age, as Dewey conceives it: the problem of the broken authority of traditional codes of conduct and the absence of anything to replace them. Once again, too, the culprit is science, or rather the fact it seems to reveal about nature—that nature is ultimately indifferent to human concerns. "The source of regret which expires from Arnold's lines is his consciousness of . . . his isolation from nature. . . . No longer, he seems to say, may man believe in his oneness with the dear nature about him: the sense of a common spirit binding them together has vanished" (EW 3: 115). Dewey offers a quote from Arnold to make his point:

> Thou hast been, shalt be, art alone:
> Or, if not quite alone, yet they

> Who touch thee are unmating things,—
> Ocean and clouds, and night and day,
> Lorn autumns and triumphant springs.
>   (EW 3: 115)[26]

There is no genuine connection possible with nature. For, as we have come to see, "nature lacks the element of purpose which alone could give joyful response to man's needs. . . . Nature goes her own way and man must return to his" (EW 3: 115).

With man thus fundamentally isolated, no amount of patchwork will make the connection. No reason can be found in nature, perhaps not even in our own nature. In truth, for Arnold, we have nothing to fall back on to find a home but our instincts and feelings, since human thought and science present so thoroughly inhospitable a world. Thus poetry and not science should be our guide in life. We have lost all faith in science, which has treated mankind's real needs so roughly. Only by withdrawing into poetry—a more emotional discipline—can we find a vital response to our innermost needs and feelings.

For Arnold, we cannot even turn for aid to other people, to a sense of community, for the old creed of community too has been destroyed by science. Science destroys our belief in the spiritual bonds that once united the majority of human beings in the West, and as a result it leaves us with only our own dear, animal selves that we seek to take care of above all else. "The life of common brotherhood, the struggle and destiny of Christianity has given way to the old isolated struggle of the individual" (EW 3: 116). Thus Arnold writes:

> No man can save his brother's soul
> Nor pay his brother's debt.
>   (EW 3: 116)

Each man is thrown back solely on himself. Neither in nature nor the social world can a person find meaning. Thus, Arnold's "last message is one of weakness and despair" (EW 3: 117). The individual is completely withdrawn and helpless. He is totally isolated and can find no meaning outside of himself. But it is precisely here, on the other hand, that Arnold does offer some solace, in Dewey's reading. There is a melancholy beauty in his poems, after all (EW 3: 114). The beauty comes from the sorrowful realization that, precisely because of his total isolation, the individual has only himself to trust and may even find an uncanny strength in himself.

> If man is isolated, in that isolation he may find himself, and, finding himself, living his own life, lose all his misery. . . . Isolation is translated into self-dependence. Separation throws man farther into himself, deepens his consciousness of his own destiny and of his own law. (EW 3: 117)

Isolation shows man the strength of his own law. Withdrawn, impotent isolation now becomes the experience of man in opposition to nature, the experience of man relying entirely on his inner strength and, in this reliance, finding himself able to create a new and potent direction to take.

Now, according to Dewey, it is precisely to the isolated individual that poetry, in Arnold's conception, responds. Poetry allows our full, inner expression free reign, and thus it responds better as a medium for conveying our isolated, inner strength. Poetry lets us evoke our loss, while freeing up our individual response, our purely emotional side, and thus it speaks to us of a new strength, which legitimates our inner, isolated experiences. Thus, according to Arnold, poetry alone can be our guide in life. It alone succeeds in giving meaning and direction where science, and our embrace of the outer world of nature, fails.

Dewey himself describes this schism between poetry and science—or between human needs and the facts of nature—as a "wound" that we most definitely feel (EW 3: 123). He agrees with Arnold and modernism that this predicament characterizes our times. "We need not be detained by what our critic says regarding the existing disintegration of intellectual authority," Dewey says. "All will admit readily that there is enough of unrest, enough of doubt in modern thought, to make it worthwhile to raise this question, Where shall we find authority, the instruction which our natures demand?

Shall we cease to find it in philosophy, or in science, and shall we find it in poetry?" (EW 3: 111). These are legitimate questions; they express the real problem, on our hands today, of trying to determine how, in the face of modern science and what it tells us about nature, man is to find a place for human meaning. Dewey fully agrees with this manner of characterizing the problem of his age and ours, but he thinks that Arnold's solution to the problem—that is, his intentional withdrawal into inner life and away from external nature and fact—is deeply problematic, for it seems to condemn us forever to a separation between human meaning and nature. If we withdraw into ourselves, Dewey thinks, we only reaffirm the loss of meaning; we only render nature truly devoid of human sentiment and value and so render it a place from which we should want to withdraw in the first place. Withdrawal into the self produces no meaning, no significance in nature, which is what the modern self really longs for in the end. Instead of producing true significance, such withdrawal, in affirming that nature is devoid of meaning, only leads to "the agnosticism, the doubt, the pessimism, of the present day" (EW 3: 114). It is better to reject the modernist separation of man from nature from the very start, and to begin with the argument that nature is *already* imbued with its own meanings, if only we know how to go out to nature and affirm it in the correct manner. The "wound" of modernism, in other words, is not intrinsic; it is not a feature of reality but rather a cultural assumption that we must learn how to reject, above all, by conceiving of nature in a different way, as a sphere of reality in which value and significance already exist, that is, as a whole that includes human values within it.

Said another way, Dewey is asserting that even in poetry, there is no unmediated access to a separate self and its meaning, detached from the rest of the world. The poet, too, gets his or her meaning from an already existent scheme of meanings, and hence there are options in terms of how to regard a given poet's works. Poetry does not automatically privilege the modernist conception; it depends on the prior scheme of meaning at work. And Dewey is arguing that we need another scheme than the one the modernist has developed. In Dewey's words,

> Life is not a raw, unworked material. . . . As it comes to the poet,
> life is already a universe of meanings, of interpretations. . . . For
> good or for ill, centuries of reflective thought have been interpret-
> ing life, and their interpretations remain the basis and furnish
> the instrument for all the poet may do; he may simply use the
> assimilated results of the labors of scientific men and philoso-
> phers. (EW 3: 113)

So we can see that Dewey severely criticizes modernism. His view
is that the reasoned, intelligible world that precedes the poet is the
genuine one, the fundamental one. As he says above, the poet "may
simply use the assimilated results of the labors of scientific men and
philosophers." The poet has no special access to anything deeper than
our inherited, everyday meanings provide. He can only respond to
the intelligible world around him; to achieve anything else is to be
lost in *mere* fantasy—something that presumably is without any direction or legitimate force, "the stagnant marshes of sentiment" (EW
3: 113). To help make his case that the poet responds to the already-
interpreted world, the everyday, intelligible world, not to a private,
detached meaning of the self, Dewey contrasts the poetry of Arnold
with that of Robert Browning. The claim he wishes to make is that
each poet responds to meanings that are already present in the world
around them, but in different ways, depending on different circumstances, so that there are, in fact, options for us other than the modernist option.

Dewey prefers Browning's poetry to Arnold's, for, unlike Arnold's,
it gives us an indication that we can somehow bridge the gap between
the facts of nature and the needs of man. Browning's poetry is full of
joy and affirmation in the face of life's tensions, rather than despair.
"Browning reads a tale of keen and delicious joy. . . . [T]he trumpet
peal of an abounding life bursts from Browning" (EW 3: 119). Dewey
notes the "strenuous, abounding, triumphant optimism" of Browning, quoting him thus:

> How good is man's life, the men living! How fit to employ
> All the heart and the soul and the senses forever in joy!
>
> (EW 3: 119)

"What is the source of this note of Browning?" Dewey asks. And he answers: "Browning knows and tells of no isolation of man from nature, of man from man" (EW 3: 120). "The abundance, the intensity, the vibrating fullness, the impassioned sanity of his verse" results from the truth that Browning expresses: the "realization that the world was made for man, and that man was made for man" (EW 3: 120). As Dewey again quotes Browning,

> The world's no blot for us,
> No blank. It means intensely and means good.
>
> (EW 3: 120)

And again:

> Such a soul,
> Such a body, and then such an earth,
> For ensphering the whole!
>
> The earth's first stuff
> Was neither more nor less, enough
> To house man's soul, man's need fulfill.
>
> How the world is made for each of us!
> All we perceive and know in it
> Tends to some moment's product thus
> When the soul declares itself.
>
> (EW 3: 120)

We have here the starkest contrast with the modernism of Matthew Arnold. This contrast reveals clearly the early Dewey's overall efforts. Neither our isolation from one another, Dewey wants to show, nor our alienation from nature, is the way of humankind. Rather it is connection and belonging. "How the world is made for each of us!"—this is the early Dewey's most deeply felt and abiding intuition, which his entire philosophy will seek to justify and make good. Modernism, by contrast, keeps us apart from one another, and keeps us separated from nature, as alien beings in a foreign land. Its characteristic expression might rather be: "How nothing in the world is made for me—and how urgently therefore I must withdraw into myself alone as my only consolation!" It is precisely this sentiment and the beliefs that seem to support it that Dewey's early philosophy will above all seek to combat.

The Kantian Origin of Modernism

To delve deeper into the meaning of modernism, we must try to appreciate its philosophical underpinnings. We must try to translate it, in other words, into the general language of philosophical concepts, the better to understand what modernism is, what arguments hold it together—and what arguments might potentially dismantle it, as Dewey wants to do.

Janik and Toulmin are again instructive. At the heart of modernism they find Kantian philosophy at work. Of the modernist debate, they write: "In order to see most clearly the philosophical issues involved . . . we must place them in their historical perspective. This means seeing them in the light of the arguments put forward by the two men who did most to shape the questions under discussion in that debate—namely, Immanuel Kant himself and Arthur Schopenhauer."[27] It was Kant who first gave clearest expression to the matter at hand, while Schopenhauer, as "a Kantian revisionist,"[28] took it to its logical conclusion. The matter at hand—a thoroughly Kantian one—is the idea that the world is split into two "spheres," the human (or evaluative one) and the physical (or factual) one.

Kant had shown, as Janik and Toulmin explain, that there are limits to human reason, but that the human mind is nonetheless predisposed to reach beyond these limits and to " 'precipitate itself into darkness.' "[29]

> The whole of the 'critical philosophy' is directed toward explaining the proper limits of reason and showing how these limits are overstepped because of reason's innate tendency to pass from sensible experience itself to an explanation of that experience, although such an explanation lies beyond it in the sphere of 'things in themselves.' There is a natural disposition on the part of reason to explain the world of perception in terms of an intelligible world beyond the possibility of perception.[30]

Kant himself wished to confine our knowledge to the side of our perception, to what can be sensed by us, while discounting any claims to knowledge of what lies outside of and causes our experience. He thus reduced our knowledge to physical, tangible events, while undermining the possibility of our having any knowledge of metaphysical ideas of directly human concern, ideas such as God, freedom, and immortality. Nonetheless, Kant reserved a function in human life for these metaphysical ideas.

> Even though it is not possible for us to form a definite idea of what lies beyond experience . . . such ideas as those of the soul, of the world and of God . . . are not without a function . . . they provide the ethical theorist with notions which serve to protect him against the temptation to take materialism, naturalism or fatalism really seriously.[31]

The ethical function of these ideas is to allow us to get beyond the factual world and to posit the existence of objects of truly human (or evaluative) concern as well. Although we are not entitled to say we *know* of the existence of God, freedom, and immortality (since these go beyond any possible experience), nonetheless we are entitled to believe in their existence as forming the bases of our experience, since it is useful to believe so and since, not knowing for sure what lies beyond our experience, it is possible to believe that they do lie there.

Thus, "having started from the idea that reason has an innate tendency to overstep its limits, Kant's critique of reason thus proceeds by positing—and distinguishing—two spheres of activity . . . : the sphere of facts, and that of values."[32] Kant has legitimated, or made room for, each separate sphere. Our knowledge is confined to what we sense, objects in space and time mechanically obeying the law of causality. Our knowledge cannot pass beyond this without creating "intellectual monsters which fetter speculation."[33] And yet there must be some cause to our experience, some "thing-in-itself" that grounds it and makes it possible (or else it would not exist); and we are entitled to believe that this ground has something to do with "the nature of Man as a rational being" and can therefore "provide a foundation for ethics."[34] Thus Kant posits that there is a realm of values existing beyond our actual experience of physical objects themselves.

And here we have the very essence of modernism. As we have seen, modernism is a cultural movement in which reason comes to seem limited, and the need is felt to press beyond it to less intellectual and more irrational forces. And in almost every cultural expression of modernism, these forces amount to a hidden source of values, as in Kraus's conception of the "creative fantasy" that gives birth to aesthetic and moral considerations, or in Arnold's concept of man in isolation from nature who gains a hidden source of moral strength in his isolation. Here, in cultural terms, we have the equivalent of Kant's separation of facts and values—and the impulse to move away from the factual world to its evaluative basis beyond.

The picture becomes more complete when we turn to the philosophy of Arthur Schopenhauer, who was himself, by his own admission, a Kantian thinker, accepting the core of Kant's philosophy as true and vital.[35] Schopenhauer's innovation, according to Janik and Toulmin, consisted of having sharpened even more the Kantian separation of fact and value, and of drawing his famously dark and pessimistic conclusions from the separation.[36] With this move, Schopenhauer became a virtual patron saint of modernism. The cultural heroes of modernism were confirmed Schopenhauerians, drawing on his pessimistic version of Kantianism to fuel their resignation from the natural world and their move into the realm of vague, poetic fantasy.[37]

What Schopenhauer adds to Kant, more specifically, is the idea that although we cannot know what lies beyond the world of facts, nonetheless we can *feel* it. Our own willing, Schopenhauer thinks, lies closest to what exists in itself, first, because we ourselves, in our innermost nature, must—like everything that is—be part of the in-itself; and second, because willing, unlike rational knowledge and perception, involves less representational cognition—cognition that would tend to separate our knowing from what is known. Our willing, which we directly feel, is less representational, less removed, much less of a copy, than our other modes of cognition. Hence, our feelings of willing correspond more closely than our perceptions and cognitions with what exists in its own right, beyond all merely human representation of what exists.[38]

For Schopenhauer what this means is that our willing gives us a fairly good sense of what exists in itself, of the nature of reality. Underneath all of our representations, behind all cognition of facts, there is a blind "striving" force (similar to our willing) that makes up the true character of the world. This blind force is a kind of erotic energy, a perpetual hunger and desire, that surges like a mad current beneath all surface phenomena and conditions our behavior in ways we cannot always understand. Our own wills are but the product of this one Will, this blind, universal striving at work in all things.[39]

Schopenhauer's philosophy led him to conclude that the proper response to reality is resignation. The factual world, grounded in the irrational (and insatiable) blind striving Will, could be no source of human comfort and reasonableness. It is better, he argued, to withdraw from nature and the world and to take a detached and disinterested stance towards things. Only in retreat into our own disinterested contemplation of the pointless striving of things would we find any solace.[40]

The modernists who were smitten with Schopenhauer saw in his concept of the Will the source of all creative energy, behind all reason, which we must tap into to be truly authentic. We must part company with the physical world of objects, the world of the push and pull of cause and effect, which is a mere illusion of our cognitive faculties; underneath lies the true reality, even though this reality, too, is ultimately fleeting and inconsequential.[41]

Moreover, it is only when we thus withdraw from nature that we can attain a genuine moral sense. For in Schopenhauer's view the factual, everyday world, being grounded in the Will, is a scene of endless egoism and rivalry, the "striving" of each creature's will against the other's. But beneath these individual creaturely agonies there is the one Will, fighting with itself in its various manifestations. Realizing this, Schopenhauer thinks, is the source of compassion (or "'feeling-with'")[42]: we realize that the other's will is our own will; we each share the will, and so a genuine response to the other (a more authentic response) consists in denying my own will on behalf of his will (and his denying his will on my behalf). To truly resign from the Will, in other words, would mean to resign from my own willing in the face of the other. Only by resigning from the factual domain of my separate ego and its objects, in which the Will is at work, am I capable of ethical action. Only by denying myself do I deny the Will in me and attain any value beyond cut-throat nature.[43]

Janik and Toulmin explain how Søren Kierkegaard—who also greatly influenced the artists and thinkers of modernism—completes the philosophical picture of the modernist tradition. Kierkegaard locates meaning in life solely in the human subject or "'inwardness.'" Locked wholly in itself, without an external world it can relate to, our inward sense can only hope for an objective correlate to its inner needs. There is absolutely no guarantee that objective conditions will meet our spiritual needs. All we can do, in despair, is take a "'leap into the absurd'" and hope that they will do so. We thus believe despite all—an absurd position that, for Kierkegaard, stands at the basis of faith.[44]

The philosophical underpinnings of modernism should now be clear. Modernism begins with the Kantian idea that facts and values are separate; it continues with the Schopenhaurian resignation from the realm of facts and his belief in the irrational basis of value that exists beyond all facts; and it ends with Kierkegaard's total enclosure of all meaning in isolated, despairing inwardness. Any rational endeavor to connect spirit to world is abandoned. All of these philosophers agreed that the factual world (nature) could contain by itself no real value, at least not for human beings. To attain genuine value, they argued, we must stand outside of nature, in a separate realm—a more distinctly human realm, in which we ground our values, such as compassion and love, despite the world's indifferent and merciless course.

It thus turns out that modernism has its origins in Kantian philosophy. It was Kant who first (and most persuasively) argued that values can come only from outside facts, from outside of nature and its happenings. While Kant certainly would have disagreed with Schopenhauer and Kierkegaard that there is an irrational basis to morality (Kant found that basis in the rational will), nonetheless for Kant the source of value is beyond overt human experience of the natural world. It comes solely from our autonomy as rational beings, from something therefore beyond physical nature and its bare mechanical occurrences. And this is precisely the core idea of modernism: that we have nature on one side, and human spirit on the other.

If we return now to Dewey's response to modernism as demonstrated in "Poetry and Philosophy," it is interesting to note that he, too, was keenly aware of the Kantian roots of the cultural revolution that had closed in around him. In this essay of 1890, after having laid out Arnold's modernist position in detail, Dewey observes: "This is . . . precisely in the vein of Kant" (EW 3: 118). What Arnold and modernism give us is what Kant gives us: "the individual as shut off from real communion with nature and with fellow-man, and yet as bearing in himself a universal principle . . . within himself finding the secret of a new strength, the source of a new consolation" (EW 3: 118). The early Dewey, it must be said, had a very clear idea of the modernist tradition that had become part of his cultural milieu. He understood readily that this was a Kantian tradition; that it was, in fact, Kantian philosophy that led us to despair of ever finding a truly human connection to nature; and that, as such, it was Kantianism in general that we must combat if we would overcome this despair and affirm natural life as compatible with human interests.

To combat Kantianism, Dewey first makes a move that has important consequences for his entire approach. He translates the whole problematic of Kantianism, modernism, and pessimism into a technical philosophical vocabulary, the better to handle its claims. The agreed-upon terms are *fact* and *thought* (or sometimes *reality* and *ideas*; EW 3: 126). The word *fact* is meant to convey, in compressed form, the natural world in its otherness. Fact is the way nature is, regardless of human wishes and ideals. *Thought* means not only our cognition but, even more importantly, the vast complex of uniquely human, or even spiritual, meanings that humans entertain. It means the human mind or spirit, and thus includes values, norms, warmth, human kindness, compassion. It designates the specifically human part of our nature.

These terms must be kept firmly in mind because of the way Dewey chooses to address the problem of pessimism, that is, largely in terms of its philosophical equivalents. The previous chapter gave some consideration to one of Dewey's most important essays in this regard, namely "The Present Position of Logical Theory"—a text with an innocuous-sounding title. Logical theory, Dewey explains in this text, is the theory of "the relation of fact and thought to each other" (EW 3: 126). We miss Dewey's point entirely if we fail to appreciate the fuller meanings behind his technical use of the terms *fact* and *thought*. It is a mistake to view his efforts to relate facts and thoughts to each other as purely philosophical (in the pejorative sense), as dealing only with abstract considerations of how thinking can hook onto the world—considerations that for all apparent purposes have no larger implications than solving a difficult epistemological puzzle. In truth, when the early Dewey wonders about "the relation of fact and thought to each other," what he really wants to know is how it is possible, if it is possible at all, to understand nature in such a way as to make room for human value and feeling, for spirit or "personality." How can we overcome our extreme despair in the face of an alien nature and find a human meaning within it? How can we overcome pessimism—the conviction that we shall never be at home in life—and affirm life instead? How can facts, in short, relate happily to our thoughts, if at all—how can the reality of things relate to our human meanings?

We know what modernism (i.e., Kantianism) answers. It says that no such connection is rationally possible. To secure specifically spiritual meanings and values, we must flee from the natural world into our essentially removed subjectivity.

But for Dewey this answer only exacerbates the problem, as we have seen in the case of Matthew Arnold. With this idea in mind, we will only confront nature again and again as an alien entity, inhospitable to our desires; we will continue to feel the homelessness and

loss. To see whether a better answer is possible, one with a more satisfying result, the early Dewey turns to the philosophy of Hegel. He
uses Hegel to overcome Kant and thereby to confront the despairing
pessimism of his age, the pessimism of modernism; or as he himself
puts it, he aims to "heal this unnatural wound" that is the separation
of thought from fact in our culture (EW 3: 123).

With this advance to a Hegelian solution, we arrive at the early
Dewey's own constructive effort and solution to the modernist problem. Through Hegel, he will try to refute the Kantian separation of
facts and thought. He will endeavor to show how facts themselves are
able to develop into thought, into spirit and meaning. He will show
how to heal the wound of pessimism by demonstrating how our explicitly human meanings can belong to reality after all.

Hegel over Kant

Dewey begins "The Present Position of Logical Theory," as we saw in
the previous chapter, with an introduction to the contradiction affecting contemporary society—its simultaneous affirmation and denial of facts. We affirm the facts insofar as we accept science and what
it teaches us about the world, while we also deny their reality by taking flight from them in isolated spirit or thought. We thereby keep
meaning apart from actual existence; we deny meaning to existence.

Dewey then shifts grounds to logical theory, to seek there relief
from the contradiction. Logical theory studies "the relation of fact
and thought to each other, of reality and ideas" (EW 3: 126). Dewey
resists identifying logical theory with formal logic, which he refers to
as a "superstition which . . . holds enthralled so much of modern
thought" (EW 3: 127). "It is true enough," he says,

> that nobody now takes the technical subject of formal logic very
> seriously—unless here and there some belated "professor." . . .
> But while the subject itself as a doctrine or science hardly ranks
> very high, the conception of thought which is at the bottom of
> formal logic still dominates the *Zeitgeist*. . . . Any book of formal
> logic will tell us what this conception of thought is: thought

is a faculty or an entity existing in the mind, apart from facts,
having its own fixed forms, with which facts have nothing to do.
(EW 3: 127)

Dewey's objection to formal logic is that it conceives of thought apart
from facts. It cleaves the world in two, thereby perfectly embodying
the problem of the age.

"The Present Position of Logical Theory" is crucial to the young
Dewey's entire philosophical approach.[45] The core idea of the essay is
that, following Hegel, we should understand thought not as a kind of
"apriorism" (EW 3: 136), something forced upon facts from without
in order to make them fit our ideas, but rather as something the facts
themselves are capable of, something developed out of facts when
they are understood (EW 3: 136–39). Facts become amenable to
thought in their own development; they become meaningful. We are
speaking, Dewey says, about "the evolution of fact into meaning"
(EW 3: 133).

According to Dewey, it was Kant who forced thought on facts.
Hegel went beyond Kant by holding that we can never force thought
on facts, only let facts themselves develop as they do and then perceive the thought working in them (EW 3: 136–39).[46] This, in truth, is
what science does; it demonstrates the laws, the rationality, at work
in the actual world, and for this reason Dewey explains that "I conceive Hegel . . . to represent the quintessence of the scientific spirit"
(EW 3: 138). Both Hegel's philosophy and the scientific spirit seek to
show the rational interconnections of events, to demonstrate that
facts can be systematically grasped, rather than merely lying about in
unorganized pieces (EW 3: 139). The question, therefore, is not
whether Hegel has forced forms on facts, but whether the facts, as
systematically arranged and grasped by science, actually do lead to
these forms in specific details. Hegel's own position stands or falls
with what we can say about the facts that science discovers about the
world: can we say they amount to order and significance, as Hegel
contends, or only to chaos, disintegration, and indifference to human
concerns?

This approach to Hegel, incidentally, poses a challenge to some more recent Hegel scholarship, most notably Alison Stone's *Petrified Intelligence: Nature in Hegel's Philosophy*. Stone develops "an interpretation of the *Philosophy of Nature* as composed according to the strong *a priori* method."[47] She endeavors to show that Hegel *does* impose forms of meaning on facts, and that this is indeed a good thing, since it helps us to "identify a determinate a problem with the scientific approach: it rests on inadequate metaphysical assumptions."[48] By arguing for the imposition of different forms from those of science, forms such as spirit and purpose, Hegel, in this reading, seeks to show up science's own limitations (its supposition of the indifference of matter).

Dewey, by contrast, views Hegel as much less of a Kantian; indeed, Dewey sees the philosopher as someone who eschews all forms of apriorism. In Dewey's view, Hegel in a sense depends on science to corroborate, not this or that special claim about reality, but the general trend and development of reality itself toward rationality. In this view, it is not that we impress *a priori* forms on facts, but rather that facts themselves can be described in such a way that they can be said to *allow for* the development of human meanings and values out of themselves. From Dewey's perspective, Stone simply reasserts the main problem of the age, which is that human significance is divorced from real, true, actual events, which require *our* forms to take on meaning; and she makes Hegel culpable in this modernist error as well, when in fact Hegel's great achievement was to show the way out. In Dewey's reading, Hegel

> denies not only the possibility of getting truth out of a formal, apart thought, but he denies the existence of any faculty of thought which is other than the expression of fact itself. His contention is not that "thought," in the scholastic sense, has ontological validity, but that fact, reality is significant. (EW 3: 138–139)

As a result of this, even if Hegel could be shown by science to be in error in specific details, "his main principle would be unimpeached until it is shown that fact has not a systematic, or interconnected, meaning, but is a mere hodgepodge of fragments." But "whether the scientific spirit," Dewey continues, "would have any interest in such a hodgepodge may, at least, be questioned" (EW 3: 139).

Dewey thus rather deftly shifts the ground from idealism to science, or the systematic rendering of observable and verifiable facts. He makes the truth of idealism dependent on scientific insight, or what we can legitimately say about facts. He claims that no matter how objective, how much within the facts, spiritual meaning may turn out to be—as idealism maintains it will be—"yet to man this objective significance cannot be real till he has made it *out* in the details of scientific processes, and *made* it in applied science, in invention" (EW 3: 140). Dewey's own philosophy thereafter, at least his early philosophy, becomes an attempt to answer a single question: "Has the application of scientific thought to the world of fact gone far enough so that we can speak, without seeming strained, of the rationality of fact?" (EW 3: 140). In other words, do science and its inventions actually lend themselves to showing that facts are rational, that existence is significant and meaningful, as Hegel contends?

If it were so, we would have a solution to the problem of the age. The dread of indifferent nature would lose its grip. Facts would be shown to lead to meaningful qualities, to spiritual values, and life therefore would be shown to be meaningful, something worth living. Pessimism would be defeated. And so also a new, more coherent culture beyond modernism would become possible.

Dewey's attempt in these early years to answer this fundamental question—does science lend itself to thinking of facts as germinating into spiritual meanings?—centers most principally on the science of psychology, and finds its fullest expression in his major work of this period, the *Psychology* of 1887. The same question has implications for ethics also, and for the issue of the emergence of a culture beyond modernism. Dewey's principle early ideas on ethics and culture are found in his *Outlines of a Critical Theory of Ethics* of 1891. I will analyze each of these texts in the following chapters, after which we will have gained a detailed understanding of Dewey's early philosophy and its implications. We will then be in a position to appreciate its merits as a response to pessimism.

Conclusion

This chapter has described the culture of pessimism that arose in the nineteenth century in the wake of the widespread assumption that the human mind is separated from nature and fundamentally opposed to it. Nature—or the view of nature that science supposedly presents to us—came to be conceived of as indifferent to human concerns, while the mind was conceived of as the source of feelings and values, which could be maintained and preserved only through the mind's withdrawal from indifferent nature into its own meaningful inwardness.

Gustav Klimt's paintings, for example, give us a pictorial representation of this cultural assumption, for Klimt tries to show us the realm of mind and feeling set free from the constraints of the external world of life and nature. However, his paintings also reveal some of the problems with this modernist cultural assumption, for some of Klimt's works are almost pathological. As Carl Schorske has said, Klimt's works can become nightmarish, since in them the imagination and the emotions have been freed from any substantial basis and allowed a wild, unconstrained play all their own.[49]

In Dewey's terms, modernist culture foists on us an "unnatural wound" (EW 3: 123). By assuming that nature has no meaning, and bidding us to withdraw into the hidden, inexplicable resources of our isolated selves to find meaning, modernism prevents us from finding meaning in nature and from others around us as well. The modernist picture is best expressed, philosophically, by the Kantian tradition, and especially by the work of Schopenhauer, which insists that reality in itself is devoid of significance and value and that we should resign from it. Modernism in this way condemns us to philosophical pessimism and bids us to give up all faith in outward life. The liberatory promise of Klimt's break with external constraints, or of Matthew Arnold's isolating withdrawal into self alone, amount, in the end, to a disgust and "nausea" (EW 3: 41) with existence, on the grounds that it is inherently devoid of any meaning worthy of a human being.

It was to help us overcome this nausea and pessimism regarding life, to reject the modernist assumption of the world of facts as thoroughly un-ideal, that Dewey wrote the major work of this period, the *Psychology*. In this book, Dewey seeks to show, above all else, that facts themselves are always meaningful, always idealized in some way, and therefore always possibly conducive to the deeper needs of human beings. The aim of the *Psychology*, as we will see in the next chapter, is to present us with a picture of nature, not as alien and indifferent, but as consistent with human meaning.

THREE

REHABILITATING DEWEY'S *PSYCHOLOGY*

The Major Early Work

Dewey's *Psychology* is one of the great, underappreciated works of nineteenth-century thought. The book has been consistently derided and ignored since its publication in 1887, and its merits are still underappreciated today, even by otherwise sympathetic Dewey scholars.[1] And yet the *Psychology* is a masterwork of philosophical synthesis, providing a general framework that seems to account well (and sometimes beautifully) for every phase of human experience. It offers a compelling account of everything from the nature of knowledge and wonder to what it means to feel malice or hunger, or to be religious, or to appreciate a great work of art, and so on. Dewey's *Psychology* is his *Phenomenology of Spirit*. It can be compared to Hegel's magnum opus in its scope and ambition, in its sheer philosophical breadth.

In this chapter I will first examine the main criticism that has been leveled at Dewey's *Psychology* since its inception, and that to this day keeps readers from appreciating the book's insights; and I will show why this criticism is invalid. I will then turn to a consideration of the book's merits. As we will see, the *Psychology* is significant for two reasons: first, it argues that there is an infinite ideal, or Absolute, pertaining to facts that renders them meaningful to human beings, so that the threat of meaninglessness posed by modernism can be overcome; second, it argues that the infinite ideal is not a substance, an accomplished entity, but rather a force that disrupts all finite determinations and forever generates the possibility of new and better meanings in life—a conception of the ideal that enables Dewey to go beyond traditional readings of Hegel and offer a significant new version of idealism. In short, the *Psychology* teaches us how to overcome modernism, and it establishes Dewey's early work as a new version of philosophical idealism. Before these points can be established, however, we must first unburden ourselves of the main criticism of the *Psychology*.[2]

The Main Criticism and Why It Is Invalid

The *Psychology's* initial reception was cold, even chilling. Robert Westbrook records it well. As he shows in *John Dewey and American Democracy*, the main complaint leveled against the work from several quarters, including from Dewey's own students, was that it pretended to be science when in fact it was speculation.[3] "Even though his book was larded with references in several languages to the latest experimental work," says Westbrook, "he failed to meet the empiricists' demand that he show how experience revealed an absolute consciousness realizing itself in the individual."[4] Dewey failed to prove that empirical science realized the Absolute. "The Absolute was not a fact of experience but it was—if one was a neo-Hegelian—logically implied by it. Dewey's book was less a discussion of developments in scientific psychology than a deductive argument grounded in controversial idealist premises."[5]

It was on these grounds that Dewey's contemporaries perceived the book to have failed. As Westbrook relates, G. Stanley Hall thought "the book would be a hit with adolescents," who tend to like ideal-ism, "but would be direly disappointing to mature minds."[6] Hall thought that Dewey read into the facts far more than they warranted, never letting the facts "'speak out plainly for themselves'" but always interpreting them according to his idealist framework.[7] William James likewise complained that the book failed to offer "'something really fresh,'" and more importantly, when it did present psychologi-cal facts, failed to do justice to them in their particularity.[8] Westbrook notes that H. A. P. Torrey, the teacher under whom Dewey had begun the serious study of philosophy and who was initially very supportive of him, had a similar problem with the book. In Westbrook's words, "Even H. A. P. Torrey could not resist a similar dig at his former pupil. 'Psychologically speaking, the world is objectified self; the self is objectified world,' Dewey had written. This, Torrey corrected, was not psychology but metaphysics speaking."[9] Dewey's students also found problems with the book, expressing these problems in the form of a poem, which Dewey biographer George Dykhuizen reproduces as follows:

> But first let me say, I'm not myself to blame
> For wearing a mask that should put me to shame.
> But man, daring man, of my folly's the source
> Man,—aspiring to be a Colossus, of course,
> Having one foot in heaven, the other on earth.
> And in lieu of real seeing, his fancy gives birth
> To wild speculations, as solid and fair
> As water on quicksand, or smoke in the air.
> With these fancies he clothed me and called me a science,
> And I—proud of the title, lent him alliance.[10]

Clearly, many of the initial readers of the *Psychology* felt that the book's approach to its subject constituted its major flaw—a view that appears to be shared by Westbrook. Dewey had not treated his subject scientifically, but rather had dressed the facts up to fit the needs of his idealist position. His critics assumed that his aim was to present the facts of psychology, and Dewey had not really followed the facts. Therefore, these readers concluded, he had failed in his project.

These are formidable charges, especially coming, as they do, from so many different sources, including important contemporaries. We should take it into account, however, that both James and Hall were very much concerned at the time to establish psychology as an empirical science independent of philosophy; moreover, James's own *Principles of Psychology* was at the time already being written, with James's own approach perhaps already being established. Both James and Hall may well have had an agenda in their criticisms of Dewey's book. In fact, William James, for his part, did not really read Dewey's book—he simply pronounced upon it "halfway through" and condemned it.[11] Hall probably also had an agenda; namely, as a man of science, he sought to champion "the facts." The critics wanted to overcome idealism, but this does not mean that Dewey's book was a bad one. The *Psychology* went through many editions, implying that there were readers who saw something in it.[12] Moreover, it must be said that when one *does* read the book through carefully, piecing together its many details into Dewey's grand vision of life and the world, one begins to feel that the main criticism somehow misses the mark.

When one considers the matter carefully, it becomes clear that the problem with the main criticism is that it results from failing to take Dewey's work on its own terms, from not understanding clearly what the book itself intended to accomplish. Westbrook, for example, nowhere examines Dewey's stated method of procedure in the *Psychology,* nor does he consider what Dewey means by *science* (and by giving a *scientific* accounting of the facts) in the work itself. Instead, Westbrook prefaces his account of the *Psychology* with an analysis of Dewey's article "Psychology as Philosophic Method."[13] Here Dewey claims that idealists must begin with the science of psychology to show how to reach the Absolute. Westbrook (and Dewey's other critics as well, it seems) takes Dewey to mean by this that "experience," as it had been tested by "experimental work," was supposed to reveal "an absolute consciousness realizing itself in the individual."[14]

If one looks to the *Psychology* itself, however, especially the section on Dewey's methodology, one sees straightaway that Dewey does not mean by *science* what Westbrook and the other critics mean, and that his method is far different from the ones they themselves presuppose. What has happened here is that the critics have read their own terms into Dewey's work, and have therefore missed its real aims and intentions, which are, strictly speaking, *philosophical*, not experimentally scientific. In other words, Dewey never intended to let the facts simply "speak for themselves." This was not his stated approach; it was not what his book was really about. *Psychology* was never intended as a book of experimental science. The main criticism of Dewey's work therefore amounts to a straw man argument: his critics have described a position that differs from Dewey's own, and then skewered that position as if it were Dewey's. The main criticism of Dewey's *Psychology* is therefore off the mark.

In the book Dewey explicitly treats psychology as science in the older and more technical sense in which Hegel understood the term, namely as a comprehensive knowledge of the real, and not in the more limited sense of experimentation, which the word has come to mean in our own times. Indeed, in the section on method, he makes it clear that to treat a subject "scientifically," as he understands the term, means ordering it according to "principles," which may include some level of experimental testing, but which ultimately relies on a rational ordering and organizing of the facts as they present themselves. Dewey puts the point in this way: "the subject-matter of psychology is the facts of self. . . . These facts, however, do not constitute science until they have been systematically collected and ordered with reference to principles, so that they may be comprehended in their relations to each other, that is to say, explained" (EW 2: 11). This is clearly not experimental science as his critics understand it, namely, as a matter of letting the facts "speak for themselves" without comment.

Having explained what he means by *science*, Dewey next considers the appropriate method for doing the science of psychology. "The proper way of getting at, classifying, and explaining the facts introduces us to the consideration of the proper *method* of psychology" (EW 2: 11). The way to get at the facts of mind, Dewey explains, is primarily though "introspection" combined with other valuable techniques, such as the experimental method, "the comparative method," "the objective method," and the method of "self-consciousness," which are designed to compensate for introspection's limitations. Dewey explains his use of the term *introspection*; it does not mean "a special power of the mind. It is only the general power of knowing which the mind has, directed reflectively and intentionally upon a certain set of facts," namely the facts of the self, which, after all, must form the main material of any science of psychology (EW 2: 11–12). Introspection is simply the reflective investigation of the facts of self.

Introspection does have its limitations, however, in that the facts by themselves do not always reveal their true meaning. One cannot simply consider a fact from the perspective of the one who experiences it and renounce all analysis from the external point of view. "Correctly to perceive a fact . . . is a work of analysis. To feel angry is one thing; to give a critical analysis of that feeling is quite another" (EW 2: 12), Dewey writes. Indeed, "there are certainly many mixed and subtle emotional states, states of half-fear and half-hope, for example, which it is as difficult to identify as it is to identify a rare species of bird-life. Even as to anger, persons are not unknown who, the angrier they get, the more earnestly they assert themselves to be perfectly calm" (EW 2:12). Introspection alone, or the reflective consideration of the mental state one is having, can lead to mistakes and misinterpretations. The internal, reflective engagement with an actual mental state, therefore, must be supplemented by external forms of interpretation. Indeed, all such facts of self must in the end receive their meaning from correct and careful interpretation. As Dewey explains the point,

> It is well understood that external observation is not a passive process—that it demands active attention and critical thought, and that its correctness will depend largely upon the ideas with which the object is approached. . . . To perceive with no ideas in the mind to which to relate the object is an impossibility. It is not otherwise with psychological observation . . . There is no such

thing as pure observation in the sense of a fact being known without assimilation and interpretation through ideas already in the
mind. (EW 2: 13)

Critics of the *Psychology* wanted Dewey to let the facts "speak for
themselves"; they felt that he should have refused to interpret them
in one way or another. But it is precisely Dewey's position that
through science facts *never* speak for themselves. They must always
be interpreted in the most coherent and compelling way. In his view,
this means they must be interpreted in the idealist way; but in any
case, they must be interpreted. This analytical and careful process of
interpretation is what Dewey meant by science, and it is this type of
science that he explicitly set out to offer in his *Psychology*.

Regarding the external methods that Dewey says we must also employ, experimental testing occupies only a small and partial place
among the available options. Experiments have their import in that
we can make changes in the physical body and note how these
changes affect the psychic states that eventuate (or vice versa). Such
an approach has "yielded ample results," Dewey says, especially relative to the "composition and relations of sensations, the nature of
attention, and the time occupied by various mental processes" (EW
2: 14). But Dewey notes that this approach has strict limitations. It
cannot tell us *directly* about the facts of self. It takes only an external
perspective, noting the connections between body and mind, but tell-
ing us too little about the mind itself, its psychological laws and processes. It provides us only with facts about certain connections that
exist between body and mind, which of course require interpretation
to gain their actual meaning for psychology. "The mere knowledge of
all the functions of the brain and nerves does not help the science,
except so far as it occasions a more penetrating psychological analysis" (EW 2: 14).

The more penetrating psychological analysis that Dewey's psychology demands is further aided by the "comparative method." Here the
facts disclosed under introspection, and sometimes with the aid of
experiment, are "compared with the consciousness (1) of animals, (2)

of children in various stages, (3) of defective and disordered minds, (4) of mind as it appears in the various conditions of race, nationality, etc." (EW 2: 14–15). This approach obviously has the advantage of allowing the psychologist to gain valuable insight concerning the nature of mind and self as such, and not only the individual mind under consideration at any one point during introspection.

A further method Dewey employs is what he calls the "objective method." The mind has created things, impressed itself upon reality, and the products of such creation can be studied to teach us about the nature of the mind. Dewey places great emphasis on this method. "The broadest and most fundamental method of correcting and extending the results of introspection," he says, "and of interpreting these results, so as to refer them to their laws, is the study of the objective manifestations of mind" (EW 2: 15). It is evident, Dewey argues, that

> science, religion, art, etc., are all of them products of the mind or self, working itself out according to its own laws, and that, therefore, in studying them we are only studying the fundamental nature of the conscious self. It is in these wide departments of human knowledge, activity, and creation that we learn most about the self, and it is through their investigation that we find most clearly revealed the laws of its activities. (EW 2: 15–16)

This is a unique kind of psychology, indeed. Far from relying only on experimental testing, it also draws on and analyzes the external manifestations of the mind such as language, science, art, and religion. For truly these must also reveal something fundamental about what or who manifested such things and what features this creator must have possessed in giving rise to just these manifestations.

The last and most fundamental method is that of "self-consciousness." Here the meaning of objective facts is realized in the actual experience of some actual self, the investigator. Such a process is crucial for understanding, for without it the investigator possesses only a detached, external grasp of an objective process, but lacks an understanding about what these objective processes truly mean to an actual mind. "The ultimate appeal is to self-conscious-ness," Dewey explains.

> None of these facts mean anything until they are thus interpreted. . . . [T]hey . . . must be interpreted into *individual* terms. What, for example, would language mean to an individual who did not have the power of himself reproducing the language? . . . So the phenomena made known in physiological psychology, would have no value whatever for the science of psychology, if they were not interpretable into facts of consciousness. As physiological facts they are of no avail, for they tell us only about certain objective processes. (EW 2: 16)

The psychologist must interpret the facts of self, not simply by reflecting on them directly through introspection and then also employing experimental testing, comparative analysis, and objective reference to build out a fuller interpretation, but also through the self-conscious experience of undergoing these facts of self (and their interpretation) for himself. The psychologist must feel his or her way into the interpretation, in other words, becoming not simply an external investigator but also an active participant in the investigation, seeing just where the interpreted results square or fail to square with his or her own experiences as a self.

These various methods, then, are the ones Dewey will employ in offering his account of the facts of the self. His explicit employment of each of these methods to "do psychology" saves Dewey from his critics' charge that his book is a work of experimental science gone wrong. Dewey never intended to show that empirical facts by themselves would somehow prove the Absolute. But Dewey's approach does raise another possible objection: that Dewey is the practitioner of a bizarre kind of science, indeed, one that hardly resembles anything that goes by that name.

I am inclined to exonerate Dewey from this charge, however, by pointing out that what he is involved in is actually *not* what we usually mean by science at all, but is, rather, philosophy. Dewey's *Psychology* is not a scientific text in the standard sense; it is a philosophical work focusing on the mind. Dewey makes this clear in the preface when he writes that he has sought "above all, to develop the philosophic spirit" (EW 2: 4). To be sure, Dewey uses the name of science in the work, but he uses it in the older, broader, Hegelian sense of complete knowledge, not in its narrower modern sense, whereby science is closely associated with experimentation. For Dewey, science is knowledge. In offering a psychology, Dewey is offering knowledge of the self. He employs several methods to gain this knowledge, only one of which is the use of experiment. He is not engaged in experimental science in any fundamental way as part of his task of explaining the self; experimental science is only one small part of his overall philosophical effort. We must get over the idea that Dewey's book endeavors to be scientific in the way we customarily understand that term today. The *Psychology* does not show Dewey engaged in bad science, forcing facts into a Hegelian mold; rather, it shows Dewey utilizing the various methods of insight available to us and trying to determine with their aid what it is that we can know about the self. It is a philosophical project. The project should therefore be judged not on scientific but on philosophical grounds, which critics so far have consistently failed to do. Dewey's *Psychology* still lacks the appraisal as a philosophical work that it deserves.

Key Ideas

To better understand Dewey's philosophy in the *Psychology*, consider its key ideas. The book centers on the finite self or "consciousness" and examines philosophically what it is and how it functions. Dewey explains early on in the *Psychology* that the facts under consideration in the book are "the facts of consciousness," by which he means an individual's "cognitive, emotional, and volitional" acts (EW 2: 18). Knowledge, feeling, and will, he holds, are not separate and detached functions but rather "the three aspects which every consciousness presents" (EW 2: 20). We feel something, that is, we take an interest in an object, which produces in us the will to learn about it, and this will to learn can result in our acquiring knowledge of the object. All three aspects of the mind—knowledge, feeling, and will—are in some form or other at work in every conscious experience (EW 2: 20).

Beginning from here, Dewey eventually moves on to the crucial idea that "it is the characteristic . . . of the subject-matter of our psychical life that it has meaning" (EW 2: 78). Knowledge, feeling, and will together reveal to us objects that are meaningful. *The facts of self,* in other words, do allow for meaning, and they do so because of rupture—that is, because any potential fact has already broken off from itself, so to speak, and become more than a fact. The basic picture that Dewey tries to defend can be seen at work in the claim that "we not only have sensations, but have an intelligent life and intelligible experiences" (EW 2: 78). We always go beyond facts merely present (e.g., the facts of present sensations, such as green and smooth) and transform them into intelligible meanings (e.g., the perception of an object, such as money). Dewey puts the point this way: "Whatever appeals to the investigation of intelligence, offers it material upon which to exert its activities . . . we call *significant,* or possessing *meaning*" (EW 2: 78). There is no *given,* as we might put it today. Anything that gives itself to our consciousness is already something that has allowed our activities to work upon it and in relation to which those activities have produced some meaning or other. (As we will see, this is also true for any apparently given sensation, such as green or smooth, as well). Dewey goes so far as to say that "whatever is meaningless has no point of contact with intelligence. . . . The main-spring of our cognitive experiences is the more or less conscious feeling that things have meaning" (EW 2: 78).

To say that something has meaning, for Dewey, is to say that the objects of consciousness are organized in relation to one another, and it is relative to those relationships that they acquire their significance. So, Dewey holds that knowledge, feeling, and will are activities that above all establish *relations* between objects, relations that are meaningful, significant, and valuable. Knowledge, feeling, and will transform facts into meanings by putting the facts into relationships relative to which the facts have something to say, or take on the properties of being noteworthy, important, or momentous.

Dewey's position is that the self builds up an entire universe of known and felt objects out of facts. And the facts permit these meanings. We do not know, of course, whether the facts will ultimately bear out our meanings, but we are able to idealize the facts to the point where they actually do take on our meanings to a great extent.[15] Even so, a critic might insist, if the facts ultimately do not (or might not) correspond to our meanings, then we have the dilemma of modernism all over again: our meanings are separated from the ways things really are. As Jennifer Welchman puts it, "this new position" of Dewey's "is only partly worked out and on occasion collapses into just the sort of dualism *Psychology* was a protest against."[16] For when we build up meanings conducive to ourselves, this of course in no way guarantees that the facts themselves—prior to our efforts—really bear those meanings. We would therefore seem to be left with the very separation of facts and meanings that the *Psychology* seeks to overcome.

However, it is at this point that Dewey introduces his concept of faith. He believes that we can have faith that the facts could ultimately lend themselves to a perfect and complete harmony with our idealized meanings. This view may sound simple–minded, until we realize that by placing faith at the center of his account, Dewey is actually insisting upon the unsurpassed power of rupture. He is privileging disruption over unity as the condition of meaning-making. In Dewey's words, "Reason must be that which separates itself, which differentiates, goes forth into differences" (EW 1: 44).[17] The movement towards the Absolute occurs as the difference from what is, as the movement toward the ideal, and although we seek higher unities in this difference—and if we are lucky can make these higher ideals real in the process—reason cannot guarantee this outcome, cannot secure its end point in some finally attained Absolute ideal. Only faith can come close. But such faith is not reason; it does not prove our ideals to be so; rather, faith is something we maintain in order to avoid "a contradiction" in our search for meaning, so that "the universal which is its goal" (that is, a world of fully idealized facts) does not remain "a blind postulate, impossible to account for" (EW 2: 363).

We feel compelled to render the facts ideal; and the way to make sense of this feeling—that is, to justify it and our effort to try to make the facts more human and ideal—is to believe that through our effort the facts will lend themselves (under the right circumstances) to our ideals. The possibility of the reconciliation of our higher, ideal meanings with ultimate reality is asserted to exist, in other words, to goad us on to continued idealizing action, in order that we might continue moving past the given and continue to build up more ideals and more and more of a meaningful universe. Dewey is affirming the primacy of rupture here as opposed to the traditional Hegelian privileging of unity; and this means affirming the importance of our continuing to try to render the facts ideal.

What Welchman's objection misses, therefore, is that in Dewey's account of things, we must work to secure the ultimate union of facts and meanings by pursuing ideals. This union is in no way given to us, but neither is the fundamental unbridgeable separation of facts and meanings of modernism given to us. Instead, there is a deep and vague lure at work in our experience that keeps us creating actual, real-life meanings that, though imperfect, would reach toward the ultimate union. This avoidance of both modernism as the separation of facts and meanings, and of the old picture of Hegelianism as the *guaranteed* subsumption of facts under meanings, is precisely the innovation of Dewey's early philosophy. It is a philosophy about creating the kind of world in which we think we ought to live, rather than assuming that this kind of world either does or does not exist.

A close reading of the *Psychology* reveals Dewey's innovation. Dewey holds in the *Psychology* that the self negates the given, seeking to transform it into ideal patterns of meaning (EW 2: 126). The self also does this to itself, which means that it grows, or constantly expands to try to include ever-more-universal aspects as part of what it is (EW 2: 137–38). For example, I first try to identify myself with my body, then with objects, then with other people and society, then with all of humanity, then with nature, and so on. This attempt at expansive self-identification never ceases. Our identities continue to expand, as we seek to identify ourselves with wider and wider aspects of the universe. We may have faith that these expanded versions of ourselves culminate in the Godhead, of which we are a part, but such faith, Dewey makes clear, is in place to keep us striving in action. We want the fullest, most complete self, but "what this . . . self as complete is, it does not know. It only feels that there is such a goal" (EW 2: 358). An endless, vague yearning to unsettle all of our previous versions of ourselves, to grow beyond ourselves, is what Dewey means by the Absolute, not the reconciliation of ourselves with any aspect of reality.[18]

We can begin to see, therefore, that Dewey's philosophy aims to help us have confidence in life by providing an account of how meaning develops in the universe. The meaning, it turns out, is in the movement—the movement from form to form, in a tireless search for perfection that refuses to rest in any of its stations. The meaning amounts to a passion for life, the desire to go on, to live, and to strive for ideals, but also, at the same time, the attainment of some idealized meanings along the way and our enjoyment of them.[19]

This is a new version of idealism, as I will show in chapter 8, going beyond the typical understanding of Hegelianism's commitment to unity and the inevitable return of reason to itself. With its emphasis on ongoing disruption, caused by a missing goal, this idealism comes close to the *Bildung* tradition that Jim Good identifies, defined "as an organic model of education as growth" and a tradition "the goal of which is the development of the higher humanity within ourselves."[20] However, the fact that the goal is missing, or at least is unclear and waiting to be created as the search for meaning itself is pursued, would seem to take Dewey beyond this tradition into new areas. As Dewey emphasizes in his idealism, "the final reality for man is that which cannot be made out actually to exist" (EW 2: 292). If anything, this new idealism resembles contemporary philosophies of rupture. As with these philosophies, the lack of ultimate unity is crucial to meaning, with the "absent centre" at the heart of things, as Slavoj Žižek calls it, driving all movement and growth.[21] The early Dewey advances beyond typical Hegelianism to a more open-ended philosophy, but also perhaps to a more uncertain and dangerous one.

With this new understanding of Dewey's early philosophy in place, we can also confront another criticism often leveled against Dewey's findings in the *Psychology*. Once we see that rupture is the central concept of the book, we can overcome from another angle the charge that Dewey fails in his project. Dewey admits in the *Psychology* that "there is always a chasm between actual knowledge and absolute truth" (EW 2: 361), since Absolute truth is universal and the individual, as individual, can never have access to the universal. Westbrook, speaking perhaps for many other critics, sees this as a confession that Dewey cannot deliver what he promises, namely to derive the Absolute from experience: "This time Dewey admitted as much . . . the Absolute was not a fact of experience."[22] What Westbrook fails to see, however, is that for Dewey, there is *necessarily* a chasm between our actual knowledge as we find it and the truth of the Absolute. This is not an admission of failure on Dewey's part; it is the very point he is trying to make. As Dewey goes on to explain in the passage about the chasm, "There can be no knowledge beyond the ground that knowledge actually covers. There cannot be knowledge that the true reality for the individual self is the universal self, for knowledge has not in the individual compassed the universal" (EW 2: 361). The truth of the Absolute is something so far "transcending knowledge," although we do believe and presuppose that this truth is there (EW 2: 361). In fact, belief in the truth of the Absolute is what compels us to know: "the motive to knowledge and the energy of its realization is the *belief* that there is truth" (EW 2: 361). Dewey's point is that the way the Absolute functions—as an ideal beyond us—is precisely by creating discontent with our actual state of knowledge and experience, a discontent or disruption that is the very condition of our searching for (and creating) ideal meanings in the first place. This chasm between our actual condition and the Absolute, Dewey wants to say, is the pregnant source of all meaning.[23]

A New Concept of the Absolute

To understand this new concept of the Absolute that Dewey advances in the *Psychology* it may help to contrast it with another, competing account of the Absolute. We will examine Josiah Royce's conception of the Absolute as presented in *The Religious Aspect of Philosophy*.[24] The differences are particularly sharp and should serve to highlight what is unique about Dewey's concept.

In *The Religious Aspect of Philosophy*, published in 1885, only a few years before the *Psychology*, Royce holds that the Absolute is an eternal entity in which all finite things are reconciled. As Royce puts it, *"All reality must be present to the Unity of the Infinite Thought."*[25] For Royce, the Absolute is the ultimate container of events, bringing all the disruption and division involved in reality into harmony within itself. It reconciles all division; it renders all disunity into unity in its "Infinite Thought."

The Absolute is, in effect, "a World-Consciousness" that grasps all things.[26] In contrast to the actual events in the world, Royce refers to it as "this higher spiritual Life that includes them and watches over them as the spectator watches the tragedy."[27] Moreover, for Royce, the Absolute does not stand above actual events, but is rather inside of them. In events themselves, "dwells the higher spirit that does not so much create as constitute them what they are."[28] The Absolute is present in the events, shaping them into the events that they become. It is those same events seen from an eternal perspective and worked upon by an eternal mind.

Dewey's concept of the Absolute, by contrast, is not an ultimate container; neither does it dwell in the facts. It is not an eternal mind grasping everything, but rather an ideal of perfect harmony that eludes us. The Absolute does not reside in the facts but is, precisely, lacking in them; it is this lack in actual events that compels those events to need to develop in a more ideal fashion.

In the *Psychology*, Dewey makes finite human consciousness the starting point and focus of meaning. The title itself reveals what is innovative about his concept of the Absolute. He does not call the book, *Metaphysics*, as if he were dealing with pure being, but rather *Psychology*, because he is dealing with finite human minds. In a word, the focus of meaning is not *in* the Absolute, in some timeless, eternal entity; rather, it is in the finite, striving mind, which yearns for the

Absolute but always misses it. Dewey's Absolute is an absence, a void—the void or absence at the heart of our experience. Because we lack any ultimate harmony, we constantly seek for it. The Absolute, for Dewey, is a creative lack in our lives.

Thirteen years after he first published the *Psychology*, Dewey wrote an interesting review of another book by Royce, *The World and the Individual*. In it Dewey argues that if we are capable of understanding anything like the Absolute at all, as Royce contends, then the Absolute cannot be something eternal and timeless; rather, this Absolute must center (or perhaps de-center) *in* our experience and must be understood in relation to *us*. If we in our finitude can grasp an infinite Absolute, then we are more than "mere fragments or parts" of it; what must be happening, rather, is that "it is in and through us, and in such an organic and pervasive way that the contrast between us and it . . . is contradicted" (MW 1: 255). The Absolute becomes defined relative to us, relative to a lack of ours, not relative to an eternal totality. "What we need is a reconsideration of the facts of struggle, disappointment, change, consciousness of limitation, which will show *them*, as they actually are experienced *by us* (not by something called Absolute) to be significant, worthy, and helpful" (MW 1: 255–56). In Dewey's view, the idealizing function of the Absolute, rendering things significant, should not be thought of as a unity occurring somewhere in which all finite reality is present and reconciled, but as the very process of our own struggling, finite experience becoming significant. Our own activities, insofar as their disrupted and disjointed parts are developing into meanings that are significant and worthy, is what defines the Absolute. Rupture is here made into the basis of harmony and meaning.

It is true that Dewey published this review over a decade after he wrote the *Psychology*. That this is how Dewey had earlier envisioned the Absolute, however, is suggested by a second review that Dewey wrote of Royce's *The World and the Individual*. This review was also written some years after the *Psychology*, but in it Dewey seems to reveal how he had always understood Hegel: in such a way as to place the center of meaning in particular, finite human life. Referring to

Fichte and Hegel, but especially to Hegel, Dewey explains, "The old transcendentalists were . . . serious with their theory of the Absolute as the meaning and reality of present experience. They worked out the idea into a logic, a *Naturphilosophie*, and a philosophy of history" (MW 2: 136). They derived the Absolute from out of the very fabric of finite, struggling human experience, rather than placing it in an eternal mind.

In pieces actually written during the earlier period, too, Dewey seems for the most part to have understood the Absolute in this way, even outside of the *Psychology*. We often find Dewey insisting that, as he says in one place, "the content of consciousness is known only in and to an individual" (EW 1: 174). This means, conversely, that it is *not* known to the Absolute. "Idealized"[29] meanings are known as they come home to us in individual, finite, and fragmented experience, and only there.

It is true that Dewey relapses at one point, prior to the *Psychology*, as he is working out this innovative conception of the Absolute, and says that "the individual self can take the universal self as its stand-point, and thence know its own origin. In so doing, it knows that it has its origin in processes which exist for the universal self, and that therefore the universal self never has become" (EW 1: 142). This certainly sounds as if Dewey's Absolute is a timeless harmony unto itself. But Dewey quickly recovers himself and goes on to say, "It must not be forgotten that the object of this paper is simply to develop the presuppositions which have always been latent or implicit in the psychological standpoint. . . . It must also be remembered that it is the work of Psychology itself to determine the exact and concrete relations of subject and object, individual and universal within consciousness" (EW 1: 142–43). In other words, whatever the claim about the Absolute, it comes from psychology, and can only be grasped in and through the study of human consciousness.

In a similar fashion, in a review of William Wallace's translation of Hegel's *Philosophie des Geistes*, Dewey praises Wallace's text because "it will introduce Hegel to many in a new aspect—as among other things a psychologist, and, according to his lights and the state of knowledge when he wrote, a physiological psychologist" (EW 5: 344), just as Dewey himself had been. Dewey, it seems, had all along understood Hegelian idealism as situating the Absolute and its worthwhile meanings in the finite life of the individual, even in his physiological life.

My position is that when the early Dewey is at his best, at his most original and compelling, he advances beyond his Hegelian contemporaries to the idea of the Absolute as "only the most adequate possible construing" of the "ultimate meaning and worth" of "'us men,'" that is, of finite human beings (MW 2: 137). Hegel himself believed that "[e]ach of the stages [of life] . . . is an image of the absolute, but at first in a limited mode, and thus it is forced onwards to the whole."[30] What seems to have happened is that the young Dewey's contemporaries focused on the first part of this belief (that finite life is an image of absolute, eternal life, which is most real), while Dewey, at his most original, focused on the second part of the belief (that each stage is forced onwards to the whole). For him, the Absolute becomes merely a prod to compel us beyond any given state to the deeper and richer meanings of which that state is capable (EW 2:358). The focus of meaning is entirely on the actual state struggling to become more ideal, or being forced onwards due to its own insufficiency, its own lack of ultimate harmony. And it is in the *Psychology*, I hold, that Dewey achieves this position most completely, and that his early philosophy comes most fully into its own. It is in this text that Dewey both attains and sustains this insight about the Absolute as the ultimate harmony that escapes us, but that nonetheless gives life meaning, to its fullest and most coherent extent.

What is needed to bring this point out is, above all, a close reading of the *Psychology*. We must move beyond speaking in generalities and engage in a detailed and thorough investigation of Dewey's book. Only then can we fully appreciate what the book is trying to do and what is significant about it. The text is a significant work in philosophy, and it will take several chapters to bring out the complete ideas of the text. In the chapters that follow, therefore, I offer such a reading.

Outline of the Psychology

Before we turn to a fuller analysis of the *Psychology*, it may be helpful to review the book's basic structure and what each part is trying to accomplish. The *Psychology* consists of introductory material about method, discussed above, followed by three parts. The first is titled "Knowledge," the second "Feeling," and the third "Will" (EW 2:xxi–xxii). Each part shows how rupture is at work in producing the kinds of meanings peculiar to each of these activities.

Part I identifies the two basic conditions of knowledge, namely *apperception* and *retention*, or the unifying and the preserving of sensations in such a way that we are able to build them up into coherent objects and their relations (EW 2: 78;130). Part I shows us how these conditions of knowledge function to generate ever-wider and more universal meanings through activities such as "perception," "imagination," "thinking," and "intuition" (EW 2:138; 169; 177; 205). The path charted here is from less rich meanings to more rich ones. Perception pertains to objects, but memory adds past content, thereby enriching our grasp of the objects. Imagination adds richer possibilities to perceived and remembered objects, and so on. Eventually, Dewey will maintain, we are capable of arriving at a conception of the universe of known objects as a whole, a single unity, which nonetheless allows for the differentiation of parts within it (EW 2:137–38; 200–1). We create the idea of a cosmos to which we belong; and to the extent that we approximate such a cosmos in our knowledge, feeling, and willing, modernism will be defeated.

In part II of the *Psychology*, Dewey addresses the role of feeling in human knowledge. He asserts that we never simply know objects, but rather grasp them always in terms of how we feel about them, or in other words, in terms of what they mean to us personally. Hence, contrary to the modernist world view, facts are always meaningful for us. Moreover, the facts can become ever more meaningful. Here, too, there is development (never to be completed) from "sensuous feeling," to "formal feeling," and then to the "qualitative feelings" of the intellect, the aesthetic, and the social (EW2: 218; 228; 239). Sensuous feeling is our basic bodily feeling; formal feelings are feelings of action and reaction, or of the body in motion; qualitative feelings are feelings we have about the content of things we encounter in our activities, such as the content of our thoughts, or our art works, or our relationships with others. We can see the development: feelings move from the merely given, raw sense of something happening, all the way up to the highest refinements of social interaction. The function of the feeling in all of these cases is to help us to develop—to give us a sense, in other words, for the ways we are relating to things and whether our relations assist our development, in which case feelings of pleasure occur, or hinder our development, in which case feelings of pain occur. The highest pleasure is social interaction, or the feeling of community, which ultimately takes on a religious quality. We feel that we might possess unity with all things, although in the end this feeling is ungrounded, for reasons we will explore in chapter 6. In any case, feelings, in Dewey's account, guide us toward better, more ideal ways of acting, and steer us clear of worse ways. There is a development to feelings. In short, feelings are part of the way we idealize the world and grasp it in terms of our sense of things, in terms of what things mean or signify for us, rather than purely intellectually, in terms of some supposedly basic facts of the world. And because of this, once again, modernism, which holds that facts are devoid of meaning, will be defeated (EW 2:216; 291).

Part III is about the will, or the various modes of intention we posses. The will combines knowledge and feeling, in that we understand the way objects relate to one another (knowledge) and we grasp what these mean for us (feeling), which in turn entails a certain desire or action on our part—an intention or tendency to act a certain way (EW 2:20ff). The pattern of development seen with knowledge and feeling repeats itself in will as well. Our will develops from basic impulses, which always contain at least a rudimentary meaning, to acts of "physical control." It then develops into modes of "prudential control," and finally to "moral control" (EW 2: 321; 332; 342). Again, there is increasing idealization, increasing development of the self's meanings, rather than simple repetition of what is given. We gradually learn to control ourselves rather than let external forces control us. In all of these willing processes, our own actions are coming more and more under our control and so they are becoming more and more meaningful, that is, more idealized and dignified than mere brute activity; and once again modernism is defeated. The final instance of this development of willing is moral control, where we have a sense of what it would mean to complete the will and attain the perfect ideal of action, since in *willing* the moral thing we at the same time are *doing* exactly the thing we should. The early Dewey is a deontologist. And yet, for him, the moral will is incomplete in the end, because we never do completely achieve the moral will and will what we should. In the total character of our life as we have lived it up to any given point, we always come up short. Only faith—the assertion that our ideals can always still be realized if we try—keeps us striving to bring our will in line with the will it ought to be, which in turn keeps us producing meaningful intentions and good willing.

These are the vital ideas of Dewey's major early work, the *Psychology,* to be explored in detail in subsequent chapters. In chapter 4 I explain Dewey's account of the nature of knowledge in the *Psychology.* In chapter 5 I discuss the kinds of things we can be said to know given this understanding of human knowledge, including our sense that we belong to a single, interconnected universe filled with meaning. Chapter 6 deals with Dewey's account of feeling and will, in which the universe comes to take on ever-deeper and richer meanings through our idealizing activities. In chapter 7, I discuss how Dewey applies this philosophy to ethical and social issues, especially in such a way as to combat modernist culture. Finally, in chapter 8, I consider the extent to which Dewey's early philosophy is a new and original form of idealism.

FOUR

THE NATURE OF KNOWLEDGE

How does knowledge occur? What are the conditions that make it possible? In the *Psychology*, Dewey holds that at the root of all knowledge there are not objects out there that we must come to know, but rather, vague, amorphous "motions" (EW 2: 30), or processes of some kind, that lend themselves to creative development and reshaping. Instead of starting with objects, we start with motions, with malleable processes that are indistinct and waiting, as it were, to be developed into a world to be known.[1] The method by which these original motions are developed into a world to be known is what I have called, after Adorno, the method of rupture—out of the original motions, out of the potentiality for something, a rudimentary form of the self appears and creates sensations, and then out of its sensations it creates perceived objects, and then out of its perceived objects it creates objects in their relationships (it creates a world), and within this world the self struggles to find itself.

At no point in this development of knowledge do external objects exist at the root of what we know. Objects are rather only reshaped motions or processes that we systematically organize into a world according to our sensations, conceptions, judgments, and acts of reasoning (EW 2:29; 178–9). But, paradoxically, we are entitled to think that these original motions, though we have broken away from them in decisive acts of rupture (in the sudden creation of sensations, in object-formation, and then in world-formation), are nonetheless compatible with our creations, are ultimately conducive to them, since these original motions allow our creations in the first place. The hope and the faith in knowledge is that as we move toward the creation of an ordered cosmos that we can know, and within which we can recognize ourselves, this cosmos will not be our own arbitrary invention, but will be what the world itself progressively enables us to say about it and what it will, in fact, become.[2]

Let us see in more detail how Dewey's conception of knowledge is supposed to work. In the first section of this chapter I will explain more fully what Dewey means by *motions* and show how they relate to our sensations. In the second section I will explain Dewey's arguments against materialism and the externality of objects, and in the third section I will discuss in general terms his alternative, idealist account of how sensations are created, if they are not created by matter. In the fourth section I will examine the two special processes by which Dewey thinks knowledge emerges out of our sensations, "apperception" and "retention" (EW 2: 78), and then in the last two sections I will explain Dewey's general account of the nature of knowledge and self-knowledge. As we will see, in Dewey's view, by moving away from external forces, creating sensations, and working on these sensations in various ways, the self is able to create knowledge. This is how knowledge arises.

In the Beginning Was Motion

The immediate task at hand is to explain more fully what Dewey means by *motions* and to show how they relate to sensations, the building blocks of our knowledge. What, then, does Dewey mean by this strange term? And what evidence does he give for the existence of motions at the root of all our knowledge?

For one thing, according to Dewey we cannot begin an account of knowledge with external objects, for, were there an object out there complete with its own structures and entirely devoid of motion, it would never affect us; it could never reach us and make its mark on us. It could never, therefore, give rise to a sensation in us, and hence could never become knowledge. In Dewey's words,

> The motion may be of the whole mass, as when something hits us; it may be in the inner particles . . . as when we taste or smell it; it may be a movement originated by the body and propagated to us through vibrations of a medium, as when we hear or see. But some form of motion there must be. An absolutely motionless body would not give rise to any affection of the body such as ultimately results in sensation. (EW 2: 30)

In the beginning was motion, not a world of objects. For it is not objects, but objects in motion (or maybe even just motions themselves qua objects), that alone can provide the impact on our organism required to affect our senses and give rise to sensations. The senses must be affected. A pure object, entirely disconnected from anything else, could not affect our senses; hence, it must be in some sense in "motion" in order to affect us, that is, it must bear a relation to us. Hence, only motions, or movements, or relationships of various kinds can be the stimuli to sensations. "For psychological purposes," therefore, "the world may be here regarded, not as a world of things with an indefinite number of qualities, but as a world of motions alone. The world of motion, however, possesses within itself various differences, to which the general properties of sensations correspond" (EW 2: 30).

So, as the motion varies, it varies in such a way that the senses are affected differently, giving rise to different sensations. The various motions by themselves, however, do not give rise to a sensation until they affect the organism in a certain way (note that all talk of bodies, organisms, and brains here is talk of certain recurring motions or processes, not talk of external objects; there is, for Dewey, an ongoing process of motions that interacts with itself in various ways until these interactions become complex enough to form brains, bodies, and selves, which can split off from motions in sophisticated ways, as we will see). For sensations to occur, "extra-organic" motions must trigger a physiological motion in the body, and ultimately in the brain— namely, the motion of "nerve action" in the brain (EW 2:30; 20). For there are plenty of cases in which a sense seems to be affected in a limb that does not exist, or in which the brain alone can be energized to create a sensation, so that ultimately the site of affectation must be the nerve-action motion in the brain (EW 2: 33–34). The basic picture of sensations, therefore, is that "a world of motions alone" (EW 2: 30) of varying degrees affects the body; the bodily motion thus produced ultimately affects the nerve action of the brain, that is, it causes motion in the nerve centers of the brain; and when the nerve centers in the brain are affected in certain ways there somehow arise sensations, which are not, however, reducible to the brain activities themselves.[3]

We will see in a moment just how Dewey thinks the nerve centers in the brain relate to sensations. It will not be through a direct, causal connection (as I have said, he thinks sensations are the result of rupture, of sudden, novel experience). For now, however, it is important to realize that, in Dewey's view, sensations themselves are not originally given to us as distinct entities, or "atoms" of experience, although it may at first seem so. To become distinct entities, such as the sound of something falling or an alarm clock ringing, they must be worked up into these entities through the interpretive mechanisms of the mind or self. What comes first is "a certain original continuous substratum of sensation out of which the various apparently distinct sensations have been slowly differentiated" (EW 2:34–35). Extra-organic motions originally affect the body only in such a way as to produce a massive, single sensation, which the creative mind then divides up and separates out into distinct sensations of its own making, again through the inventive power of rupture. The variation in motion does eventually allow for different sensations to be possible, but in order for motions to become fully distinct sensations, we must *do* something to the motions as they affect us. Originally they affect us more or less *en masse* and we must separate them out and distinguish them. Dewey gives four different arguments for the position that our primary sensations are indistinct and vague conglomerations of sense, waiting upon our activity to become separate sensations: a "historical" argument, a "physiological" argument, an "experimental" argument, and a "psychological" argument (EW 2: 35–36).

Historically, he says, evolution seems to show that the further we proceed down "the animal scale," the more we see organisms without sense organs at all. "At this point, sensation must be one palpitating homogeneous mass of consciousness, with no breach of continuity of kind or number, but simply expanding and contracting in intensity" (EW 2: 35). This suggests that originally there was a continuous form of sensation common to all life, since we all evolved from this same material.

Physiologically, it seems that the brain functions as "a single . . . organ," unifying all the sensations into a single feeling state (EW 2: 35). To be sure, there is a "localization" of sensations in specific regions of the brain, but the brain still seems to function so as to link together all the sensations: they "are all interwoven into one larger whole" (EW 2: 36). For example, "while . . . the auditory centre may be constantly gaining in distinctness of localization, it is also gaining in multifariousness of connections with the other sensory centres" (EW 2: 36).

Dewey notes that experimentally, tests have shown the influence of sensations on one another. Some people experience synaesthesia, for example, while all of us to some extent associate certain sounds with colors, or certain colors with tastes. That is, some senses feel to us connected with other senses, whether more or less firmly (EW 2: 36).

Psychologically, the opposing theory, "the atomic theory of sensation," creates more problems than it solves (EW 2: 36). For, if we accept that our sensations occur as distinct units, we have to explain how they get connected into the single experience that we do have of all the various senses flowing and working together. Atomists must make recourse to some special power of connection, which seems to multiply entities, whereas the sensation-continuum view does not. In addition, we make a common mistake in our experience that helps explain the allure—but ultimate falsity—of the atomistic position: we commonly attribute the distinctness of the objects of our sensations to the sensations themselves, such as attributing a table-cloth to a particular color or a bell to a particular sound, to use Dewey's examples. In actuality, however, the sensation is not a distinct mental state, but one flowing insensibly into, and intermixed with, the vague total mass of sensations that we are experiencing, which then gets broken up in various ways through our experience (EW 2: 36–37).

The existence of an original sensuous continuum is important for Dewey's position, for if it exists it strongly suggests that objects are not original but are formed out of the activities of the self (and so are conducive to at least some of the meanings the self can recognize). Along with the idea that the self must convert extraorganic motions into a sensuous continuum, this idea that the self must also convert a vague homogenous continuum of sensations into distinctly perceived senses forms the first crucial step in Dewey's overall argument. For if these ideas are true, then Dewey has already to some extent made his point that facts grow into self-recognized meanings, and what remains is to show more fully how these meanings develop into ever-richer forms. In any case, these ideas would already put materialism on the defensive by showing that there is little reason to believe that at the basis of things lies indifferent matter, shut off from conversion into meanings enjoyed by the self. There will exist a vague mass of sensation that waits upon our activities to shape and mold it, that waits for the self's efforts for it to become actualized or realized in a way conducive to the self.

Against Materialism

A further step in Dewey's argument is to address the question, which naturally arises in this discussion, of exactly how the motions relate to the sensations that arise. Do the motions cause the sensations? A dualist will answer *no*, a materialist *yes*. Dewey's view differs from both, so it is worthwhile lingering over the precise difference between three different solutions to what Dewey calls "one of the most difficult problems of psychology" (EW 2: 37).

Dewey defines a dualist as someone who holds that there is no connection between the motions (i.e., the motions of a nerve discharge) and sensations (considered as mental states). Dewey easily refutes this view, because there is obviously some connection between the two. A damaged brain affects the nature of the sensation, and so on (EW 2:38). It is the materialist with whom Dewey more forcefully contends.

Dewey defines a materialist as someone who holds that the sensation is caused by, and is reducible to, the nerve discharge in the brain. More specifically, the materialist holds that the same law, "the law of the conservation and correlation of energy" (EW 2: 39), applies to both entities. The materialist position maintains that a wave of light, for example, neither loses nor gains any energy, so that when it hits the retina, say, "it is converted into an equal amount of energy known as nervous action, which is conveyed along the nerves to the brain, where it sets up another equal amount of energy, which results in the state we know as a sensation. It holds that along this line of changes there is no breach of continuity. Each process is the mechanical result of its antecedents" (EW 2: 39).

Against this view Dewey levels two arguments, "physical" and "psychological" (EW 2: 39–42). The physical argument is that there is a difference in kind between nerve actions and sensations. A nerve action is a motion, whereas a sensation is not. A sensation is a product of rupture, or what Dewey calls "a chasm" (EW 2: 39); it is not itself a motion any longer, but a new creation deriving from a motion, splitting off from it, as it were—an implosion from out of the motion itself, resulting in something entirely new. Strictly speaking, a sensation cannot be a motion, because a motion (or any external force) is supposedly objective; it must exist in space, it must have form, size, and number, whereas "the sensation is subjective, existing only in the mind, having no spatial nor numerical relations" (EW 2: 39). The sensation is a new creation. A sensation is certainly related to motions, but it is not the same as a motion—it *has* no motion itself, nor does it have size, or frequency, or any other such property. Instead, a sensation is "a unique psychical state," a mental entity, sharing no properties with the motions that were presented to the senses to give rise to the sensation (EW 2: 39). The sensation of red, to use Dewey's example of a color, is tied to motions, but "as a sensation it is its own unique psychical state, having no motion, no vibrations, no spatial length nor form"(EW 2: 39). The sensation of red is a mental event, not something out there in the brain activity sharing certain properties with it. In fact, there is no similarity whatsoever between the brain activity and the red sensation. Hence, the law of the conservation and correlation of energy reaches a block when it arrives at the end of the nerve action; a quantity of energy is not carried forward into the mind. The physical nerve action cannot by an unbroken flow of energy give rise to the mental quality of the red sensation. "The law holds only of motions; to apply it to sensations is to commit the absurdity of supposing that a sound or color is a movement occurring in space" (EW 2: 39). Actually, for the sensation to occur, it must break off from the material element and arise as a new, sudden creation that is irreducible to the material cause, although the variations in the motion can be the occasion for (though not the cause of) our splitting off the sensations in one way or another.

Because of this difference in kind between the nerve discharge and the sensation, the materialist position loses its explanatory power. That is to say, it cannot explain the sensation, cannot demonstrate the causal link between the nerve discharge and the sensation that results, for a causal link presupposes identity, and here there is only difference. The materialist explanation presupposes like being caused by like—some kind of equivalent, self-same "stuff," some quantity of something, being caused by another quantity, the equivalent force of which is simply transferred from the one to the other. But "consciousness is not a quantity" (EW 2: 40). It is different in kind from the thing that is supposed to cause it by a transfer of energy. Energy cannot be transferred, and preserved in a thing, if the thing to which it is being transferred is different in kind from the thing transferring.

Moreover, materialism fails to explain why just the one specific form of motion should give rise to just the one specific kind of sensation to which it supposedly does give rise. It is "incomprehensible why one mode of motion should give rise to that psychical fact which we know as color, and another to sound. So the knowledge of the difference of rates of rapidity in the musical scale does not enable us to explain why one rate should result in a low note and another, more rapid rate, in a higher" (EW 2: 41). If you know that the color red always occurs at a certain frequency of light waves, nonetheless this tells you nothing about why this frequency gives rise to the sensation of the color red. Once more, an identity in kind seems to be lacking between the motion and the sensation. Or, as Dewey puts it, in even stronger terms: "No identity between the conscious facts and the various forms of physical motion can be discovered which will enable us to explain one by the other" (EW 2: 41).

Dewey augments his physical argument against the materialist view with a psychological argument. The psychological argument is that material motions are never known independently of the mind; they exist only as known phenomenon. "The fact of motion . . . is not a fact which precedes knowledge and can be used to account for it, but it is a fact *in* knowledge" (EW 2: 41). Motions are something whose existence we seem to have knowledge about, especially since they help us to account for the origin of our knowledge, but we never really get outside of our own minds to grasp the motions pure and simple; hence, the motions cannot serve as the external cause of our knowledge, its ultimate explanation. The object does not explain the subject. The reverse rather is the case: the subject explains the object; the knowing mind explains the thing known. What needs to be shown is "how the subject, as knowing, is involved in all those facts which the physical sciences treated merely as existing facts, overlooking that they are in reality facts *known* to exist, as facts in relation to mind" (EW 2: 41–42). The idea of external motions has explanatory power, but it does not follow that we can ever know external reality in its own externality and know that its features are the cause of our knowledge.

Having discounted materialism to his satisfaction, Dewey pushes on to give his own account of the relation between nerve discharges and sensations. There is a connection, obviously, but what is it? The sensation cannot be a copy of the nerve discharge, the result of a similar feature passed from one to the other, for the quality of the sensation qua sensation is not *in* the brain activity—color, for example, is not in brain activity in the same way as it is in sensation. Brain activity has no color. Again, the two are different. Hence, one cannot be a mere copy of the other.

The connection seems to be, rather, that the one occasions the other. The brain stimulates the mind into action. The mind responds, in its own unique fashion, and creates sensations as its own "virtual" product, one not reducible to the brain charges that occasioned the mental activity, but a product that "the facts" of the brain charges themselves allow (EW 2: 42). The nerve action is not the cause, but merely the occasion, for the mind to spring forth with its own creations of meaning beyond the brain activity. In Dewey's words, "a sensation is not the simple affection of the soul by some bodily change, although the affection is a necessary prerequisite to sensation. The sensation is the state developed out of and by the soul itself upon occasion of this affection" (EW 2: 42–43). As he sees it, the mind is creative—engaged in a kind of virtual production of reality—when the brain activity stimulates it into action. "The soul, when thus incited to action, responds to the stimulation with a characteristic production of its own, whose appearance, relatively to the physical phenomena, is a virtual creation; that is, cannot be in any way got out of them" (EW 2: 42).[4] And again: "Physical energy is always external; it never acts upon itself, but is transferred beyond itself. . . . But the mind has the power of acting upon itself and of producing from within itself a new, original, and unique activity which we know as sensation" (EW 2: 43). The brain activity serves, in effect, to elicit what is an original response, but also what is a mechanical response, in that the brain activity elicits the response without our direct awareness and always with certain definite responses of characteristic sensations. The *forms* of the mind, in essence, are awakened into their own mindlike activities of sensory production upon the occasion of nerve activity. The facts of nerve activity occasion the virtual productions of mind, which go beyond the facts in their meaning, and yet the virtual productions grow out of these facts in the sense that the facts permit the meanings they occasion to be true of the facts. The brain activity in no way *resists* the virtual production of the sensation of red, for example, or the concept of love or justice, and so on, even though the concept is irreducible to the brain activity.

This is a remarkable view. We will have occasion to assess it in more detail later, but for now it is important to note that Dewey here avoids both dualism and materialism in accounting for sensations. Dewey may appear to be a full-fledged dualist, since he speaks about the mind as something different from matter, with its own unique mental productions, and so on. But he does stress that the mind or self is only really a process or activity. As he puts it, the "self is, as we have so often seen, *activity*. It is not something *which* acts; it is activity" (EW 2: 216). His basic view would then be one in which the self is a swirl of motions that congeal into rupturing pulses that, somehow, create meaning; in which case the self is not a substance, not a distinct entity imposing its forms, but rather part of one overall developing process, in which the part to be played, as it were, by the self is to break off from the original motions and to develop them beyond themselves. We may well have a process philosophy before us, with a process view of the self, which complicates the simple identification of Dewey's position with dualism, not least because dualism is the view that reality consists of two distinct kinds of *substance*. Dewey's view seems to be that there is really only one stuff, motions, some portion of which—call it *minds*—forms into patterns with their own distinct responses, which invent, as part of their virtual creations, sensations for themselves that are distinct in quality from the original motions themselves.

The Birth of Sensations

The next step in Dewey's argument is to explain how the mind develops its sensations. In particular, we need to see how Dewey thinks the original sensuous continuum gets differentiated into distinct sensations. Thereafter we must explore how he thinks these distinct sensations get further developed into our knowledge of objects, as well as into our knowledge of ourselves, the subjects who are and who know. How is it that the mind, once it produces the vague sensuous continuum, differentiates it into actual sensations, such as red and cold and so on? How does the mind then take up these distinct sensations and use them to build up its knowledge of the world, that is, of the actual, real objects that exist, and of our own self that knows them? And how does it do this, all the while, in such a way as to show that the world is in fact meaningful, full of significance for us, and not simply a barren desert of indifference?

We have seen that according to Dewey, motions awaken the mind into its own distinctive activity. At first the result is a vague sensuous continuum, already quite separate in quality from the motions themselves. The sensuous continuum represents how I at first take in and process the motions, what they mean *for me*, at the lowest level of my experience of them. "The original sensation has a maximum of mere feeling or emotional quality, and a minimum of intellectual value. It is simply the condition, the inner affection of the organism itself; it tells or reports practically nothing. It gives us no qualities of objects. Going on from this point, we may classify our present sensations" (EW 2: 46). But the sensuous continuum serves as the medium from which I can draw out and begin to separate distinct sensations. The mind learns to take another step away from the motions by breaking up this sensuous continuum into separate sensations and gradually learns to give them intellectual or abstract value as well.

We can begin to break the continuum into separate sensations because "no special sense organ can be purely passive, even physically speaking, in sensation. It must adjust itself to the stimulus. . . . We must sniff with the nostrils. The tympanum of the ear must be stretched; the eye-lenses must be accommodated, and the two eyes converged" (EW 2: 47). The structure of our bodies already lends itself to the breaking up of the continuum. The mind, by its own effort in certain directions, as we will see, discriminates these sensations even more through its own interpretations, referring one sensation to another to give it a sense of its import in relation to the others. The sensations then take on intellectual value in addition to vague emotional value, and we gradually form our sensations into objects, and eventually a whole world, that we know.

The original sensuous continuum, Dewey tells us, can be compared to our overall "organic or general sensation" as we are experiencing it at any given time; or to the experience of drifting into sleep, when one by one the various senses fade out and we are left with a hazy, fading, homogenous state of awareness; or to the experience of an infant before it learns to differentiate things (EW 2: 45). Using these analogies, "we can form some idea of what a shapeless, vague, diffused state a sensation is to, say, an oyster or a jelly-fish" (EW 2: 46). Such is the kind of sensation that underlies all of our experience and forms its basis. It is indistinct. But it can become richer and more detailed through our different activities, just as seeing is more refined in its efforts than smelling (EW 2:46–47). "The eyes are constantly on the lookout for sensation. Instead of a mirror waiting for impressions, like the lower senses, they are a dark lantern rapidly moving and focusing here and there" (EW 2: 47). This higher level of sophistication, moreover, is achieved not by the sense organs alone, but by higher forms of intellectual discrimination. To have distinct sensations, we must first divide up the sensuous continuum; we must intellectually discriminate it into separate parts. The sense organs already push us in this direction, and the "discriminating" power of the mind completes the process. The eye may lead me to slightly distinguish the color of red, for example, from the sensuous continuum, but the concept of red is needed to identify a sensation that is definitely and distinctly red and to complete the process (EW 2:47; 44). We may think we simply open our eyes and possess ready-made sensations. "But, in reality, this is a complex psychical product, formed by judgments which are the interpretations of the sensuous material and not the material itself" (EW 2: 65). The sensations we experience are the product of our own activities and develop along the lines of our activities.

In general, sensation develops from the original sensuous continuum into particular, distinct sensations, into objects in space and
time, and then into objects with definite connections to others, objects in systematic arrangements, and eventually into "an ordered,
harmonious world, or cosmos; not . . . a chaos" (EW 2: 76). The self
further adds its own ideal contents to the system in a gesture that
adds significance to life. "The epic of Homer, the tragedy of Sophocles, the statue of Phidias, the symphony of Beethoven are *creations*.
Although having a correspondence with actual existences, they do not
reproduce them. They are virtual additions to the world's riches; they
are ideal. Such creations are not confined to art, nor are they remote
from our daily existence" (EW 2: 77). Our idealizations transform a
flower into a symbol of love, for example, or certain modes of action
into kindness, or a handshake into friendship, and so on. Our idealizations are the source of all the deeper meanings of life, all that
makes a life worth living. The meanings never derive from sensations
by themselves. "When shall we *see* justice? Who has touched righ-
teousness? What sense or combination of senses gives us the idea of
the state or the church; of history, as the development of man; of
God, or the source and end of all our strivings?" (EW2: 77). The idealizations of life are the basis of meaning, not sensations or given particulars. The self shapes the world as meaningful; it does not find
meaning already there. It seeks harmony; it does not find harmony in
things themselves as they are.

Lastly, the self also shapes itself through the development of the
sensuous continuum. A knowing self evolves; it learns about itself
through its actions and affections, through how its sensations occur
and respond in the world; this is a self that grows and develops along
higher and higher cycles of meaning, as we will see—a self, in addition, that becomes more and more real in the world as it injects,
through will, its own creations into the heart of things (EW 2: 75–78).

Apperception and Retention

There are two mental processes by which all this occurs: "apperception" and "retention." *Apperception* is the process whereby the mind

acts on "sensuous material" and structures it after the mind's own pattern. *Retention* occurs when the structured, "apperceived" contents that make up our experience "react upon the mind and develop it," giving the mind new meaning and direction pertaining to itself (EW 2: 78–81; 131).

In terms of strictly intellectual content and processes, only that which is meaningful occurs to the mind. In other words, all "inquiry," or "investigation," all thinking, is of what is "*significant*." "Whatever is meaningless has no point of contact with intelligence or the apperceiving activity of mind. The main-spring of our cognitive experiences is the more or less conscious feeling that things have meaning" (EW 2: 78). This meaning occurs, moreover, when some sensation "is connected in an orderly way with the rest of our experience. The meaningless is that which is out of harmony, which has no connection with other elements." And again: "Relationship is the essence of meaning" (EW 2: 78–79).

There is, therefore, no one, first, particular sensation. A sensation becomes particular in and through its relation to other sensations. And sensations get into relationships with other sensations through the ordering and connecting power of the mind—through apperception and retention—so that we grasp the intellectual meaning of sensations through relating each sensation (either all at once or sequentially) to other sensations *that we have already experienced*. The key to the formation of intellectual meaning is the use of our past experience of some sensations to inform our present understanding of some new sensation, that is, to connect it up with other sensations of ours and hence to understand the new sensation in terms of its relationships. The relationship occurring between sensations—the essence of meaning—is provided by the self and its grasp of past events, not by a mind-independent world of external objects. Dewey gives the following example to support this position. Suppose that a child is presented with an orange, which is new to him. The child will have several separate sensations, such as tangy (when he tastes it), a certain texture when he touches it, and a visual sensation of the color orange.

Cognitively, the child must connect these sensations into a unified whole to understand that they all refer to a single object, the fruit we know of as an orange. But this is not enough. The child must also recognize the object as an orange to be able to really know it, and the only way he can do this is to connect it with other objects that he already knows, for example fruit, apple, banana, and so on (EW 2: 79–80).

There are at least two objections to this position that Dewey entertains. The first is that, as a matter of fact, we *do* know about things without past experiences, and we learn everything we need to know about such things simply by investigating them for the first time. The second objection is that there must be *something* we know at first, a first experience, if we are going to be able to base all our knowledge on past experiences; for otherwise, we would never know anything. All of our experiences would be referred back to a previous one and this to a previous one before that, and so on, without any one experience gaining the support of a known thing to begin with. To make sense of any one known thing, it seems there must have been a first knowledge, in infancy, say, on which all of our later and adult experiences are built up (EW 2: 80–81).

But the first objection, Dewey maintains, is a real mistake. For with any new item presented, we must first at least know that it is a thing, in order to be able to recognize it (if we did not know that it is a thing, we would never even be able to grab it or pick it up to try to gain more information about it)—that is, we certainly must base our grasp of it on *some* past experience, an experience with "things," or something that exists. And the same goes for its other qualities. If "a strange fruit" were presented to us that we had never experienced before, we would have to touch it and taste it, and so on, and refer the touch and taste to other fruits that we had known, in order to place the strange fruit in the order of fruits and come to understand the kind of fruit it is (EW 2: 80).

The second objection appears to be more serious, but Dewey makes short work of it. The objection simply misses a key feature of what it means to know. Knowledge "is a matter of gradual growth. The first years of childhood are spent, not so much in knowing things, as in getting experiences which may be brought to bear in the future, and thus enable him to know. . . . The child spends his early years in *learning* to know" (EW 2: 81). There does not need to be a first known thing in order for one to connect any would-be known thing with past experiences. All there needs to be is some past experience, and this the child acquires before he or she actually comes to know anything in particular.

Let us now consider in more detail the actual processes of knowing and see how they function to transform sensations into ordered objects in their relationships, that is, into intellectually meaningful objects. In other words, let us consider in more detail how apperception and retention work.

The power of apperception takes three different forms: "association," "dissociation," and "attention" (EW 2: 81). *Association* is the process whereby "*the activity of mind never leaves sensuous elements isolated, but connects them into larger wholes*" (EW 2: 83). *Dissociation* is the process whereby the mind separates some part from the whole. *Attention* is the process by which the mind focuses on the separated parts and "*attends*" to them for itself (EW 2: 81–82).

There are two forms of association: "presentative" and "representative" (EW 2: 85). *Presentative association* is the mechanical bringing together of simultaneous sensations into a unity. "The mind's hunger for the fullest experience possible," "the maximum of significance," leads it, for example, to unite "a rod striking a surface at certain intervals" with "a noise," even if the two are unrelated and not causally connected (EW 2: 85). The mind nonetheless puts them together as it puts together all its separate sensations (a sensation by itself is unimaginable). All of the simultaneously occurring separate sensations, given separately through the different senses (as they must be), are brought into a whole, "*into one total maximum experience*" (EW 2: 85), as for example the different properties of an orange—its taste, smell, sight, and so on—are brought into the single experience of the fruit.⁵ We then have the perceived object of an orange that sits there before us.

Representative association, or the mechanical association of present sensations with past ones, takes two forms, "accidental" and "intrinsic," which Dewey also calls "external" and "internal" (EW 2: 87–88; 97). *Accidental association* is the mechanical bringing together of present and past through an arbitrary connection in our experience, as when the smell of an orange reminds me of a certain person, since the person happened to be eating oranges when I met him. The present experience of the orange enlarges its meaning due to the inclusion within it of my past experience with the orange and who ate it. The present experience is now not just of the orange, but also of this person who ate it. *Intrinsic association* is the mechanical conjunction of present and past based on some real similarity between the sensations, for example the connection of the experience "dog" to the various dogs that I encounter, whether a poodle, German shepherd, mutt, or other type of dog (EW 2: 95).

What happens in both accidental and intrinsic association is fusion of past and present experience into a single new idea, into one idea, not several disconnected ones. "If the perception of a flower recalls the spot where I picked it, it is because the flower and the place are members of the same whole; they are organically united in the same activity of apperception; one has no mental existence without the other" (EW 2: 90). The past experience is dragged along into the present one, becoming an essential part of it, and "the train of ideas is formed" (EW 2: 88). Ideas begin to move and flow as connected parts of the same overall experience, as opposed to separate ideas chopped up and unrelated to each other. Through both these processes, accidental and intrinsic association, the mind is freed from the unified sensations of the given moment and is able to expand to include wholly new ideas that combine present and past, thereby enriching the experience. The mind is thus able to grow and enlarge itself. "It enriches its present experience by supplying the results of previous experiences" (EW 2: 87). It is able to create new, enlarged experiences that are supplied by it and that take it well beyond any given, determining fact.

The crucial feature of all forms of association is that they are mechanical. We can see that the mind imposes unity upon its sensations; Dewey notes that in hearing someone speak, for example, "I do not apperceive separately each sound, and then piece them together. I take in the idea of the whole sentence. . . . [T]he synthesis precedes analysis" (EW 2: 90). But this imposition is mechanical. I do not consciously think about it. It is the result of habit; and the great function of habit is that it frees the mind to function in other ways. One of these other ways is by dissociation.

Dissociation is the power of the mind to separate its given sensations in the train of ideas one from the other, so that any divisions that come to exist in our experience are the result of the mind's own activity (just as are any unities that come to exist in our experience, as we have seen). The mind does not do this based on any inherent differences in the sensations—for taken on their own terms, "each is worth as much as every other" (EW 2: 108). Rather, the mind places its own "*interest*" into the train of sensations, and this interest is what divides up the sensations and makes some stand out over and above others.

> We have to recognize that the meaning of psychical life is determined largely by the differences of *value* that its elements possess. This difference of value is not due to their existence as data, for as existences each is worth as much as every other; it is due to their relation to the mind, that is, to the *interest* which the self takes in them. The interests of the self are the factor which is influential in breaking up the hard rigidity of psychical life governed wholly by the principle of association, and introducing flexibility and perspective into it. (EW 2: 108)

Dissociation is the mind's ability to part ways with habit, once habit's patterns of association have provided enough stability for mental life to build upon. This ability is the result of the self's own interests. Relative to the interest the self takes in certain sensations, our sensations—already unified by presentative association and enlarged by representative association to include past experiences—can grow even further, and along the lines of what is important to the self. Certain parts of the field of sensations can stand out for special consideration. This then frees the mind to utilize the additional power of attention, which, as we will see in a moment, will empower our mental life even more, allowing us to attend to, concentrate upon, and reshape the train of experiences we are having.

Dissociation divides into two forms, based on the type of interest the self takes in its sensations: "natural" and "acquired" (EW 2: 108). Dissociation based on natural interest further divides into two kinds, "quantity" and "tone" (EW 2: 108–09). The self naturally tends to take an interest in sudden or intense quantities of sensation, and certain tones are either "agreeable" or "disagreeable" to it, and it takes an interest in them accordingly. These elements of the experience are then separated out from the stream of experience and are noticed and dwelt upon, while the other elements recede into a kind of background. This shows again that the mind, and not the bare fact of a sensation, plays a crucial role in the sensations that we come to know.

Dissociation based on acquired interest is very important; indeed, "advance in psychical life depends largely upon the power of advancing from natural values to acquired" (EW 2: 109). Because of this advance—that is, because the self is able to take an interest in experience over and above what is only naturally conducive to it, in things that it learns to be interested in throughout its life—the self can advance beyond mechanical association and render present experience even more meaningful, placing in the present experience some *significance* relative to what the self has learned in the past. "Acquired interest . . . necessarily leads the mind beyond what is actually present to other elements in our experience which give what is present its attractive power. The mental life of an animal always remains upon a low plane, because it is taken up with the interesting features of the *sensations* as such," whereas due to the power of our acquired interests, which we learn to adopt beyond only natural interests, we can be "led beyond" our sensations "to relate them to each other in a meaningful way" (EW 2: 109).

Acquired values are of two types, familiar and novel (EW 2: 110–13). Familiar values are of two types, the more recent and the repetitious. The more recent experience figures more prominently in our psychic life, whatever that experience happens to be (whatever its acquired content is), and likewise an experience repeated over and over again begins to form our bedrock, familiar basis for having any experiences at all. It becomes what is near and dear to us, a part of our lives; while things less related to it fade out into experiences we are more removed from and less interested in. Novel values are those that are acquired through their sheer novelty. "It is the new, the unfamiliar, that attracts notice, and that is especially emphasized in consciousness" (EW 2: 110–13). Familiar and novel values work together to produce developing experiences for us, in that familiar experience lets our past inform our present, while novel experience lets us see the present as different from the past (EW 2: 114).

Dissociation in all of its forms is a step toward allowing the mind's power of attention to set to work. Because some elements of experience are highlighted in dissociation and made the focus of our mental life, the mind can attend to them. That is to say, due to dissociation, some sensations are released from the routine and mechanical ordering of association. Here Dewey stresses the power of "the negative function" of the mind: "If left to itself," mechanical association would create "bonds which tie the mind down to objective data, without allowing it free play according to its own interests" (EW 2: 115). He explains: "The perfection of the principle of association would be reached when the mind was governed by purely mechanical principles, and its activity controlled by external considerations. The negative function of dissociation is to break up this control" (EW 2: 115). Thus, the negative power of the mind, which breaks the chains of objective order, is an essential asset. It sets "the mind or self free from its subjection to purely objective influences . . . causing it to act for *ends of its own,* that is, for *ideal or internal ends.* In short, dissociation paves the way for *attention,* which is simply this mental activity for self-regulated ends" (EW 2: 115). Freed from having to obey the mechanical order of sensations by the power to select some of them at the expense of others, the mind is "set free" to pursue "its own ends," to go with the direction of its own interests. When it does thus go entirely in the direction of its own interest, this is *attention*.

It is with attention that the mind truly begins to introduce idealizations into its experiences, and to complete the process of rendering known objects as things that occur in relation to the mind, not independently of it. Attention is the process of actively selecting some sensations to focus on relative to some aim or purpose we have. "Attention always selects with reference to some end which the mind has in view, some difficulty to be cleared up, some problem to be solved, some idea to be gained, or plan to be formed" (EW 2: 119). This end is supplied by the self, which organizes sensations according to its interests. More particularly, sensations are selected that may serve as "signs" for future experiences, for what to expect; sensations that do not serve this function get dropped. They are not even noticed at all, and form no part of our knowledge of a thing. Sensations that may serve as signs of things are selected (EW 2: 120). The sense of how to interpret a sensation as a sign is provided by our past experiences. Our past experiences direct us to pick one thing as a sign of things and not another. The sensations selected in this way are taken up, moreover, in terms of their relations to other sensations. It is only when a sensation of a thing occurs in a relation to other such sensations that it has any intellectual meaning and purport. A bare sensation, one that cannot be related to another sensation, has no intellectual value. If you are doing a logical proof, for example, and you are given only the symbol S, you cannot precede with the proof; the bare symbol has no significance. It gains significance only by being connected to other symbols and its function relative to them. It gains this connection, moreover, only from the self bringing its past experiences to bear on the symbol S and its relation to other symbols. For a person with no familiarity with formal logic, the symbol has no connection to the other symbols.

So, the self selects the sensations that will matter for it—the ones that can be taken as signs of something relative to achieving its interests and ends, and the sensations gain their significance as signs in relation to the other sensations with which we are familiar, which we bring to bear on the sensations from the resources of our past experiences. In doing these things, the self is, in effect, idealizing its bare sensations. By *idealization*, Dewey means "the process by which the self, *acting upon the basis of its past experiences,* interprets sensations" (EW 2: 131). In knowledge, no fact or sensation exists by itself; it exists only as it is interpreted by the self. "Knowledge always consists of *interpreted* sensations: elements which have gained meaning by their connections with other elements, of which they serve as signs" (EW 2: 120). As an actual existence, a sensation has no meaning. Its meaning consists in how we take it up in its relationship to other sensations, and this relationship is supplied only by the self and what it has been. To use Dewey's example, the act of swinging your arm has, as its actual existence, only the felt muscular sensation. But its meaning consists in the *reason* we are doing it, the end to be achieved by doing it (EW 2: 120–21). Its meaning is ideal. It goes beyond the actual existence of the felt sensation to something else, to an aim and understanding of what we are doing, which we acquire because in the past it has meant this same thing. We might also go further than Dewey here and observe that the meaning behind the swinging always exists in relation *a wider system* of other sensations and their meanings supplied by past experience—for example, that swinging your arm is the act of throwing a pitch in a game of baseball. We can then grasp Dewey's point. Considered by themselves, the swinging of your arm, the people positioned a certain way on a field, the crowd, and so forth— these bare sensations do not mean baseball. Considered as idealized meanings beyond what is actually present, and relative to how I have taken these experiences before, that is, as throwing a pitch, playing a game, scoring a point, striking out, and so forth, these sensations gain meaning. And they gain this meaning only in relation to each other. You understand what throwing a pitch means only because you understand what scoring a point means, and so on. "*Meaning* always takes us beyond the bare presentation, to its connections and relations to the rest of experience" (EW 2: 121).

Another way to put this last point is to say that knowledge occurs when we unify our sensations into a whole. We must relate each of the parts to the others if we are to understand any of them. But if our only action was to unify our sensations into a total, homogenized whole, all things would blend together and we would have no knowledge of anything in particular. We must also differentiate our sensations at the same time. That is, we must be able to distinguish one sensation from the other in the whole of sensations that we grasp. Knowledge occurs when a unity of sensations occurs alongside a keen discernment of the differences between the elements that are unified. "While the goal of knowledge is complete unity, or a perfectly harmonious relation of all facts and events to each other, this unity shall be one which shall contain the greatest possible amount of specification, or distinction within itself" (EW 2: 130). In essence, knowledge is an understanding of how things fit together, grasping the role specific things play in the overall system of known things as well as possessing thereby an understanding of the overall system. The mind relates its sensations to each other in this way, and there is knowledge.

The Nature of Knowledge

As soon as we define knowledge in this way, as the mind's relating of sensations to each other into a unified system of distinct parts, we can see clearly that knowledge is a process of idealization, and that its features are provided by the self, and not the object. We might state the argument in something like syllogistic form. "Attention . . . is a relating activity, and . . . there is no knowledge without relation"; therefore "there is none without attention" (EW 2: 130). In other words, knowledge requires relations; it is attention that organizes and provides the relations; and so knowledge requires attention. But attention is an act of idealization. So, knowledge requires an act of idealization.

The upshot of this view of knowledge is that "experience . . . or the world of known objects, is not a colorless copy of what actually exists, stereotyped or impressed upon us, but is an experience produced by the mind acting according to the interests of self in interpreting sensuous data" (EW 2: 120). The self always shapes the mass of sensations in its own way, so as to grasp and master them in an orderly, intelligible fashion, relative to its interests.[6] The result of this shaping, and not a mere passive reception of something external, constitutes knowledge. "We know with what we have known" (EW 2: 125). And we know with our interests in mind, with our own acts of attention shaping the product of what is to be known.

But this means, in effect, that all knowledge is about "self-realization" (EW 2:216). We know in order to become. Attention, as we saw, is relative to the interests and ends of the self, and is organized to help us fulfill these interests and ends. "The various activities of attention" [namely, selection of sensations, their interpretation based on past experience, and the relation of sensations to one another]

> are based in the interests of the self, and directed towards ends which will satisfy the self, by fulfilling these interests. Its process is such a direction of its own contents that these ends will be reached. Starting-point, goal, and way are all found in the self, therefore. Attention is thus a process of self-development. (EW 2: 118)

We pay attention in order to realize our interests, that is, in order to realize ourselves. Acquiring knowledge is one of the ways we pay attention in order to realize our selves. We gain knowledge in order to learn about the world in which we live; and we want to learn about the world in which we live in order to realize our ends within it. Since, in the process of knowing, we are shaping and constructing what we know relative to our selves, all knowledge is a phase of our self-realization.

Moreover, knowledge is always about "self-knowledge." Since to know an object means, in effect, that "the mind puts itself into it," when we know an object we know ourselves (EW 2: 125–26). Dewey puts the point in this way:

> The fact known is not a bare fact, that is, an existence implying no constructive activity of intelligence, but is idealized fact, existence

upon which the constructive intelligence has been at work. That which is not thus idealized by the mind has no existence for intelligence. All knowledge is thus, in a certain sense, self-knowledge. Knowing is not the process by which ready-made objects impress themselves upon the mind, but is the process by which self renders sensations significant by reading itself into them. (EW 2: 126)

In coming to know the world, I come to know myself. I learn how I organize my experiences and to what end. I meet myself, and become familiar with who and what I am, through engagement with the world. Now we can see the implications: there is no alienation from the world of objects; I am at home among them, for they are what they are through me. The self is putting its own significance and order into its sensation, "which as bare existence it does not have" (EW 2: 122). What the self knows, therefore, in coming to know a sensation and its meaning, is its own self. It comes to know an organized world of objects—an intelligible ordering of things, which meets its own need for intelligibility and order and in which it can find its own distinct place.

Self-Knowledge

We have considered the three forms of apperception, or the way the self organizes its sensations: association, dissociation, and attention. The next step is to explain *retention*, or the way the apperceived material will "react upon the mind and develop it" (EW 2: 131). For in gaining knowledge, the self does not simply impose its structure on sensations; the structured sensations also inform the self and allow it, in effect, to enlarge itself, to become different, relative to the knowledge gained (EW 2: 130ff.).

The important point about retention and how it functions is that it is not a process by which contents are somehow added to the mind, as if the ideas had independent existence and the self were a mere container, as the dualist might maintain. Nor is retention comparable to the self having in mind "faint or unconscious copies of its original experiences" (EW 2: 134), as some realists would hold. What happens

instead is that the ideas we have once experienced become totally in-
tertwined with who we are; though the original sensation of the idea
has passed, the idea has had an effect on us, molding what we pres-
ently are. We therefore carry on the existence of the past content in
our very selves (EW 2:132).

The process works in the following way. At first, as infants, we have
no ideas, no organized sensations, no knowledge, no character or self.
We do have certain capacities for experiencing things, however, and
these we use to have experiences. One of these capacities is the power
of retention. Retention is the power to preserve apperceived content,
to infuse it into ourselves. A simple example will help explain the
process:

> The infant comes into the world with no *definite* tendencies and
> abilities except some inherited ones, which are instinctive. These
> he uses to gain experiences with, but these experiences once got,
> immediately react upon the mind and develop it. They organize
> it in some particular direction. The mind of the child which has
> apperceived his nurse is not the same that it was before; he has
> formed an organ in his mind for the performing of like appercep-
> tions in the future. (EW 2: 131)

The mind itself expands, so that from an original capacity to apperceive and on the occurrence of a new sensation (the sensory elements related to the nurse) apperception occurs, and then a first
vague experience is had. Due to the power of retention, the first vague
experience determined by apperception does not disappear from the
mind. Instead, the mind has already changed, and has become more
than it previously was. It is now a mind with a further capacity to
apperceive, one that can apperceive sensory elements related to a
nurse, and can begin to know the nurse therefore, and act eventually
in relation to the nurse in a fuller way.

The process can be likened to what happens physiologically. Physiological growth is "not preservation of copies of the original molecu-
lar motions, but such a change in the structure of the nervous system
that, in responding to future stimuli, it acts in a more complex way,
containing elements due to the former motions" (EW 2: 134–35). So,

too, with the mind: "The mind grows, not by keeping unchanged within itself . . . copies of its original experiences, but by assimilating something from each experience, so that the next time it acts it has a more definite mode of activity to bring to bear, one which supplies a greater content to whatever is acted upon" (EW 2: 134).[7]

Or the process can be likened to the growth of a tree. Just as the tree is not passive in its reception of the materials of the earth, "but reacts upon them and works them over into its living tissue," so, too, with the self (EW 2: 132–33). The mind or self takes the apperceived content, which it has already idealized, into its own "living tissue," that is, into the sphere of its own mind, and transforms it yet again by making it part of the self. The self, accordingly, is changed and enlarged by the process as well and will experience new things.

Moreover, it follows from what has been said that retention is an activity of the mind in which idealization is added to idealization. Dewey explains the point as follows:

> In attention, as soon as the mind is brought to bear upon the sensation so as to read itself into it and give it meaning, the apperceived content becomes a condition which determines how the mind shall act in the future. Every element thus apprehended and absorbed into the mind gets an ideal existence, and becomes the means by which future idealizations, that is, acts of attention, are exercised. Attention forms *apperceptive organs*, in short. (EW 2: 132)

Retention is simply the capacity for increased apperception. An added capacity to apperceive in a new way is formed with every experience, and this addition is retention. This means that there is an initial idealization—when sensations are formed and apperceived—and that this idealization only grows, or advances, with the ongoing experiences of the self and its increasing capacity for apperception. We are about as far removed from any original "object," wholly unattached to the self, as we could be. "All knowledge is . . . self-knowledge" (EW 2: 126), in which the self comes more and more to realize itself, that is, to recognize itself, and not some foreign world of independent objects, as the basis of what it knows. At the basis of the facts of the world are the self's own meanings, which it alone has given to the facts. They are the meanings of an ordered and intelligible arrangement of sensations that the mind needs to possess, not simply the meanings of things in chaotic juxtaposition with one another.

We can begin to see, therefore, how Dewey's philosophy of rupture responds to modernism and the predicament it holds for humankind. In contrast to the modernist view of the rigid separation between human meaning and the facts of the world, Dewey's view renders the facts of the world meaningful. The self negates the given, goes beyond the external motions that are presented to it, and transforms them into meanings based on its own ideals, its own version of things, ever hopeful that these ideals are not simply its own but are one with the original external motions that occasioned them and from which the ideals broke off. To be sure, the ideals we seek for and create in some sense remain elusive to us, in that they operate unconsciously in our minds to shape external motions in a certain way. But in any case, in our construction and pursuit of these ideals, the external motions gain more and more meaning on a tentative basis, objects become known, and ultimately, Dewey will say, we realize that the meaning of known things lies in their pursuit, not in their attainment. The meaning is in the progress we make away from external motions, away from the given state of things, toward ideals. The meaning of the world comes to rest, not in a complete realization of the ideal, but in the drive that inspires us to realize it and thus to create ideal meanings and known things.

We turn next to a fuller consideration of how our knowledge itself conforms to this conception, that is, to how *what* we know (not only *how* we know) demonstrates that known objects are our own creations, the creation of which helps to give our lives meaning.

FIVE

WHAT WE KNOW

W e saw in the previous chapter how Dewey conceives of knowledge. We will now consider what it is that we know, in his
view. Dewey maintains that when we have knowledge we never grasp
facts in their pure, given state, but always construct and reorganize
them to render them more idealized. We will see in this chapter how
our aim in this endeavor, for Dewey, is to *know* the facts—that is, to
relate them together into a systematic whole, so that each becomes
intelligible. What we would like to achieve as inquirers is complete
knowledge. We would like to justify an intuition we have of there
being a whole world, an ordered cosmos, to which we and everything
else belong and in which everything can find its place. But the full,
rational justification of this intuition is a hard-won achievement, not
yet attained, the desire for which drives us on to discover more and
more things about the world and to organize it more adequately. As
we grow in knowledge, we approximate the final state of all knowing,
the achievement of a complete understanding of the universe as an
interconnected whole. But we have yet to achieve this result. The ideal

of this complete understanding, however, drives us on to negate, and then to idealize, every isolated fact, placing it in an ordered system of known things. And as a result our knowledge grows, even if we have no ultimate guarantee that in the end we will know everything (EW 2:200–1; 212).

All knowledge involves idealization, in other words, and it occurs in stages. We begin, not with mind-independent facts, but with our sensations, and we try to organize these into objects, which we then try to arrange in a systematic fashion, which in turn allows us to grasp the objects (or "the facts") in their true relationships. Thus, at one stage of knowledge there are sensations that are less idealized, and at another stage there are sensations that have become more idealized, more systematically arranged, and so are more firmly known. In between these two stages are varying degrees of idealization (EW 2: 137). The different stages of knowledge, in order from less idealized to more idealized, or less systematically known to more systematically known, are "Perception, Memory, Imagination, Thinking, Intuition" (EW 2: 138).

External Objects

Perception is knowledge of particular things, or of actual objects in the world. Such objects as they occur to us in perception are 1) different from the self; 2) distinguishable from one another; and 3) out there in space (EW 2: 139–40). Dewey tries to account for these features of perception wholly in terms of the conditions of knowing that we have seen so far, and hence wholly in terms of the form of idealism that he has so far advanced.

Perceptual objects are apparently different from us and exist out there independently of us. But Dewey notes that the perceived world, contrary to our first assumption, is not entirely an external, wholly real world existing "out there." "The perceived world is more than an *existent* world; it is a world existent for the consciousness of the individual, a *known* world" (EW 2: 140). Perceptual objects are always perceptual objects *for* someone. They must, therefore, be explained on this basis. Sensations by themselves cannot account for the externality of perceived objects, because they do not tell us anything by themselves, least of all that an existent world is there, distinct from me and my perceptions of it (EW 2: 140–41). In fact, the self has to *do* something to the sensations to make them yield an (apparently) external world of perceived objects. The self appropriates sensations and "takes them and projects them" out into a sphere of external things (EW 2: 141). The sensations of red and sweet that I experience, for example, must be held together by my knowledge of them as features of an apple, an object that I perceive to be out there in the world and that I can eat.

Dewey claims that the unity of the object, what makes it a single entity distinguishable from other objects, comes about in this way, which, as he notes, we have seen already at work (EW 2: 141). Presentative association occurs among our separate sensations and unifies them into the perception of an object along with the "redintegration" (or representative association) of previous sensations, which enlarges our understanding of what the object is there before us; attention then allows us to recognize that the unified sensations refer to an actual, specific thing, which we can use or respond to in some way based on our needs and interests (EW 2:88). The sensations of orange and round, occurring together, are associated and taken as signs (through redintegration) of something I can eat and get nourishment from (an orange), and distinguished (through dissociation) from other things I cannot (EW 2: 141).

The perception of objects in space also happens partly through our own activity; "all objects, as perceived, are projected in space, and given definite position" (EW 2: 142). Spatial relations are not presented to the mind at first; we do not have immediate knowledge of them. "If an adult lays his hand upon something he has a vague perception of space relations, while it requires movement to explore the outlines and make it definite. Infants, however, have not even such a vague perception. It is, therefore, the result of a process by which tactual sensations have become symbolic of motor" (EW 2: 143). We must learn the shape of things, learn to perceive things as spatial objects. Our perception of objects in space arises, more specifically, from the association of our movements with certain perceptions, which we are then capable of having even when we do not move. We come to "see" the experiences associated with our experience of certain movements, which we afterwards perceive as depth and the specific arrangement of objects even when we are not moving (EW 2: 144–45).

As Dewey puts it, "to say that an object is seen to be at such a distance, means that so much muscular sensation must be had before it can be touched; to say that it is of such an outline, is to say that certain muscular and local sensations would be had if the hand were passed about it, etc." (EW 2: 144). This is George Berkeley's argument, as Dewey notes, and in its wake everything concerning spatial relations militates against materialism and stays in the realm of sensations that are constructed by the self. "According to this theory, originally propounded by Bishop Berkeley, spatial relations are not originally perceived by the eye, but are the result of the association of visual sensations with previous muscular and tactual experiences" (EW 2: 144). Dewey adds, "[T]he adult comes to *see* all that he could touch if he tried. The visual sensations immediately and instantaneously call up all the tactual perceptions which have been associated with them, so that the individual has all the benefit of his previous experiences without being obliged to repeat them, or in this case actually to touch the objects" (EW 2: 144–45).

The process occurs in the following way, at least in the case of touch, on which I will focus. From out of a mass of indistinct sensations, we first isolate specific sensations, then associate them with the experience of our movements, and thereafter "intelligence . . . interprets" these specific sensations, now associated with our experience of movement, "into spatial order" (EW 2: 142). In other words, we feel our way into spatial relations, with the help of the mind.

First, we isolate specific sensations. Suppose we had two or more tactile sensations happening at the same time. They would not by themselves tell us anything about how any objects were arranged in space. "The mere presence of simultaneous sensations . . . is not identical with perception of spatial coexistence. The mind must recognize their distinction, and construe them spatially" (EW 2: 142). We must first distinguish the sensations from one another and then interpret them in spatial terms. The way the mind comes to understand the distinction between the two sensations is through the use of what Dewey calls a *local sign* (EW 2: 52). A local sign is a sensation, which we have come to "localize" somewhere specifically on our bodies, that results from a certain pressure on some part of the body, as well as from our own intellectual activity (EW 2: 52). We learn by contrast. Given a variety of pressures on the body, we learn to distinguish between different pressures of this kind, on different parts of the body, as an "*exercise* in discrimination" (EW 2: 52). If two different pressures are "sufficiently differentiated in quality," there will be two different experiences, or local signs, that we recognize as such because the self is able to discriminate between them, to keep them distinct, or to make them local to each sensation, based on the self's attention to the difference in quality of the sensation that is experienced (EW 2: 52). Through intellectual discrimination, we thus come to identify different experiences with different parts of our body.

But we still do not have an experience of a spatial relationship, only sensations that we make out to be separate and distinct from one another and that are therefore "kept from fusion with others" by reference to the local signs (EW 2: 143). The second thing that needs to take place is that we must associate the different local signs with the experience of our movement, so that, when we move, the "muscular sensations" we undergo are tied to different experiences of different local signs (EW 2:143). As I experience the movement of wrapping my hand around a cup, for example, different local signs will occur on my fingers and hand as I move around the cup. I associate the experience of this movement with the different local signs. The movement, in fact, gives rise to "certain fixed associations" between the local signs (EW 2: 143). The local signs thus come to be associated with these movements, but in such a way that they are coordinated, brought into one fluid experience of holding a cup, with the experience of the movement involved in rendering the cup more definite tied to the local signs that are experienced and coordinated. The cup takes on depth. Moreover, after these associations have been fixed, even when my hand is at rest on the cup, I have acquired something like a spatial perception of the cup, because I now associate the local signs with the experience of the movement of my hand around the cup, even when I am not moving my hand.

Lastly, the mind fills out this perception and reads into the world the perception of objects in space. "Intelligence . . . interprets these local signs, through their association with muscular sensations, into spatial order" (EW 2: 142). It advances my own experience as something that is actually going on out there, my own anticipation of resulting local signs being read into the world as a perception of objects with depth.

To show how it all works, Dewey uses the example of "the infant, as his hand is at rest upon some object" (EW 2: 143). Thanks to local signs, he can experience different qualities of sensation on different parts of his hand, instead of only one massive sensation. When he moves his hand, a certain motor sensation is experienced, and this experience will alter depending on the local signs and what it takes to experience them. "It will not give the same kind of sensation to go from the little finger to the thumb as from the latter to the wrist" (EW 2: 143). These different experiences of movement will produce different local signs, but the sum of the experience of movements will gather the local signs into a coordinated relationship with the experience of the movement. The infant will eventually be able to experience the depth of the cup, even when the infant is not moving his or her hand, for the touch stands in for the movement, which was definite in the past. The mind then interprets this experience of depth as a spatial relationship existing among objects. "The perception of spatial relations is due to the association of muscular sensations with others, interpreted by the apperceptive activity of mind" (EW 2: 142).

Differentiation between "self and not-self" in spatial perception also occurs by the very activity of the processes that Dewey has so far laid out. To unify separate sensations into distinct objects and project them into space is already to jettison into the world the not-self, and to distinguish it from the self (EW 2: 150). Here the mind excels at its power of dissociation, which becomes uppermost (EW 2: 151). The reason this occurs is to be found in the will. Only by the exertion of muscular movements (occasioned by the will) can the unified objects become projected into space. And indeed it is only through such acts of will that we can distinguish subjective from objective sensations at all—as when, to tell if an object on the wall we sense as red really is red, we move our eyes and bodies to see if it stays red under varying circumstances. If the object stays red, it is objectively red; if its color alters, it is subjectively red (EW 2: 151). "Were there no will to origi-nate these movements, there is no reason to believe that we should ever come to distinguish sensations as objective or referred to things, or as subjective, referred to the organism" (EW 2: 151). There would be no distinction between self and not-self, but only one unified, fuzzy, massive sensation. There would be no perception of objects. But precisely because of my activities, the perception alters; and I am able to perceive certain objects as being out there in a more real and enduring fashion, and others as originating more from my own sub-jective states.

Knowledge of the Past

Memory is the next stage of knowledge. Perception alone cannot be complete knowledge, because it supplies us with awareness only of particular things here and now, and there is more to what can be known than this. We can also know the past. Said another way, we can have "*knowledge of particular things or events once present, but no longer so*" (EW 2: 154; italics in original). But how do we do this? Just because we have had the experience, it does not follow that we would still have it and remember it. For the experience is gone; it exists no more (EW 2: 155). The answer is that the mind must actively assemble the past experience.

> Memory is not a passive process in which past experiences thrust themselves upon the mind, any more than perception is one where present experiences impress themselves. It is a process of construction. In fact it involves more of constructive activity than perception. In perception the objects, at all events, do exist before

the perception construes them [that is, they do refer to some sensations that are occasioned by some actual external movements]. In memory they do not. Our past experiences are gone just as much as the time in which they occurred. They have no existence until the mind reconstructs them. (EW 2: 155)

In memory, the mind's idealization of things becomes even greater than in perception, for the remembered object exists entirely in the mind and through the mind's construction. The remembered object has no actual existence, although it may correspond to a particular thing or event that *did* once have existence.

To see that the object in this case is entirely ideal, the product of the mind's constructive activity, consider that association alone cannot account for it. At best, association will give us "the *presence* of the object" (EW 2: 156). But we must also be able to "*re-cognize*" the object as having been "a previous" part "of our experience," and so we must situate it in terms of "temporal" relations: "the mind must actively take hold of the idea and project it into time, just as in perceiving it takes hold of the sensation and projects it into space" (EW 2: 156).

We do this in the following ways. First, we form a mental image. This occurs primarily through association. Representative association ensures that some past object is linked up with some present object; disassociation, however, also makes manifest the differences between the present object and the past one. The image of the past object then stands out in its own right, as occasioned by the present object but distinguished from it, its own object, an image of the past event (EW 2: 158–59). Attention further allows us to focus on one such image; rather than letting association drag up random chains of past events with respect to that image, attention allows the self to recall specific moments as it needs to. This process Dewey calls *recollection* (EW 2: 160).

The image must also be related to other past experiences in succession, however, if it is to constitute a remembered object proper (EW 2: 160). We always remember an event as occurring at some specific time in relation to other events occurring at other times; we situate the event temporally. This happens, according to Dewey, primarily "through the sensation of hearing" (EW 2: 161). Sounds occur one after the other; moreover, they are associated with muscular movements, as in rhythm (EW 2: 161). Indeed, rhythm plays a crucial role in time perception, in this account. Rhythm is so essential to human life that "all the early traditions of the race are expressed by its means," and dance, which accompanies rhythm, "may, in some way, be considered more natural than walking, which is, after all, but a more regular dance" (EW 2: 161–62). Through rhythm we acquire the rudimentary, the fundamental basis of the perception of things in time. "In rhythm every sound points, by its very structure, both to the past and future. Every part of the sound is at once a continuation of the old sound . . . and a transition from it" (EW 2: 163). This is a prelude to what happens in our perception of time: we recognize some event as "changed from some previous event, and still connected with it" (EW 2: 163–64). Moreover, in rhythm there are repetitions and changes, the sense at once of both permanence (a temporal stretch that continues) and elements that fade away (the actual moments of time that pass). The basic emergence of time can be seen in the rhythms of the hungry child: "hunger and satisfaction . . . are exceedingly different from each other, and yet one succeeds the other. They may, accordingly, form the rudiments of the perception of succession. . . . The very tendency of the child, while hungry, to recall his previous satisfaction, and to anticipate the coming one, is the beginning of the recognition of time" (EW 2: 164). We project our lived rhythms into things, and temporal succession is born. It becomes more orderly and definite when we consciously link up events with other events and speak of their relationship: which came first and which later, and so on (EW 2: 164).

Lastly, memory involves, not simply the placement of distinct events in a successive order, but also the distinction of the self from these successive events. This seems implausible at first, since one could argue that the self must actually be identified with its passing moments, but Dewey's argument is that memory involves the necessity of a self who is remembering, a self-same self in both past and present, who *has* memories, and so consequently is not to be identified fully with them. There must indeed be a present self (if there is

to be someone who has a memory), and the present self must be having a past idea (if there is to be a memory). There must be "a now
and a then," and a self who is aware of the now and the then. But this
means, according to Dewey, that the self must recognize itself as present both now and then—that is, as the same enduring self, who is the
link connecting present and past experience (EW 2: 165). In Dewey's
words, "memory requires a now and a then—the recognized difference between past and present; and this is not possible without the
recognition of the difference between a self which is present both now
and then, permanently present, and the idea which changes, and consequently *was then*, but is not now" (EW 2: 165). Memory requires a
present self aware of itself as the enduring connecting link between
present and past experience.

At this point in his argument, Dewey notes that his account of
memory only confirms what he said earlier about knowledge requiring both unity and difference. Knowledge of remembered things requires the unity of all times to be part of the same time; and it
requires each point of time to be its own point, different from every
other point (EW 2: 166). The aim of all knowledge is "the complete
unity of perfectly discriminated or definite elements" (EW 2: 151–52).
For this reason, perception and memory are not everything that
knowledge can be. Perception cannot be all of knowledge, because
there are connections between things (and their unity) that exist beyond the mere grasp of immediately present things, as we see in the
case of memory, for example, where a relation of a *succession* of
events (and unity in succession) is also possible (EW 2: 152). Likewise,
memory excludes some important relations between things, particularly the relations of the self to things, since, though in memory the
sensation is more internal than in perception, yet it still wears an external aspect, excluding the self as different from the succession of
events, as we have seen. With the relations of self to the world (and
to itself) at a minimum, we do not have a complete picture of all the
connections of things in their peculiarity. Higher stages of knowledge
are therefore necessary.

Imaginary Objects

The next stage of knowledge is *imagination*. Here what is known is a particular thing, as in perception and memory, but one without any reference to actual existence, unlike in perception and memory, where some particular real event is still referenced, or may be, as in memory. Imagination, accordingly, is the grasp of a particular thing without existence, that is, existing completely in the mind (EW 2:168). As Dewey puts it, in imagination, the image gets "independent, free existence, severed from connection with some facts actually existing, or some event which has really occurred" (EW 2: 169). Through this process, the self breaks out of routine, selecting its own activities; its aims are made ends in themselves, which the self can engage in for its own purposes, in reference to nothing outside of itself. "Imagination has no external end, but its end is the free play of the various activities of the self, so as to satisfy its interests" (EW 2: 173). In imagination, the self thus gets closer to itself, at least in the sense that it becomes free to exercise itself, without reference to anything else but itself. It is freer than in other modes of thought to work upon itself and its sensations (and their relations to each other).

The imaginative process occurs in the following way. Dissociation separates the imagined object from any real existence, and attention then shapes it according to the direction of the self. "Dissociation disengages the image, and prepares it for free recombination; attention transforms into novel and unexperienced products" (EW 2: 169). Through the experience of "varying concomitants," the image gets dissociated: this happens when you experience something in so many different and varying contexts that you are able to frame an idea of the thing as such. Dewey uses as an example the idea of a man, which "occurs under so many different circumstances" that finally the idea, separated from any special spatial and temporal circumstances, occurs to you, and "thus gets an independent and ideal existence" (EW 2: 170). The image suddenly breaks out of the actual, normal round of experience and becomes an independent something.

Once isolated, the image (or imagined thing) undergoes a process of "recombination" in one of three ways. In *mechanical imagination*, some everyday, unimagined object (the result of association) is separated off from its usual circumstances and placed in some imagined setting (the result of dissociation; EW 2: 170). A writer imagines that his book is published, for example, so that he imagines himself as an accomplished author—that is, in a set of circumstances different from those he is currently in.

In our *fancy*, or *fantasy*, "the formation and connection of images is controlled by an exceedingly vivacious and receptive emotional disposition" (EW 2: 170). Here an excess of imagined content abounds, a fantasy world is created—Dewey gives the example of "A Midsummer Night's Dream" (EW 2: 170)—and everything becomes imbued with the emotions of the particular self who fantasizes. Fancy "affords keen delight," but it is "not revealing in its nature" (EW 2: 171). For this, a higher stage of imagination is required, one that does not express the emotions of the individual self, however lively and entertaining, but captures the situation and truth of all human beings.

This higher stage is *creative imagination* (EW 2: 171). In this type, the separations and recombination serve a higher purpose, giving us access to deeper meanings about ourselves. In perception and memory, the occurrence of meaning depends entirely on some particular existence (or its memory), but in creative imagination "existence is subordinate to meaning" (EW 2: 172). Everything is about the meaning that can be revealed; the sensations are made to exist solely for this purpose. Here meaning develops into something far exceeding the bare connections of sensations, one with the other. In terms of form, the sensations now exist in such a way that all the parts fit into one whole, and the whole is in the parts. No part is introduced without meaning something in the totality of what appears, and no whole is devoid of its appropriate parts (EW 2: 171). In terms of content, imagination when it is creative takes on monumental proportions—meanings far transcend our sensations and tell us something that everyone needs to hear. Creative imagination has, in fact, a universal component, as Dewey sees it. "It sets the idea of memory or perception free from its particular accidental accompaniments, and reveals it in its universal nature," so that others may experience it as well (EW 2:172).

Of course, creative imagination can pertain to one's own peculiar interests as well, as when its meanings are subordinate to "the individual and peculiar tastes and experiences of their authors" (EW 2: 174). But this risks becoming fancy, and in any case it is "ephemeral," passing in significance as the generations pass, or else "morbid and unhealthy," too involved in the life of a narrow self (EW 2: 173). And here we find the first expression of a theme that is subtly at work throughout the *Psychology*: the theme of unhealthiness (and its equally important opposite, healthiness). This theme will appear again and again in the book, especially in the section on feelings. It reveals a core interest of Dewey's—how to remain healthy, steadfast, and alive. In this first manifestation, Dewey uses the concept of unhealthiness to identify an improper use of the creative imagination. He says, "The product of the imagination may also be the result of morbid and unhealthy feeling. It then falls into what Ruskin has well named 'the pathetic fallacy'" (EW 2: 173). In this misuse of the creative imagination, the artist's personal state is read into nature, as when "the hero attributes his own feelings to the rose and the lily" (EW 2: 173). This is morbid and unhealthy because it treats the individual self as so important, so infused with meaning, that nature must answer in response; indeed nature must become the self. Said another way, the individual, with all of his peculiarities, is taken as the main principle of things, regardless of his *actual* connections to others and to nature. This is a kind of sickness—a kind of narcissism, if not megalomania. The individual is actually set apart from nature and from others, made to stand on his own, as his own peculiar, isolated, completely distinct self. We have here the first example of the unhealthy, modernist type of self that Dewey will later make the object of intense criticism, which I will discuss in more detail in chapter 7.

The healthy use of the imagination, on the other hand, is the expression of what is "true" and of interest to all human beings. "The poem of Homer, the art of Michael Angelo, and the drama of

Shakespeare are true to the universal side of humanity, not to the individual and peculiar tastes and experiences of their authors" (EW 2: 174). These works demonstrate the "fundamental unity between man and man and between man and nature" (EW 2: 174). If this unity were not expressed in imagination, imagination would be completely idiosyncratic, nothing more than "unreal and fantastic" (EW 2: 174). But it is not so: imagination is deep. It can give us insight into how we should think of ourselves as human beings, namely as connected both with other people—possessing a "unified life of humanity, with common interests, in spite of separation of time and space"—and with nature—finding ourselves "in some way in nature" (EW 2: 174). "Not all identification . . . with nature" is unhealthy, only that kind which puffs up the individual self and his emotions to the point of being everything. In fact, we can find "joy" in nature, "in the degree in which we find ourselves therein, and are able to identify the work-ings of our spirit with those of nature" (EW 2: 174). In such cases, as in the poetry of Wordsworth, "we do not find ourselves in a strange, unfamiliar land" (EW 2: 174).

With this quote, we can see clearly where Dewey's true intentions lie. They lie in his effort to confront and combat modernism and the pessimistic philosophy that defines it. For the unhealthy and pathetic use of the imagination that Dewey identifies here is one with the modernist tradition that we have seen at work in the early Dewey's day. It is man separated from nature and from other men. And simi-larly, the healthy use of imagination that Dewey here insists upon is one that finds a connection between man and nature and between man and other men. In other words, healthy imagination must show that reality is conducive to the "workings of our spirit" and that we are not alien and foreign beings within reality, but are at home within it and among one another (EW 2: 174). Healthy imagination reveals the goal of all knowledge: the "fundamental unity between man and man and between man and nature" (EW 2: 174).

In these few revealing comments, we have the whole of Dewey's effort in the *Psychology* laid bare. This is the same language Dewey uses in "Poetry and Philosophy" when he praises Browning's poetry for its "realization that the world was made for man, and that man was made for man" (EW3: 120). In the language of "The Present Position of Logical Theory," the *Psychology* must show that facts are consistent with thoughts or meanings.

Dewey goes on in the *Psychology* to discuss the other uses of creative imagination, the *practical* and the *theoretical* (EW 2: 174). The practical use of imagination results in inventions, while the theoretical use results in scientific creations, the more so "as it advances . . . for it recedes further from the sphere of that which is sensuously present to the realm of hidden, ideal significance and meaning, while it is constantly necessary to body these ideas in concrete forms" (EW 2: 175). A scientific model of a geographical feature, for example, can tell us much more about the feature than our simple, unthinking perception of it can. By becoming more abstract in our grasp of a concrete feature, we can gain more knowledge about it. In any case, we can see how the early Dewey's epistemology is developing. We are moving from knowledge that is less ideal to knowledge that is more ideal. That is, we are moving from things we know (objects in the world) that embody human meanings and aspiration to a lesser extent, to things that *embody them more*, things that are more systematic and idealized, more rich and deep than bare facts alone. We are watching the early Dewey's deepest intuition— "*'How the world is made for each of us!'*" (EW 3: 120)—become progressively justified in philosophical terms.

With imagination, we have reached a stage between perception and memory and the next stage of knowledge, which is thinking. In both perception and memory, particular objects—that is, objects that are not the self—still function in knowledge to a great extent. In thinking, as we will see, the universal is the sole focus and reality. Imagination accounts for the transition from perception and memory to thinking by involving the grasp of a particular thing that nonetheless embodies an ideal—that is, by being of a particular thing (say, a horse), but without actual existence, with wholly ideal or imaginative existence. Like acid that eats away at the necessities of actual existence, the imagination "dissolves this ideal element out of its hard concretion in the sphere of actual particular fact, and sets it before the mind as an independent element, with which the mind may freely work" (EW 2: 175).

Things Thought Of

Thinking, as Dewey understands the term, denotes the mind's involvement with the universal as such. Through this process, the mind gains a higher knowledge—a knowledge of things not considered as this or that particular fact, but in their universal relations to other things. This is not to say that the mind disregards the facts and considers only abstractions. On the contrary, the idea here is that, in grasping the universal meaning and import of the facts, the mind encompasses and explains the facts, giving them a richer meaning even as the facts render thought's universalizations more definite (EW 2: 177–78).

It should be kept in mind in this discussion that thought, thus defined, is ideal; it provides meanings to the facts, which otherwise, as isolated particulars, devoid of any relations, lack all meaning. Thought takes up the fact, which has already been constructed out of sensations into a perceived object and its relationships with other objects, grasps what is universal about it, and relates the universalized content to other universalized contents with which it is familiar. In this, thought brings out what is truly involved in the fact, which the fact by itself, in its bare existence as a fact, cannot tell us (EW 2: 177–78).

Indeed, since the self supplies the universal content and relations by which all given facts are compared, Dewey develops the following conception of truth: "a judgment is called true when it harmonizes with all other judgments; false when it is in contradiction to some other" (EW 2: 189). The early Dewey has, in effect, developed a version of the coherence theory of truth. "The mind always tests the truth of any supposed fact," he says, "by comparing it to the acquired system of truth" (EW 2: 190). This view serves Dewey's idealism well, since it removes the fact from its own self-standing authority and gives the force of truth to the self that knows the fact. As we have seen, too, even the fact of a sensation is never given in itself, since it is only a product of the self's activity as well, namely its power of dissociation and its ability thereby to render some sensations isolated from others. The fact itself, in effect, is already ideal, so that, in Dewey's view, we are again far removed from any wholly external fact determining what is in the mind (since the fact is the result of the mind's distinguishing activity), let alone what is true about the fact (since the mind supplies the relations relative to which the fact harmonizes or not with our previous judgments, and is thus rendered true or not).

Let us look more closely at Dewey's account of how thinking is supposed to work. Thinking has four aspects: "conceptualization," "judgment," "reasoning," and "systematization" (EW 2: 178–79; 201–02). *Conception* is the process of abstracting what is universal about a presentation, that is, the attainment of "some law or principle in accordance with which a thing or number of things may be constructed" (EW 2: 179). I will use Dewey's own example: the concept of a man. "To think man," he says, "is to apprehend that universal element of ideal significance which constitutes a man wherever and whenever he is found" (EW 2: 178). When I form this concept, through the powers of attention, I notice what is "common to all men," at the same time bringing various actual men under the concept (EW 2: 177–78). Conception is thus a matter of analysis and synthesis, the picking out of some abstract feature to focus on, thus universalizing it, and the comparison of this with actual instances of the principle, thus giving the universalized feature concrete specificity of meaning as well. The universal concept thereby grows "more definite," Dewey says, and the particular thing is enriched by noting its universal similarities to other instances of its type. Conception is thus "the recognition of a one comprehending many differences" (EW 2: 182).

It is through language that the universality of concepts is applied to actual cases. A name is universal, while the thing named is particular. Language completes the conception, indeed makes it possible, by getting the universal "projected into real existence" (EW 2: 186).

Language takes the form of *judgments*; or rather, the mind's activity of forming judgments finds expression in language. When we form a judgment, we are explicitly applying a concept to existence. "Judgment may be defined as *the express reference of the idea or universal element to reality, the particular element*" (EW 2: 186, emphasis in the original). We are making a claim about reality. We are saying that some universal element—some concept—applies to it. We always do this in two ways, both by forming a judgment in which we apply a predicate to a subject (applying some ideal to a real) and by asserting that some predicate or general class of things contains a subject as one of its members (subsuming some real under an ideal). Again to use one of Dewey's examples, "when I say that 'a lion is a quadruped,' the judgment states one element of the meaning of lion, the idea of fourfootedness, and it also includes the lion in the class or number of objects called quadrupeds" (EW 2: 187). In the former case, we "idealize a real thing, by stating its meaning"; in the later case, we "realize an idea by asserting that it is one of the universe of objects" (EW 2: 187). Ideals are involved in any case, getting reference to real things through the process of judgments.

The connecting of real and ideal is at work in every activity of mind. There is always at work in our mental activities a process of connecting meaning and existence, since the mind, as we saw, contains both apperceptive, idealizing powers and reference to some actual sensations, and works up their unity of relationships (EW 2: 187). Judgment is simply this normal mental process itself, when recognized and made explicit in our minds. It is going on when we perceive, and remember, and so on. "Perception is a judgment of place; memory, a judgment of time; imagination, a judgment of ideal worth" (EW 2: 187–88). We exercise focused judgment when we explicitly direct our minds toward the assertion of some concept applying to reality, but in any case "the typical act of intelligence" by the mind is judgment-forming (EW 2: 187). The mind makes judgments; this is how it gets connected to actual things, that is, how its meanings inform and structure its sensations.

Judgments may be analytic or synthetic. And Dewey thinks that every judgment actually contains both aspects, not that the analytic and the synthetic form two distinct sorts of judgments. They are two different moments of "the same judgment" (EW 2: 188). To say that a judgment is synthetic is to say that in the mind the power of identity is uppermost: If I say, for example, that "a hog is a pachyderm," what happens is that "I identify both ideas; I form a connection or synthesis" between the two ideas (EW 2: 188). In this case, I enlarge my conception of the meaning of "hog" by identifying it with another conception. A synthetic judgment "enriches the conception by some new meaning, or refers it to some reality to which it had not been previously referred" (EW 2: 188). To say that a judgment is analytic is to say that in the mind the power of differing is uppermost. We can see this, Dewey holds, when we realize that "there can be no judgment where there is only one idea. A judgment involves duality. No one, except a formal logician, ever makes an identical judgment only. When we say, 'a man's a man,' we still imply difference. We mean that, in spite of all differences of rank, wealth, education, etc., every man *is distinguished* by the possession of manhood" (EW 2: 188–89). In this case, we are rendering two different meanings, even though they are expressed as one: we are breaking them apart into two different senses. To return to Dewey's previous example of a synthetic judgment, "a hog is a pachyderm" (EW 2: 188), consider that in this case, too, the judgment is also analytic, in that we intend to express a difference between the two concepts. For here the two concepts, "hog" and "pachyderm," do seem different, since one presents the creature from an everyday perspective and the other presents it from a more technical scientific perspective, presenting a meaning distinct from the common meaning of the word *hog*. Once again, the point Dewey is trying to make is that the mind always both identifies and differentiates. This is how intelligence functions (EW 2:187–89).

Truth

We have seen above what Dewey claims with regard to the truth or falsity of a judgment—namely, that the test of the truth of a judgment comes in asking: Does it fit with what we already know?

When a novel proposition is brought before the mind, intelligence views it in the light of what it already regards as true, or in the light of relations previously laid down. If the new relation coincides with the former, still more if the new one expands them, or *vice versa*, it is judged to be true; if there is irreconcilable conflict, one or the other must be false. (EW 2: 190)

Dewey stresses that there is no method for getting at the truth of any single judgment, taken by itself. There is no sure-fire way for testing any one judgment. All we can do is depend on the store of knowledge we have, and the more extensive this is, the greater the chance that we can gain knowledge of the truth of a judgment put forward (EW 2: 190). "There is no simple criterion or rule for determining truth which can be applied immediately to every judgment; the only criterion is relation to the whole body of acquired knowledge, or the acquired system of relations, so far as it is realized" (EW 2: 190).

It is worth lingering here to consider the argument for Dewey's position. Though he never explicitly states it this way, his position presupposes that we must accept some such coherence theory of truth as this because, first of all, there is nothing ever given to the mind in a pure, unidealized state to which our judgments can correspond, so we cannot rely on a correspondence theory of truth. We have already seen that even sensations do not amount to meanings simply given to the mind. They always requires the self's interpretation based on its past experience and knowledge. The sensations of orange, sweet, round, and so forth must be interpreted by me as "an orange," based on everything I know already about objects, colors, edible things, fruits, and so forth. Moreover, we have seen that all intellectual meaning consists of grasping an object in terms of its relations to other objects. It stands to reason, therefore, that a judgment will be true only insofar as it captures the object's relationships in a way that is consistent with everything else we know—that is, consistent with all of our other judgments.

Stated another way, Dewey's position amounts to this: "there is no such thing as purely *immediate* knowledge. Any cognition is dependent; that is, it is *because of* some other cognition" (EW 2: 192). There are no fundamental, given facts of which we have immediate and certain knowledge. There is only an extensive chain of interpretations into which a fact must fit, a process of mediation in which each fact has to be interpreted and situated in reference to the system of known things in order to become itself known (EW 2:192).

Reasoning is the next aspect of thinking that Dewey considers; and, as he sees it, reasoning involves "the explicit recognition of this mediate element involved in all knowledge" (EW 2: 192). When I reason, I move from one judgment to another, trying to determine the truth of some judgment. In other words, I acknowledge in my very activity that something is the case not because of its bare existence, but because of its reference to something other than itself, to its placement in the chain of reasons, its relation to other judgments of mine. Reasoning is "consciously knowing that a thing is so *because* of, or through, its relations, its reference to something beyond its own existence" (EW 2: 192). It is a clever argument that Dewey makes here: even to reason is to admit the primacy of mediated knowledge as he defines it. There is no immediate reasoning. All reasoning, as a process involving inferences, or a movement of judgments implying one another, already establishes that knowledge is "a going beyond what is sensuously present to its connection with something else," indeed, a going beyond of any immediate known object to its connections to other known objects (EW 2: 192). And when we reason we more or less openly acknowledge this mediated property of all knowledge, whereas in perception, for example, the same mediated process occurs without our being fully aware of it, because we get lost in the apparently external aspect of the object (EW 2:192).

We start with particular sensations, which we conceptualize. Let us expand on one of Dewey's previous examples, "man." We have various sensations, particular in nature, of various aspects of various men that we then conceptualize by bringing them under the general category of "man." We form a judgment about the concept, adding a predicate to it, such as "Man is mortal." In the judgment, as we have seen, the universal and particular work together to give us knowledge. We are claiming something about man (that is, about all men, and hence about this particular man also), namely, that man has the general property of mortality (or that mortality is a class that contains the reality of man). This judgment serves to bring meaning to the concept of man by connecting it to another concept, mortality. Again, we are far from any given, original sensation, working only in concepts or universals; and yet we have true knowledge, since we are forming a judgment about things that clearly harmonizes with previous judgments that we know to be true, namely, that every particular man is mortal; this is consistent with what we know about men, who are finite, and become unhealthy, and so forth. We arrive at this judgment, this knowledge, through a process of reasoning, and we may expand this judgment in this way as well. We may take the judgment "man is mortal," for example, and reason about it in relation to other judgments, thus:

Man is mortal.

This is a man.

Therefore, this man is mortal.

We thereby gain increased knowledge of other judgments; we come to understand that this particular man is mortal. And reasoning enriches the original judgment also (EW 2: 200). As the new judgment emerges, it affects the one it was based on, since now "man is mortal" is something that we know to include this unique person as well. "Mortal" comes to mean something that includes this particular person's death; his death has become part of what it means for man to die. The new judgment fleshes out, and gives fuller meaning, to what it means for man to be mortal.

Reasoning in this way brings "a particular under a universal," which is deduction, or, when it "starts from the particular facts, and discovers in them the universal, the law, the process is one of *induction*" (EW 2: 195–96). Some individual is always reasoned about, some specific item, which then becomes "a richer object of knowledge"; it is "becoming more universal," or is "identified with other individuals under some common relation or idea," and it becomes "more definite" as well, "for these various relations which are thus recognized are taken into it, and become part of its content; they enlarge its significance and serve to distinguish it" (EW 2: 200). Law and fact mutually reinforce each other in reasoning to produce more universal and definite knowledge.

Dewey also makes the point in this way: "Law is the *meaning* of fact; it is its universal aspect; the side that gives it relation. . . . Law, on the other hand, has no existence for us except in connection with some fact" (EW 2: 198). A law is the meaning of the fact; the fact is the existence of the law in a real case. The two are parts of the same mental process. What is known, some "concrete mental content," is therefore always "a union of universal and particular, of identity and difference, of fact and meaning, of reality and ideal significance" (EW 2: 199). In other words, to know an object is to grasp its meaning, what universal set of relations it embodies, and therefore to know it in its own specificity all the more. It is to bring this object under some general category, and therefore to know *it* with greater insight. It is to access a fact always in relation to its ideal meaning, and only thereby to know the fact. Everything thought of is "a union of universal and particular . . . of fact and meaning" (EW 2: 199). There is a universal, but it exists only in some fact. There is a fact, but it exists only in and through its universal meaning.

What follows from this is that facts never exist without meaning, just as real meanings never exist without reference to some facts (i.e., some sensations we have already idealized). Facts are, precisely, elements of knowledge that are always meaningful for us. Therefore, the given world of facts is meaningful. And so Dewey has achieved his basic purpose: to show that facts do actually germinate into meanings. They always do whenever we know an object. But if this is correct, then modernism is mistaken that facts and meanings are separate, that the world and man stand forever divided and opposed. And this, in turn, means that we are wrong to be pessimistic about this division and what it seems to say about the deadening indifference of facts, of brute matter. For in our intellectual activities—in perception, in memory, in imagination, and especially in thought—we are all the time grasping facts in their meaning. We are grasping meaning. And we are grasping a meaning that bears a relation to ourselves—namely, we are grasping an intelligible order to the facts that lets us understand and know them. But as we will see, this meaning that we grasp is never quite complete; the facts are not yet fully idealized. The best we can do is have faith that the universe will continue to allow this meaning to occur just as we construct it, in the shape of an intelligible order—a faith that in turn keeps us going and trying to produce more meaning and more intelligible order.

But though such unifying activity is at work in the mind when it knows, bringing facts into existence always in relation to their significance, the reasoning mind does not necessarily know this. It is fixated on the actual things reasoned about, lost in the actual reasoning, and does not reflect on the underlying import of such reasoning. To reflect on this import is the task of philosophy, "this higher development of reasoning" (EW 2: 201). When we reflect on what is going on in reasoning rather than merely reasoning, we find that, since all reasoning renders some individual both more universal and more definite, the complete state of reasoning, the aim of reasoning, is to achieve "unity in variety" (EW 2: 202). "A completely universalized or related individual, which is at the same time perfectly definite or distinct in all its relations, is . . . the end of knowledge" (EW 2: 200–01). When we reflect on reasoning and realize that, as we have seen, reasoning always gives us an individual in its universal relations, while simultaneously rendering the individual ever more particularly and definitely itself, then we see that the point of knowledge as such is to bring everything together into a system—that is, to show that "each is what it is, because of its connection with and dependence upon others" (EW 2: 201). When we know, we are trying to connect each single thing to the whole, that is, to its total relation to other things, and to understand it better and more fully therefore in its relations to these other things, in its relations to the whole.

Systematic Knowledge

This takes us to the next aspect of thinking, what Dewey calls *systematization* (EW 2: 201). Here the mind recognizes that systematic knowledge is the task of reasoning; the task becomes explicit for it. The mind realizes that knowledge is all about relations, about grasping them and the individuals that are related, and so the mind understands that knowledge presupposes a totality. The mind knows that knowledge "presupposes that there is no such thing as an isolated fact in the universe, but that all are connected with each other as members of a common whole" (EW 2: 201). We give ourselves this goal, in other words, whenever we try to know and inquire, namely to know everything together at once in all of its diverse interconnections. We postulate, as the ultimate object of our knowledge, "a true *universe*; a world which, in spite of its difference, or rather *through* its difference, is one" (EW 2: 202). It would be a world in which human beings, for example, are seen to be connected with all other things, but in such a way that each of us becomes a distinct individual in and through this connection.

Dewey is claiming in this section of the *Psychology* that to have knowledge at all is to presuppose this type of universe, in which each member is a distinct part of the whole. To try to know is to search for such a universe, if not in every particular act of knowing, at least in reflection on the task of knowing, in seeing what it is about, what its overall aims and intentions are.

Intuition

Intuition is the highest stage of knowledge. It is the actual knowledge we have of any given thing, "knowledge of an individual," where this knowledge is understood to be a product of both a concrete and universal grasp of what the thing is (EW 2: 205). The knowledge of any individual thing, we should understand by now, "involves both the identifying and the distinguishing activities" (EW 2: 205). All the previous stages of knowledge utilized such activities. Reasoning was

required to render perception more universal, and perception was required to provide something distinct to which the universal can pertain; "the union of perception and reasoning involved in every act
constitutes *intuition*" (EW 2: 205). In effect, intuition, as Dewey understands it, is simply the knowledge we have of an individual—
namely, that this individual is this particular instance of a universal.
When I know a person, for example, I know them as this unique instance of a human being; or, conversely, as what a human being
means in this unique instance.

Dewey thinks it should be clear by this point that any traditional
account of intuition, as simply seeing and understanding immediately
that something is the case, cannot be correct.

> Something perceived by intuition is supposed to be just what it is
> by virtue of its own independent existence. We are in a position
> to recognize that there cannot possibly be intuition of such a kind.
> Every act of mind involves relation; it involves dependence; it in-
> volves *mediation*. A thing as known gets its meaning by its sym-
> bolism; by what it points to beyond itself. (EW 2: 205)

Intuition, properly understood, is a grasp of the individual thing only
in and through many layers of mediation. The particular person that
I know, for example, is someone I have gained knowledge about because of what his particularity "points to beyond itself," that is, to all
of my past dealings with him, my own interests relative to him, and
also to a more universal understanding of him as a human being,
someone who will die someday, someone who requires food, water,
and shelter to live, and so on (conversely, of course, my knowledge
of what it means for a human being to die or to need food, water,
and shelter takes on more meaning and depth by pertaining to this
particular unique human being and his death or his needs). When I
see this particular person, I see beyond him; and only in seeing beyond him, do I really see him. This kind of "seeing" is intuition.

But if we consider, not simply our intuition of a particular person,
but of "ultimate reality" itself—our knowledge of that—then we seem
to have a problem (EW 2: 206). For "it is evident that this cannot be

related to anything beyond itself; it can symbolize only itself" (EW 2: 206). The solution to this problem is to see that "all dependence, all mediation, must be *within* itself" (EW 2: 206). Ultimate reality, considered something to be known, must be "self-related"; it must constitute a whole because of the differences within itself (EW 2: 206).

And we have an intuition of such a self-related whole, Dewey wants to say. For one thing, intuition is at work in all of our knowledge, as we have seen; all of it involves the universal and the particular. And what our knowledge does is make sense of things by organizing them in terms of a universal set of relations. It stands to reason that the more universal the whole, that is, the more relations of things the whole can encompass, the more it will give us knowledge of any particular thing. Perhaps the most comprehensive universal set of relations we can conceive of would be the world, which would then have to be a self-related thing, for we would never know it by pointing to something beyond it. As a vast cosmos of interconnected things, it would seem to encompass all things within itself. And we do seem to have an "intuition of the world," Dewey wants to say (EW 2:206–7).

In fact, our intuition of the world, or knowledge of the world as an individual thing, as an entity for consideration, occurs in several stages. At first we are aware of sensations, then of existence, or "that these sensations are objectified" (EW 2: 207). We then proceed to the idea of "*substance*," or the idea that these objectified sensations have a being, then to many objects in "coexistence," sequenced according to space and time, to the ideas of "force" and "motion," then to "cause and effect," and to the idea of "order," and finally to the idea of relations, and at last we arrive at the idea of one world, "the intuition of reality as a whole" (EW 2: 207–8). Dewey quotes a poem by Tennyson that exhibits this final stage of intuition about the world:

> Flower in the crannied wall,
> I pluck you out of the crannies;—
> Hold you here, root and all, in my hand,
> Little flower—but if I could understand
> What you are, root and all, all in all,
> I should know what God and man is.
>   (EW 2: 208–09)

The realization we come to is that all things are parts of the whole, parts of the self-same world. More importantly, "we *see* in the part the whole" (EW 2: 209). We grasp that each single element not only never stands alone but implicates all the others; that each element mirrors or reflects the whole working process of the world itself, with all of its events and history contained within it. This is the original intuition that science and philosophy then systematize and try to make more explicit and intelligible (EW 2: 209). Through this intuition, we arrive at the idea of "necessity," because we understand that all the parts of the world are interconnected and that they come to be, accordingly, only in and through what the others have been (EW 2: 209).

We then proceed to an "intuition of the self." We arrive at this intuition because, in having an intuition of the world, we are grasping a more and more intelligent organization of events—more and more of an *intellectual* meaning and order to the facts—and we come to recognize this aspect of the world. We come to recognize the intelligence of the world, its intelligent ordering, which leads to the recognition that the world's "true existence is in its relation to mind" (EW 2: 210). As Dewey puts it, quite significantly, "this intuition of the whole in a part is the recognition of *all* that the part *means*, and meaning is put into fact from the activity of the self" (EW 2: 209). Since we recognize an intelligent ordering of the world, that is, that each part means its relation to the whole, we must recognize the self at the basis of this ordering of the world, for meaning only gets into facts and their ordering from the self. So, the self must be at the basis of the world's intelligence, for nothing else could supply it (nothing else supplies intellectual meaning or ordering to facts). Especially since all relations must be self-related, taking the world by itself will not do; it cannot be the highest stage of intuition, because we then leave out one of the world's obvious and most fundamental relations, the relation it bears to the self (EW 2: 210). Hence, the self must be included in our intuition of the world, and it must be included as its basis or fundament.

We thus proceed to the ideal aspect of every individual known (and we recognize it). Normally, we only recognize intellectual meanings without seeing where they come from (EW 2: 210). In intuition of the self, however, we see where these meanings come from, namely from the "self alone." Since we realize that these meanings come from the self alone, we also arrive at "the *conception* of *freedom*" (EW 2: 211), for the meanings are seen to be coming solely from mind, without support from any other direction or force. They are a free, unsupported manifestation of the self, offered to its own sensations, and they undo our previous belief in necessity, which we had supposed was at work in the interconnection of all events of the world.

Next, and last, we proceed to the "intuition of God" or the Absolute. At this point we realize that the world, to be known, requires the self that knows it; and the self, to know, requires the world that is known (EW 2:211–12). Everything seems to work together to suggest that self and world (each a candidate for a self-related entity) in truth require one another. They must be related to one another to form the one, genuine self-related thing, given what it means to know, that is, for the ideal to become real (and the real to become ideal). The universalizing and distinguishing activities of mind would seem to assert themselves in this case also, enabling us to grasp the world as a particular entity only in relation to the universal self, and the universal self only in relation to embodiment in the actual world. Thus, Dewey asserts that "the true self-related must be the organic unity of the self and the world, of the ideal and the real, and that is what we know as God" (EW 2: 212). God or the Absolute would be "perfectly realized intelligence," the actual world regarded as totally intelligible (EW 2: 212). It would be the complete explanation, rendering every isolated fact entirely understandable to a rational mind.

But Dewey quickly reminds us that the intuition of the Absolute is mediated; it is not direct knowledge. The intuition of the Absolute, he thinks, is "the primal and the ultimate intuition," but it is still an intuition (EW 2: 212). The intuition lies at the basis of all knowledge, since all of it is an effort to fuse to the extent that we can the real and the ideal, the particular thing and universal meaning; so we always understand, in a way, that a complete knowledge of everything is something that is possible. But this understanding, again, is an intuition; it is a belief we have. Science and philosophy have yet to demonstrate it; they exist in order to try to prove what the intuition maintains (EW 2: 209; 212). And yet, it seems, they keep coming up short, for there is an inexhaustible wealth in our intuition. "There is more truth, in short, implied in the simplest form of knowledge than can be brought out by our completest science or philosophy" (EW 2: 212). No matter how complete our knowledge has become so far, it has yet to exhaust our intuition of the Absolute. Said another way, our intuition of the Absolute, of a world that is completely intelligible, is a *belief* we have, a belief that both goes beyond what our science and philosophy currently offer, but that also inspires these activities to pursue their knowledge in the first place and to keep going to try to complete themselves.

Summary and Conclusion

Our knowledge begins with amorphous, external "motions"—an indeterminate and malleable vagueness—that engender the activities of a self. The self develops these motions into sensations, and then shapes the sensations into objects. The self then connects the objects to one another in more and more coherent ways; it does this through its own acts of perception, memory, imagination, and so on. The self also reflects on the work it is doing, the systematic world of objects in their relations that it is creating, and forms judgments about it. It then reasons about these judgments, trying to see which are true and which are false—that is, trying to determine the ways some specific objects relate to others, or pertain to one another in the self's own systematic ordering of things.

"All knowledge is thus, in a certain sense, self-knowledge" (EW 2: 126), because, in knowing, the self is only revisiting the work it has already done—throughout the ages in human culture and even in its own daily unconscious operations—to produce a unified, organized world of objects. The self creates an ordered cosmos and then eventually recognizes its own work. In knowing the external world, the self apparently returns home to itself. It seems to find an intelligible, rational world that is conducive to itself, for it seems to find a world that it has already constructed and that is based on its own needs. When we look out at the world, therefore, we believe that we see a familiar face. We believe that we see something like a human face looking back at us.

But the self only has an intuition that it returns home to itself in this way, never immediate knowledge. We believe that reality must be capable of being fully understood (fully idealized), but this belief is a mediation, not a given fact. The intuition goads us on, and our science and philosophy try to justify the intuition. It provokes us to keep striving to know more, to seek a total, realized system of all knowledge. But the intuition of the whole is not the same thing as a fully worked-out, scientific confirmation of the whole, which is something for which we are still waiting. We think God must be there to complete the system, but the system does not yet show and demonstrate that God is there.[1]

And so, in the end, our knowledge is driven in its whole complex development by a basic intuition of the unity of the world. But this is just to say that our knowledge itself has not yet realized this unity— the intuition of it is the hidden force that keeps us producing known things, with higher and higher meanings. The intuition of the completion of knowledge is an ideal that makes possible the actual knowledge that we do possess. We seem to be moving closer to a complete grasp of the whole, all of our knowledge builds in that direction, and yet we cannot know for sure, for our science has not yet confirmed our primal intuition. We can, however, have faith that we are moving in the direction of complete understanding, for we do possess the intuition that this complete understanding is possible and our knowledge can become more and more systematic; and as a result we can reject the view that "ultimate reality is unknowable" (EW 2: 212). This faith is, in fact, a vital intellectual resource. It is this faith that the world *can* be known (that it is intelligible to us) that lies behind our efforts to make sense of the world from the very beginning; it is this faith that compels us to try to understand things to the extent that we can, and it is this faith, therefore, that allows us to find things condu-cive to our understanding to the extent that we do find them to be so.

SIX

FEELING, WILL, AND SELF-REALIZATION

Toward a Meaningful Universe

We have seen Dewey's arguments for holding that we are entitled to think of ourselves as belonging to a single, interconnected, and meaningful whole. We are entitled to think this, he
believes, because our knowledge all along builds towards such a result. We have now to consider Dewey's reasons for saying that we can
also *feel* ourselves belonging to this meaningful whole, and that we
should act, as well, as if we do belong to it.[1]

The crucial steps in Dewey's argument at this stage are to show,
first, that feelings are about "self-realization," and second, that they
contain a universal progression (EW 2:241–43). To say that feelings
are about self-realization is to say that we can feel our way into our
own development. The self, for Dewey, is not a static thing: its "life
is one of . . . growth rather than attained being" (EW 2: 260). The self
is able to grow, to enlarge itself. It "grows wider and deeper with
every experience" (EW 2: 241). The self is able to develop itself, and

to enrich its own meanings and interests, by adopting the meanings and interests of others into itself (EW 2: 249). Feelings are guides to this process of self-development. They help the self recognize the extent to which it is growing in a healthy direction (through feelings of pleasure and happiness) or in an unhealthy direction (through feelings of pain) as it incorporates more and more of things outside itself into itself (EW 2: 216).

To say that feelings contain a universal progression for the self is to say that there is a certain direction in which all selves must move in order to find true pleasure and happiness, although no two selves will move in this direction in exactly the same way or at exactly the same time (EW 2: 217). The direction in which Dewey thinks each self must go in order to become more fulfilled is toward feeling itself as belonging meaningfully to a whole. The self must adopt feelings of true sympathy, by which it feels at one with everything else, even as a condition of possessing its own distinct being. It must come to feel itself as part of a wider whole in order to feel that it has a place somewhere, and thus in order for it to *be* a self at all—that is, in order to have a distinct role to play in life and action that will help to define it.

I want to emphasize, however, that this apparent goal of the self is no goal; the self yearns for something, in Dewey's account, but it does not know what this something is. It feels unfulfilled with every finite determination of itself, and it desires a more complete version of itself, but the self does not have any clue what this more complete version of itself would be (not even sympathy fulfills the condition). There is something *missing* in the self—what Slavoj Žižek has termed an "absent centre"[2]—that drives the self towards a wider and wider identification of itself with other things. It is seeking itself, without a sense of what it is looking for. It keeps dislodging itself from itself, saying: "But this is not me either"; and the self's very disturbance in this regard is the impulse that creates the direction in which it moves. The impulse to grow is not caused by any determinate external goal that imposes its form upon the self, but rather emerges from the self's own finitude and feelings of isolation, its own inherent lack and poverty as an isolated thing.

In this chapter, I first explain Dewey's account of feelings and show how this account helps him make the case that feelings are about self-realization and contain a universal progression. We will see that Dewey presents a compelling argument for the view that our human feelings progress from narrow, isolated states to more and more universal and encompassing ones. Insofar as this is the case, we will see that human beings create the sense of a meaningful whole with which they can identify, contrary to the modernist insistence that the separate individual harbors isolated meanings that he must oppose to a world utterly lacking in significance. Dewey tries to show, on the contrary, that our individual feelings in their normal capacity broaden out to include, eventually, the meanings of the entire universe, meanings of the world that are at one with the self's own meanings. Modernism, with its isolated self opposed to the universe, will on this account prove to be an aberration, an abnormality and sickness that manifests itself in various problematic feelings and in other unhealthy ways .

In the second part of the chapter, I will show how, for Dewey, this same pattern repeats itself in our willing: our wills, too, are about our self-realization, about our ability to put our ideal meanings more and more into our actions. Hence, contrary to the modernist assumption, our wills also help demonstrate the meaningful nature of the universe—a universe now imbued with human meanings through our efforts, and therefore a universe that human beings can embrace.

Feelings and Their Universal Progression

To see how the individual self is able to grow and come to identify itself with ever-larger meanings outside of itself, let us briefly review what we have seen so far about how the self obtains meaning.

The process by which meaning-giving takes places is idealization, a process by which an actual event, in itself quite malleable, is given significance and value based on the self's interest and needs.[3] The engine of idealization is rupture, the negation of a given sensation in its actual elements and its connection with other sensations. "The mind," Dewey says, "is an activity which connects every fact, event, and relation with others. Nothing remains isolated" (EW 2: 131). And this connecting and relating process occurs through "the free idealizing activity of mind working according to its own subjective interests" (EW 2: 175), a process that "always takes us beyond the bare presentation, to its connections and relations to the rest of experience" (EW 2: 121). By allowing us to uproot static, isolated sensations, for example, and to put them into certain relations with other sensations, rupture produces meanings in the objects that are presented to us. For meaning is defined, quite precisely, as the significance that one thing has in relation to another. An orange, for example, *means* that object which gives me a day's worth of vitamin C, can be distinguished from an apple, has a certain color, and so forth.[4] By negating the given fact of the visual sensation of the color orange, for example, and freeing it to be put into relation with other facts, such as "gives me vitamin C," "can be made into juice," and so on, our powers of rupture allow us to establish certain relations between facts based on our needs and interests, to establish, therefore, idealizations of things—that is, to make things possess meanings in connection with one another conducive to ourselves (in this case, the collection of meanings comes to signify orange juice), and we are therefore able to find and to create a world ordered according to elements of significance and value for us.

We have seen in the preceding chapters how this process of meaning-giving is supposed to work in the case of knowledge. Through the powers of apperception and retention (special forms of rupture), the self negates the brute, given fact of some raw, sensuous material, freeing it to be organized into new and different forms. Through the power to unify present sensations, as well as to bring our past experiences to bear on present objects, the self establishes new patterns and connections between things—patterns and connections that can only be called ideal because they are the result of the mind's own activity. An orange, for example, is a perceived object, or in other words, a unified series of different sensations, and this unification includes in its meanings the whole extent of my past experiences with oranges.

Because knowledge, for Dewey, is a construction in this way of ideal meanings, he is able to conclude that known objects are "the objective side of self" (EW 2: 243)—that is, the outward presentation and manifestation of activities that the self has been engaged in all along as it has constructed its idealizations of vague motions by negating them and turning them into perceived objects.

It is essential to realize that the process of idealization that occurs in the construction of our knowledge of objects is also occurs in the self. The self negates its present version of itself and thereby enlarges itself, growing into a new self. Rupture lies at the heart not only of the self's relation to objects, but also of its relation to itself. Perhaps the best way to think of this point is to say that the self, for Dewey, is not a substance: "It is not something *which* acts; it is activity" (EW 2: 216). It is activity, moreover, that builds on itself. The self does take on various forms, but then it moves away from these, negating them, as the activity that the self *is* pushes forward. Through the process of rupture, by negating its previous versions of itself, the self is able to organize itself in relation to things and to other selves in more and more meaningful ways. It is able to expand itself to include these others as part of what *it* is and what it means to be a self. In the early Dewey's basic picture, the universe is moving; it is a universe of events and activities, some of which form into selves, or self-replicating activities that may be at first quite rudimentary, but that grow into more complex forms, and that are, in any case, more and more purposefully advancing. The self is an activity that builds on itself, that learns to become more than itself, until eventually it develops the complexity that enables it to take an interest in itself and to actively promote itself, to realize itself, where and when it can. For example, the self begins as an organic body, but "the self is something more than a body. It enlarges itself, grows wider and deeper with every experience" (EW 2:241), developing into higher states of perception, feeling, and the awareness of meanings, such as consciousness, which then enable it to monitor its own organic states and to use these to measure how well it is developing itself. The self evolves and continues to grow; and it grows into a self that can to some extent shape and construct its own growth. And this process of self-development, of the self coming to realize itself more and more, is endless, as Dewey sees it; it is an unceasing activity. The self, for him, is never a static thing: "our life is one of progressive realization, not of completed development, of growth rather than of attained being," and so, as a result, there always arise for us "feelings of dissatisfaction and of limitation" (EW 2: 260). The self feels uneasy and modifies itself; it tries out different versions of itself. The self, this tireless searching for itself, keeps moving toward something, keeps moving toward itself, in ever new directions and variations.

Dewey will seek to show that what I am, in essence, is something drawn out of itself by a vague longing into or toward something else. What I feel is a longing after a more and more complete and ideal version of myself. With every new version of myself I attain, I feel that it is not enough. "Every relation known brings with it a dim sense of others with which it is connected, but which are not known" (EW 2: 261). I feel a lack at the heart of what I have so far attained, "the vague and indefinite feeling of this universal self as not realized," as what I have not yet become (EW 2: 261). The Absolute Self, the ideal of a complete and perfect version of ourselves, draws us forward, draws us out of our particular, given selves; it is the secret source of rupture and hence of the growth of ideal meanings, of meanings beyond myself, which I strive after but have never yet attained. The self "is taken beyond its limitation to its immediate sensuously-present experience, and transferred to a realm of enduring and independent relations," but these enduring relations are never our final resting point (EW 2: 245). We continue on; we keep seeking through an "infinite variety of concrete ways" to realize ourselves (EW 2: 319).

Such is Dewey's basic conception. Let us turn now to how he argues for this conception. The self acts, Dewey holds, and its actions either help it to realize itself or not. Feelings are the mental states that accompany this self-realization or its opposite, the self's lack of realization. Feelings tell us how we are doing in our actions; they help us sense the extent to which we are realizing ourselves through our acts, or failing to do so. Nothing in this process is guaranteed; Dewey offers no easy optimism here. There are clear cases of failure of self-realization, as, for example, when one's acts lead to "permanent break-down" (EW 2: 236) or to a sense of loss or unhappiness (EW 2: 253–54).[5] And as we will see, Dewey sees modernism itself as a special version of the self's failure to realize itself, characterizing it again and again as a kind of "emotional suicide," noting that "there has probably never been a time when this unhealthy employment of feelings was so prevalent as it is now" (EW 2: 259). The isolated, separated self of modernism generates a distinct set of unhealthy and problematic feelings, ranging from "cynicism" to "*aestheticism*" to "*malice*" towards others. Unhealthy acts are committed, and they are accompanied by unhealthy feelings—unhealthiness here being characterized by the failure of the acts to help engender the self's realization, the failure of the self to fulfill itself in a world beyond its own narrow, given confines (EW 2:253; 279; 282; 288).

Although for Dewey there is no guarantee that one will act and feel the right way, nonetheless there is a normal course of progress that one's feelings can take, although he notes that there are no two ways alike by which different selves will realize this progression. "[A]n infinity of directions" with "an infinity of contents" are inevitable, since feelings are subjective states and every subjective state is personal and unique (EW 2: 217). Nonetheless there are phases of feeling that every healthy self must go through to be itself, although each self goes through these phases in different ways and at different times. "There are, in other words, universal and essential realms of experience in which the self must find itself, in order to be a self at all" (EW 2:243). Healthy, normal experiences and their accompanying feelings are, first of all, those that are absorbed in their objects: we do not normally experience a sense of separation between our feelings for objects and the objects themselves, but rather a fusion of the two.

> The connection is not an external one of the feeling *with* the object, but an internal and intimate one; it is feeling *of* the object. The feeling loses itself in the object. Thus we say that food *is* agreeable, that light is pleasant; or on a higher plane, that the landscape *is* beautiful, or that the act is right. (EW 2: 239)

Only a detached, overly self-conscious self tries to distinguish itself and its feeling for an object from the object itself. Normally, the feeling is one with the object; we feel, not our own feeling, but a feeling of the object itself. In normal feeling, in other words, we already exist outside of ourselves to some extent; we exist out there, in the object, with which we emotionally identify. "Normal feelings, in short, are regarded as real *values* in the objects which excite them" (EW 2: 251). The feeling we have when we taste a delicious orange, for example, is regarded as a real property of the orange: we call it a delicious orange. We say that the orange is delicious, that it has this value as part of what *it* is.

Secondly, this feeling outside of our selves is something that can grow and develop to incorporate greater reaches of material with which we feel and sympathize. Indeed, one can chart the course of this ever-enlarging "feeling with" into higher and higher meanings until we seem to reach, in the end, a feeling of the universe's own meanings. More specifically, Dewey identifies three different types of feelings, and he develops in minute detail the manner by which each type makes possible higher and deeper degrees of feelings—feelings that continually progress to include an emotional attachment to aspects of ourselves beyond our narrow and merely private selves, an attachment, indeed, to the universe itself in its full and comprehensive nature.

The three types of feeling are *sensuous, formal,* and *qualitative* (EW 2: 217). We can cover sensuous and formal feelings rather quickly, as they are easier to grasp, while qualitative feelings, being more complex and with more important results, will require fuller treatment. Sensuous and formal feelings are feelings regardless of the contents— that is, regardless of what we are having feelings about. As such, taken just by themselves, they are abstractions, but they serve to indicate definite modes of feeling that we possess, and even here we can see the way feelings reach out beyond themselves. Qualitative feelings are feelings for objects wherein we definitely consider the content of the feelings, or that for which we feel (EW 2: 217).

Sensuous feelings are feelings of the body, or those we possess in merely having sensations—namely, the bare intensity of feeling something (whether too intense, not intense enough, etc.; states that are accompanied by pleasure or pain in themselves)—and also the feeling of merely being alive, which is the basis of all feeling (EW 2: 217–21). "This vital sensation remains at all periods . . . the substructure of every feeling," although it seems to be "much more vivid in childhood than afterwards" (EW 2: 221). We simply feel alive and vital, especially if we are well and not thinking about it. Indeed, here we can see especially clearly what is true of all feeling, namely, that when it is functioning best we are not aware of it. "The healthy workings of the organism give us our most fundamental feeling," but normally "we are not reflectively conscious of it. . . . The healthier the feeling, the more we are absorbed in it, and the less we recognize it, even as a feeling" (EW 2: 221). In normal, everyday life, we are lost in the objects of our concern, and our feelings of well-being only serve to promote our continued unconscious engagement with the world.

But that is not all. There is also a progression of this normal vital feeling of being alive that also ensures that the self who experiences it gets outside of itself. The feelings occurring with our various senses, from taste and smell to hearing and sight, seem to move from relatively private to more public. Taste and smell, for example, are bound up with our own subjective states and are not easily transferrable to others. The sense of touch, however, along with our motor activities, begins to engage us with the wider world, until at last, with sight and sound, the qualities are objective and shareable and much less subjective, for which reason they are able to serve as the basis of language and music and to convey more universal meanings shareable by all (EW 2: 221–25).

Dewey provides an interesting discussion at this point in the text, about how

> terms expressive of moral qualities and such as name activities are derived rather from touch and muscular activity. A person is

sharp, acute, or obtuse. He has smooth, polished manners, or is rough and coarse. Character is firm or yielding. An upright man is said to be square. . . . Some men are slow, others fast. An act is right and of a high character, or is base and low. Good elevates a man, bad degrades him. (EW 2: 224)

Harmony and disruption work together to produce meaning, for the bodily states are harmonious with or still retained in some form in "higher feelings" (EW 2: 224). But notice that for the early Dewey, it is only by drawing on senses that move us away from our bodies that feeling becomes more developed. "The more immediate it is," he says about sensuous feeling, "the less developed it is. The more we are absorbed in the feeling as such, and the less we are absorbed in the object or activity to which feeling clings, the more undefined and undeveloped is the emotion" (EW 2: 225). If we want to get beyond feelings such as high and low, smooth and coarse, we apparently need to take the cue from "feelings of sight" and begin to develop feelings that are more "objectified." We will then be able to develop more "mediate intellectual feeling," which will make up for "what is lost in the way of direct sensuous feeling" by enabling this sensuous feeling to turn up again, but in a higher form, through the mediation of intelligence (EW 2: 225–26).

Formal feelings are those that "take us beyond" the "immediate presence" of bodily feelings (EW 2:217; 228). "They are psychical experiences which extend beyond the intrinsic qualities of the sensation to the emotional value which it has from its connections with other experiences" (EW 2: 228). Formal feelings derive from the way our experience hangs together, from the fabric of our experience. Here we are talking about our experiences of struggling with and against the objective world. In the course of such struggles, "we have feelings of *harmony*, of *conflict*, and of *reconciliation*, or harmony after conflict," not to mention further conflict, and a new reconciliation, and so on (EW 2: 230).

It is important to realize that this basic pattern of our feelings in relation to things (harmony-conflict-harmony-conflict) is driven, above all, by conflict. Indeed, as Dewey stresses, "The more conflict the better, provided the conflict does not become actual opposition—that is, provided all the conflicting activities are capable of being unified in one whole—for such conflict only calls forth more activity and results in more complete adjustment, that is, in more complete development of the self" (EW 2: 231). As with all the other modes of idealization that we have discussed so far, here, too, rupture and harmony work together to produce meaning, in this case the meanings enjoyed by a "more complete development of self." But conflict is the driving force. Conflict, or the disruption of our harmonious activities, is the necessary condition for the emergence of our effort, which tries to control or "to adjust present factors" and take them in new directions (EW 2: 230). And the process is endless. Notice that Dewey does not mention "the most complete" development of the self, but only "more complete" development, for, as we will see, there is no end to the pattern of conflict and self-development. To be sure, he thinks that we will arrive at a place where we might have faith that our development can be complete at some point, and that we side then with the deepest and best sources of meaning in the universe, but the fact that this conclusion is reached by the result of faith means that it is not based in actual fact—that it is an ideal, in other words, and serves only to lure us on to further endless developments of the self. It helps us to deal with future conflicts. But conflict, in any case, is the recurring force that drives us on to the development and enjoyment of new meanings. Paradoxically, the dismantling of significance is the mechanism of its realization, just as death, as some people see it, entails a new birth.

Formal feelings take on three definite patterns, based on our relations to the present, the past, and the future. In the present, we respond to conflict by "the putting forth of energy so as to adjust present factors" (EW 2: 230). If the conflict is something to which we can successfully respond, and we do so respond, we feel "*triumph* or *exaltation*" (EW 2: 230). If the conflict is too much for us, we feel "*impotence*, which may amount to *discouragement* or *depression*" (EW 2: 230). If the conflict is too prolonged and taxing, "there results the feeling of *fatigue*" (EW 2: 231), while if the conflict involves "such activities as bear a purely external relation to the end sought . . . this gives rise to the feeling of *drudgery*" (EW 2: 231–32). Indeed, a whole catalogue of feelings can be defined in terms of the basic structure of our responding to some activity:

> There is a feeling of *clearness* when each element in the activity is appropriately directed towards its object. . . . When each interferes with some other, and there is no evident way of reconciling the conflict, although this does not amount to entire opposition, there is the feeling of *confusion*. When there is conflict of various activities going on, and no resolution of them is at hand, there is the feeling of *suspense* or *uncertainty*. (EW 2: 230–31)

Every conflict provokes a response from us; and our response to the conflict generates a feeling—a feeling related to how adequate our response to the conflict is, in terms of our own well-being and self-realization.

Some cases are more complex and recurring, and they, too, bear out the general principle: we do not know what to call such emotions, but "we *rarely* make a decision which is not followed by a mixed feeling of content for that which is attained, and regret for that which is foregone" (EW 2: 231; emphasis added). Something happens; we respond; a decision is made. As a result, we feel both contented and regretful. For some part of us has been realized by the decision, while another part has been closed off and denied. Hence, there exists the complex feeling-state of contentment-regret, which may well define a good part of our life experience. For the most part, life is bittersweet. Only rarely, it seems, when "the conflict is ended, not by the repression of any element, but by the harmonious inclusion of all in some comprehensive activity, there is the feeling of reconciliation, which may become *joy*" (EW 2: 231).

Another pattern of formal feelings arises from our relation to the past. Our past experience is retained in a way that affects our present activity (EW 2: 232). When the present situation is consistent with our past experience, for example, we have "a feeling of familiarity," which "is pleasant because the energy which occasions it is put forth in a well-worn groove, and it requires no overcoming of obstacle and resistance" (EW 2: 234). When the past experience overwhelms the present situation, there is "*brooding*,"

> the feeling of dwelling or lingering upon a subject. . . . If the dwelling is upon some supposed wrong done, there is *sullenness*. If upon some past agreeable experiences in contrast with present painful ones, it is *melancholy*. The opposite feeling, induced by a pleasant transition, is *gladness*; while opposed to sullenness, which looks for occasion for pain, is *cheerfulness,* which is the feeling which arises from a constant tendency to find pleasure in the change of experience. (EW 2: 233–34)

Again, a whole range of emotions becomes intelligible when we understand emotions as following the harmony-conflict-reconciliation model, this time for experiences specifically oriented to the past.

The same goes for our response to expectations of future activities, which likewise elicit certain responses from us, responses always accompanied by feelings. "The typical feeling of this class is *expectancy*, which is the feeling that accompanies the stretching forward of the mind. Its acute form is *eagerness*," and so on continuously (EW 2: 237). Hope, anxiety, courage, timidity, yearning, aversion, the "feeling of *success* or *failure*," "*satisfaction* or *disappointment*"—all these feelings can be accounted for in terms of Dewey's model of feeling as an "accompaniment of adjustment," or self-realization (EW 2: 237). One feels hope at the prospect that the future will conform to one's desires, and anxiety at the prospect that the future will not (EW 2: 237). "*Courage* is the feeling with which one faces a future to which he feels equal" (EW 2: 237).

In all of these cases, the objective world confronts us and creates a conflict with our settled self, which elicits our response to the conflict; and in general we feel good when our efforts can reconcile the conflict, and bad when they cannot. We feel good or bad, that is, depending on whether or not our unsettled self becomes a new self, one that has been able to reconfigure itself in an enlarged, more harmonious way.

So far, however, we have said nothing of the content of any feeling. We have only discussed the bare form of our feelings. To include the content is to discuss what Dewey calls *qualitative feelings* (EW 2: 239ff.) which, as I have mentioned, are the most important in his account. There are three types of qualitative feelings: intellectual, aesthetic, and personal (EW 2:256ff.; 2: 267ff.; 2: 281ff.).

Two points should be noted right away about qualitative feelings, as Dewey understands them. First, these feelings are normal when they go out to their objects; they involve a healthy "forgetfulness of self" (EW 2: 293). With intellectual feelings, for example, we are "lost in the objects known"; with aesthetic feelings, we are lost in the aesthetic values we contemplate; and with personal feelings, we are lost in the ends of the actions we are pursuing relative to other people (EW 2: 251). "Normal feelings, in short, are regarded as real *values* in the objects which excite them, or exist only as springs to action; they subserve conduct" (EW 2: 251). Such feelings become abnormal when they no longer seem to pertain to actual objects and their values, or the ends of some action, but only pertain to our mode of knowing and regarding our feelings. We focus excessively on our awareness of our feeling with regard to the objects. "Feeling is unhealthy . . . when set free from its absorption in the object or in the end of action, and given a separate existence in consciousness" (EW 2: 250). Such feelings, "cut loose from their connections . . . occasion what is called 'self-consciousness' in a bad sense of the term, when the individual is unduly conscious of the reference which feelings have to him as an individual" (EW 2: 251). This is unhealthy because the feelings then serve only one, detached aspect of our self, which never gets negated and never goes beyond itself; it prevents our full self-realization, which, to be achieved, requires that the self is ruptured or goes outside of itself to form a new self, a self formed by acquiring a new set of relations to some object in the world other than itself. It should be clear by now that such abnormal, self-conscious feeling almost defines modernism. Withdrawing wholly into subjective experience, lingering not on objects in the world but on our subjective apprehension of objects in the world, detached, isolated, lost from the world, the modernist self is unhealthy by definition. Its feelings are perverse, too limited and estranged for what an actual self is capable of. Some singular, superficial aspect of the self is taken as what the self is, and it is frozen in that aspect, regardless of what the world offers and occasions. The example of the character Mersault in Albert Camus's novel *The Stranger* comes to mind. For no matter how many events in the world demand an emotional response from him—such as his mother's death or his killing a man—he refuses to be affected by them.[6]

The second main thing to note about qualitative feelings is that when feeling becomes isolated in one's individual consciousness, there is a "conflict of feeling," in that one feels one's fuller self to be blocked by some isolated element (EW 2: 251). There is, in fact, "a more or less permanent conflict of feelings resulting from the opposition of some particular individual interest to some more universal one" (EW 2: 251). One has a constant feeling of conflict between one's individual self and one's larger self, the "someone else" and "someone better" one is capable of becoming. If a person partakes too much in bodily pleasures, for instance, he opposes his better nature and feels bad as a result. "Even in purely organic matters, he has a universal side. His body should conform to *law,* and law is universal. The result of a constant neglect of this universal side is pain, disease, possibly destruction of the organism" (EW 2: 252). Mersault, for example, ultimately gets himself killed. As Dewey puts the point in more detail, "in gratifying the purely particular side of his nature, he gets pleasure; but, as this gratification disorganizes the universal side, that which connects him with the laws of the universe, he gets ultimate pain. There is conflict of feeling" (EW 2: 252). The alcoholic, for example, may gain pleasure from his drink, but this pleasure is accompanied by a feeling of pain, in that he is neglecting the rest of his body and person. He goes against "the law" of his own nature by isolating one feeling, the pleasure, and focusing all of his energies on that, instead of focusing on the total pleasure of his body as a barometer of how he is developing overall as a person (EW 2: 252). He may therefore become diseased, lose social standing, or perhaps even die. "Or, upon a higher plane, suppose that one has made the pleasures which come from money-getting an end in themselves; suppose he has isolated them from his integral being, and makes his life to consist in their gratification" (EW 2: 252). Such a person, unlike the alcoholic, may not feel any physical pain. "What he feels is rather loss, dissatisfaction, misery" (EW 2: 253). Isolation of one particular feeling from the rest of one's life will lead one's particular feeling into conflict with "a higher general feeling of well-being," a higher feeling that results from the fact that "the self . . . is a very complex organism, uniting physical, intellectual, aesthetic, social, moral, and religious interests. . . . [I]n acting to gratify any one of these interests, pleasure will necessarily result, but not necessarily happiness" (EW 2: 253). For the early Dewey, happiness is the result of coordinating the various feelings of which we are capable, "an active unification of various acts into a whole life" (EW 2: 254). "Happiness is the feeling of the *whole* self, as opposed to the feeling of some one aspect of self" (EW 2: 254). Moreover, a person must come to identify his or her whole set of interests with universal aspects of the self to truly be happy. For only if a person is "thoroughly identified with more universal and permanent interests, intellectual, aesthetic, social, etc.," will the person be able to accept the loss of the particular interests and pleasures that are beyond his control, a loss that might happen at any point, and in the case of death certainly must happen (EW 2: 254).[7]

What these two points amount to, in essence, is the idea that there is a difference between *"the actual and the ideal self"* (EW 2: 254). The actual self is lost in particulars and what they mean for the self narrowly defined, and is not as well-rounded as it could be; the ideal self is universal and completed. The ideal self is not there; it does not exist. But it is the self we could be, or perhaps should be. It is our self realized to the full extent of its capacity, which can only mean, on this account, the self that lies beyond my limited person and finds its adequate home and meaning in universal values—intellectual, aesthetic, and social. In feeling, I grope my way toward this universal self—a self, be it noted, that while universal also allows me to find my own distinct identity as an individual more clearly within its universal framework. The ideal self would not be my ideal self if it totally lacked any connection to my actual self. The ideal self must still make room for *me* to be something actual, a distinct self, even if it negates an earlier version of what that actual self was by putting the actual self into fuller connections with other people and things, intellectually, aesthetically, or socially (EW 2:254).

This is the main idea behind Dewey's account of qualitative feelings. To make more sense of this account and see whether or not it is plausible, we must examine it in more detail. Let us begin with "intellectual feelings," after which we will consider "aesthetic feelings" and "social feelings" (EW 2:256; 267; 282).

Intellectual feelings are feelings that pertain to knowledge, whether we are talking about "feelings of acquisition" or "feelings of acquired knowledge" (EW 2: 257; 260). If we keep in mind that knowledge on this account means an understanding of the connection of objects to one another, and that this connection objects bear to one another is the meaning objects have, then we can say that intellectual feelings are "feelings of the meaning of experience," feelings pertaining to what our knowledge means or portends for us (EW 2: 267). In acquiring knowledge, we might have feelings of "habit and routine," when what we come to know is already akin to us (EW 2: 258). Or we might have "a feeling of *surprise*," when the known factor goes against what we had previously believed (EW 2: 258). (Notice again the pattern of a conflict of different elements at work.) Here at once, in the feelings related to knowing, an abnormal feeling can occur, the feeling that nothing new happens under the sun.

> This is the *nil admirari* spirit; the feeling that there is nothing in heaven or earth which can surprise one, for one has gone through it all. Such a mood results from a cessation of the healthy objectification of feelings, and from dwelling upon them as experiences of self, until the entire capacity for freshness of feeling has been destroyed. (EW 2: 258)

We are talking about the world-weary cynic (EW 2: 259). By focusing on the feelings of objects that are possessed by a narrow and limited self, and regarding these as all there is to say (or feel) about the objects, one negates the real meanings of the objects and condemns oneself to an inability to be surprised and to a denuded sense of what the world has to offer. Truly, the world has very little to offer so long as a person's way of experiencing it is narrow and limited. The point with normal feelings, however, is that they meet the objects out there in the universe; they are feelings for these things. "The true self finds its existence in objects in the universe, not in its own private states" (EW 2: 259). To be sure, private states do exist, but they exist so that they might serve to inform us of what is going on outside of ourselves in the wider world. They exist in order to make apparent the meanings of the world around us. "Although it [the true self] does and must have these private states, it pays attention to them only for the sake of their universal worth. They exist not for their own sake, but as the medium through which the universe makes its significance and value apparent" (EW 2: 259). We will see that this capacity of feeling to make us aware of the meanings in the universe is especially true, for Dewey, in the case of wonder.

In the possession of knowledge, and not simply in our acquiring of it, we naturally develop a "sense of ownership and power," as if we were not controlled by external factors but in some sense free in regard to them (EW 2: 260). But the normal self feels this sense of ownership alongside its own limitations, alongside a sense of how little it still knows. The feeling of ignorance arises, which is a feeling for our universal self that has not yet been realized. We feel that we are incomplete, not fully in possession of what we would need to know to be complete. Here again an abnormal form of feeling may present itself: the feeling of the "unknowable" (EW 2: 261). To feel that something is not yet known is normal. But to feel that something will never be known, cannot ever be known, "could only paralyze all action," whereas the feeling of ignorance makes us desire to find out, propels us to action, to inquiry (EW 2: 261). Strictly speaking, the feeling of the unknowable is impossible, because it would be "a feeling of something utterly unrelated to self" (EW 2: 261). This would be "a psychological impossibility" (EW 2: 261). Those who believe they have such a feeling are abnormal, in Dewey's account; moreover, they risk experiencing alienation, the feeling of an alien world that they can never know, entirely set over against them.

We come next to the feeling of wonder, according to Dewey one of the most important feelings we can have. Wonder is basically the feeling of awe that we have in the presence of a world outside of ourselves, a feeling we might have, for example, when gazing into the night sky. "Wonder is the attitude which the emotional nature spontaneously assumes in front of a world of objects" (EW 2: 261–62). When we stand in front of the world, we feel that here is a secret we must unlock, here is something we must try to know. For the mind has "the sense that it is in the presence of a universe of objects to know which is to find its own true being" (EW 2: 262). We feel genuinely interested in external objects but also feel implicated in their meanings. In the case of wonder, it is not that our narrow, private selves want to understand themselves in relation to the world, in order, as it were, to know where they stand with respect to the world. The feeling is rather one of negation of our private selves, and of our intimate connection with what is larger than us, the sense of a shared mystery that we feel compelled to unravel, the solution of which would allow us to know ourselves as well as the world. Or, to put it another way, in the feeling of wonder the mind has the sense that its true being is *out there*, out in the world, and not simply inside itself; and the mind senses that to know our true being, we must come to know the being of things "out there."

The mind that loses the sense of wonder is abnormal. It is a mind that in some sense kills itself, denies itself as mind. To lose a sense of wonder about the wider world "is to sink back contended into one's own subjective possessions, and thus commit intellectual suicide" (EW 2: 262). One cuts oneself off, intellectually, from what one is, from what one must understand if one would understand oneself.

Dewey has the highest praise for the feeling of wonder and reserves for it the highest function, insisting that "wonder is the cause of all growth" (EW 2: 263). The normal mind wonders at facts until it feels "at home" in them and knows its own meaning (EW 2: 262). This effort requires going out to the facts, genuinely wanting to understand them, whereas in its degenerate form, where wonder clings to its subjective meanings and uses, we end up with mere *"curiosity,"* or else knowledge for the sake of "vanity," or "power," or "self-culture," and so on (EW 2: 263–64). The normal mind, however, is comfortable with going beyond itself and takes a genuine interest in doing so. *It wants to grow.* It is interested in extending itself through an encounter with what is outside of itself, and feels that to know this wider world would be, in an essential sense, to know itself as it really is.

The last point to consider about intellectual feeling is the precise way in which it relates to the world outside of itself. The key notion here is *"presentiment"* (EW 2: 264). What comes first, for the early Dewey, are not the rules of logic, but the actual practice of thinking in some situation. Actual thinking is guided not by rules but by presentiments of what the mind is seeking, and how it should seek. One has a vague feeling of what one is searching for; one does not know in advance. Indeed, the "intellectual genius" is the one who hits the mark most successfully without really knowing, guided by "intuition" rather than the application of pre-given, formal requirements (EW 2: 265). Said another way, the end we are seeking is not known, but felt (EW 2:264). Feeling here has an immense amount of intellectual power. It guides us in our explorations as we grope along. Afterwards, we when look back on the path we have traversed, we can formulate the standards of our movement and specify the route we have taken. But we must not confuse the secondary formal rules for the actual living inquiry. In intellectual matters, we are guided forward by a feeling that draws us onward—a vague feeling of finding ourselves outside of ourselves, a feeling of coming to know more and more of what we are beyond our narrow selves. We are drawn outside of ourselves into something that may be our higher selves (EW 2:264–65).

Aesthetic feeling, the second type of qualitative feeling, pertains to the worth of any experience relative to how close it comes to "the ideal of mind" (EW 2: 267). The closer our partial selves come to the universal ideal, the more those selves appear beautiful, and are judged to be so by us. Aesthetic feelings occur to the extent that we experience the world as it is shaped by our best and highest ideals. In other words, what is essential is that our ideals be embodied in outward form (EW 2: 268). The sensuous in these cases is literally made to embody values or ideals, and not just any values or ideals, but the values and ideals of the self, so that the material seems "as one with self" (EW 2: 270). In aesthetic feelings, the mind recognizes itself in the objects in the world that are presented to it. Thus, for the early Dewey, the ideal at work in any art must be "true . . . *to human nature*" (EW 2: 271). An artwork misses its mark if it is alien to human beings and does not mirror our needs and interests, or does not at least express our meanings.

More specifically, what an aesthetic feeling conveys is "the feeling *of the agreement of some experience with the ideal nature of the self*" (EW 2: 273). Art is like a revelation to us, a revelation of "our own inmost nature" (EW 2: 273). "We find a landscape beautiful," for example, "because we find ourselves in some way reflected in it" (EW 2: 273). We then experience *admiration* for the object in its beauty (EW 2: 274). Admiration, indeed, is the key to aesthetic feeling, just as wonder is the key to intellectual feeling. The reason we make art, according to Dewey, is to give us something to admire; we want something to admire in the world, and art fulfills this need. In point of fact, therefore, "aesthetic feeling . . . is something more than passive enjoyment of beauty; it is active delight in it" (EW 2: 274). We actively pursue and interpret the object for what it can tell us about our higher selves. Thus we expect of art that it must struggle to manifest the ideal completely; that is, it must hint at, and try to express, the "completely developed self," the self that we would be at the end of an infinite process of perfection, our ideal self, which lies far beyond our narrow, actual self (EW 2: 274). But Dewey stresses that we do not know what this ideal self would be. "Art can completely satisfy admiration," he says, "only when it completely manifests the ideal—whatever that may be" (EW 2: 274).

Dewey gives an interesting account of how close the different art forms come to expressing this completely developed self—of how

close they come to presenting our self-realization in outward form—
but the details of this account need not detain us. As he moves from
an account of architecture (the art form most dependent on its material), to sculpture (material made to approximate the human body
and spirit), to painting (mere pigments that require active ideal interpretation by the mind), to music (mere sounds made to express
human emotions and aspirations), to poetry (mere breath given ideal
life), moving thus from art forms that are less ideal to those that are
more ideal (an account that seems similar to the one Hegel gives in
his *Introductory Lectures on Aesthetics*[8]), he arrives at dramatic poetry
as the crowning achievement of the arts (EW 2: 274–77).

With dramatic poetry, as Dewey sees it, art becomes almost entirely human and ideal and therefore closest to the spirit of the complete self. Dramatic poetry deals with the human predicament, and,
being poetry, does so in a manner less dependent than other art forms
on material elements; thus it "consummates . . . the range of fine
arts" (EW 2: 276–77). Both its form (less material than other arts) and
its content (the human story) are related to "personality" (EW 2:
277). Dramatic poetry tells the story of human life, not, as does epic
poetry, "as the result of any external historical forces," nor, as does
lyric poetry, with privilege given to "man's inner life," but in a manner that combines subjective and objective meanings in an ideal way
(EW 2: 277). Dramatic poetry exhibits, not simply the inner states of
human beings, nor simply the objective forces that shape us, but
"man as irresistibly pushing on towards an inevitable end through his
own personal desires and intentions" (EW 2: 277). Dramatic poetry
reveals how inner, private life comes to take on larger meanings and
significance. And with this idea, we arrive once more at Dewey's basic
claim, namely, that feeling is not simply a physiological event, though
it is this, but is also a deep, rich, complex, and nuanced occurrence
that, in the end, is about our self-realization, about our becoming
selves whose meanings are out there, present in the world. As the case
of our aesthetic feelings shows, we are forced outside of ourselves; our
feelings draw us outward into new and other versions of what we are.

The last point to notice about aesthetic feeling is that here, too, as with intellectual feeling, "the canons of taste" or rules of assessment come later and are secondary (EW 2: 279). For Dewey, all great art is natural, and says something to us of the mystery of ourselves (EW 2: 278).

> The great artists are, after all, only the interpreters of the common feelings of humanity; they but set before us, as in concrete forms of self-revealing clearness, the dim and vague feelings which surge for expression in every human being, finding no adequate outlet. Thus it is that we always find a great work of art *natural;* in its presence we do not find ourselves before something strange, but taken deeper into ourselves, having revealed to us some of those mysteries of our own nature which we had always felt but could not express. (EW 2: 278)

It is the expression of the artist that we must trust, not the critic who comes afterward and judges the art according to standards of aesthetic appreciation. For the artist is in first contact, as it were, with the mysteries of our nature, while the critic comes afterwards and notes the procedures that have worked in the past to address these mysteries. Art cannot be given a rule, since it is a creative enterprise, but rules can develop out of successful versions of art, and they can serve future artists and their admirers by steering them clear of "vain and unfertile attempts" (EW 2: 279).

In aesthetic feeling, too, there are abnormal forms of feeling that should be avoided. These occur when we feel not for the object itself but for our own personal satisfaction in apprehending the object. One then becomes a superficial admirer of art, or perhaps a superior expert snubbing everyone else. This person "prides himself upon his fastidiousness and refinement of taste rather than loses himself in the realm of objective beauty" (EW 2: 280). Aesthetic feeling then

> degenerates into *aestheticism.* . . . Feeling . . . is shut up within itself, instead of being made the key to the unlocking of the beauty, grace, and loveliness of the universe. The penalty is inevitable—loss of freshness, of healthiness, and finally of all vitality of

feeling. Feeling has to live on itself, instead of finding new food in every object of experience, and it ends by destroying itself. (EW 2: 279–80)

Once again, the abnormal is the isolated, the withdrawn (EW 2:282). In such a state, a feeling has no real inspiration and becomes the shallow instrument of a petty, self-serving taste. The standards of taste can help us avoid these abnormal forms, for example by reminding us of how the artist must connect with more universal meanings. Even so, we must always remember, according to Dewey, that the art comes first, and the critic must constantly accommodate his standards of judgment to the artist and what he does when he does his task well (EW 2: 279). In truth, for the genuine artist, the ideal is "a spur to new creation," but the critic "fossilizes the ideal into cut-and-dried formulae," which makes the ideal only "a burdensome command to produce nothing new" (EW 2: 279).

The third and last type of qualitative feeling is *personal feeling*, the feelings we have for other persons. With the process of self-realization, I am usually connected to other people; and personal feelings are those that develop within me in my relations to these others. These interpersonal relations are fundamental to our own realization. "The self has no meaning except as contrasted with other persons" (EW 2: 282). The abnormal version of this process is egoism, or "egoistic feelings" (EW 2: 282), in which the self resolves the interpersonal feelings it undergoes solely into its own personal states, instead of letting them exist between, and among, ourselves and others. But Dewey notes that egoism only makes sense with the presupposition of other people. It is never the case that we have an individual feeling first, and then a feeling (or not) for others. Instead, our own feelings always include others, an acute awareness of others, which then serves as the basis for our later embrace of or resistance to them. In this sense, there is always a "*reciprocal* relation of egoistic and altruistic feelings" (EW 2: 281). These feelings imply one another and are grounded in the more general feeling of encountering others, which is primary and ineradicable.

Dewey identifies three types of personal feelings: "social, moral, and religious" (EW 2:282). Social feelings come in two forms: feelings we have for others (e.g., "antipathy" and "sympathy") and feelings we have for ourselves in relation to others (e.g., "pride" and "humility;" EW 2: 283–88). The feelings we have for others "are feelings *which result from the identification of one's self with another*," and they demonstrate, above all, the connection we have with other people, the unity of human nature even amid our differences (EW 2: 283). As we have seen, "the self has no meaning except as contrasted with other persons" (EW 2: 282). Even antipathy, for instance, can result only from a prior identification with (and then rejection of) the other person. There are two types of antipathy: "disgust" and "indignation" (EW 2: 283). "In disgust we identify the state of mind or experience of others with ourselves, and find it repulsive to our own actual state" (EW 2: 283).When I feel indignation, I identify someone or their actions with myself and then see him (and myself) acting in a less than ideal way. Two things happen: I identify with another person—that is, I see myself as if I were him—and I judge him to be failing to live up to an ideal that we share (or should share). I am not simply angry at the other person, which would mean a blind sort of rage, but rather I am very specifically upset at him for not living up to his full potential, for coming up short, for not being his ideal self (EW 2: 283). This shows again how some feelings can take us outside of ourselves; having the feeling depends on our ability to identify with another person and also with an ideal version of how both of us should act. Indeed, Dewey argues that "could we not identify the other person with self, and then measure both by a common ideal, the feeling of indignation would be impossible" (EW 2: 283).

This condition of having personal feelings—namely, that my feelings pertain to the feelings of another, or the other's feelings pertain to mine—is even more prevalent, and indeed reaches a higher grade, in the feeling of sympathy. Sympathy requires that another person's experiences are felt to be ours: "we take the feelings of another for our own" (EW 2: 284). We can feel their emotion because we can have it ourselves. An additional feature is also required, namely, I must also *recognize* that this emotion that I could have is actually someone else's. Suppose someone feels hurt, for example. I know that feeling; I can undergo it myself. And I also understand that this same feeling that I am capable of is being experienced by another (EW 2: 283–84).[9]

What the feeling of sympathy shows is that once more we go out to others and we find the meaning of our selves outside of ourselves. Sympathy requires "the ability to forget self" (EW 2: 285). Sympathetic feelings are feelings of mine, but are felt as "the experience of some one else" (EW 2: 285). I objectify my own feelings *in* someone else. I thus enlarge myself. Otherwise I would simply watch and observe the other person and not feel what he or she feels. But to feel sympathy I cannot simply experience the person as an object for me. "We must not only take their life into ours, but we must put ours into them" (EW 2: 285). We must take an "*active interest*" in the other; we must recognize our own feeling in them *as another who is not me.* Someone else, out there, has *my* feeling; consequently, I feel for her; I feel for her as if she were I, although she is in fact someone else besides me. My feeling therefore extends beyond myself and becomes a feeling for another from whom I am nonetheless distinct. This is the feeling of sympathy.

According to Dewey, the feeling of sympathy strongly suggests that we are able to move outside of our private lives and closer and closer "into what universally constitutes personality" (EW 2: 286). For there is something shared between two distinct individuals (and so something no longer local, specific, and individual) and, moreover, there is no boundary to this feeling of sympathy. It is not restricted to the life of only this or that individual. Indeed, such a restriction is "a defective sympathy," as when we arbitrarily restrict our sympathies to only "our own family" or "our own neighborhood" (EW 2: 286). In itself, the feeling of sympathy is expansive. It continues to grow if it is nourished. Thus, as the self develops, it is able to have sympathy for more and more people and things beyond itself, until at last, the most "developed personality" would become "absolutely universal" and would have universal sympathies, if this could be achieved. This

would mean that we attain a feeling that "can . . . recognize no distinction of social rank, wealth, or learning, or anything that tends to
cut off one person from another" (EW 2: 286).

If we were to reach this point, our expansive sympathy would be a
feeling for society as "an organic whole, a whole permeated by a common life, where each individual still lives his own distinct life unab-
sorbed in that of the community" (EW 2: 286). Or, as Dewey also
puts it, in the feeling of universal sympathy, our life widens "till it
becomes as comprehensive as humanity, and at the same time deepens our own distinct individuality" (EW 2: 286–87). The more universal is the range of our feeling, the more distinct becomes our
individual personality in relation to the universal whole with which
we feel connected. This is so in virtue of the nature of sympathy itself.
As we saw above, sympathy involves both an identification of myself
with the other and at the same time the recognition that we are distinct (EW 2: 286). I feel *my* feeling, and I feel that it is also *the other's*
feeling. I feel, therefore, that two distinct selves share a common feeling. Sympathy is this third, new feeling, the feeling of the other, as he
feels something that now exists for me, a feeling which therefore takes
me outside myself even as it allows me, in my connection to the
other, to be myself.

What the feeling of sympathy reveals, then, is that "our true nature" does not simply exist inside of us as private selves, but exists in
a wider version of ourselves, in a "universal personality," in a self that
is larger than ourselves. I feel that I am a distinct self who has his own
feeling, which is at the same time a feeling beyond itself, shared with
others (perhaps, eventually, with all others, since for Dewey there is
no limit to what I can sympathize with). I might be able to extend the
feeling of sympathy to all of humanity, for example, or even, perhaps,
to the cosmos as a whole (EW 2: 286–87).

So much for the feelings I have for others: with sympathy as their
highest expression, these feelings, Dewey would say, reveal to me my
longing to find my true nature as a distinct member of a universal
whole. There are also feelings I have *for myself* in relation to others.
Dewey has in mind pride and humility (EW 2: 287). Feeling *proud*

Dewey interprets to mean "a sense of our own worth compared with a personality not ourselves," and he interprets *humility* to be the feeling of our having less worth when compared with others (EW 2: 287). There are degenerate forms of these feelings. Too much pride means "conceit" or "vanity" and indicates that the person has failed at "getting outside of himself" and is failing at his self-realization, at becoming a more universal self with more universal sympathies than his own narrow interests (EW 2: 287). At its best, pride means "self-respect . . . the feeling that we *are* personalities; that there is embodied in us the infinite value of a self which is worthy of respect wherever found" (EW 2: 287). Pride would then seem to indicate that we possess higher worth than mere particular organic bodies, to be used at will. On the contrary, each of us is a personality, which means we participate in larger meanings beyond the bare given fact of ourselves. We participate in shared social meanings and we form laws, for example, that confer on us our worth and our rights; and we reach toward even higher ideals than this for humanity. Humility, at its best, is our feeling our own lack in relation to the ideal self we could be (EW 2: 287). We are humbled by recognition of the ideal self that it is possible for us to be, and we feel the contrast between this ideal self and the self we are (EW 2: 287). But humility can also degenerate, as when "it takes the form of sensitiveness, self-depreciation, perhaps even . . . degradation" in contrast to some specific person we meet in the world (EW 2: 287). As the form of pride called self-respect reminds us, we also do count for something in relation to other people; and so the proper mixture of emotions would be pride (or self-respect) combined with humility. In the emotionally healthy person, "pride and humility necessarily accompany each other" (EW 2: 287).

Dewey notes that a whole range of more nuanced feelings, from "*envy,*" to "*jealousy,*" to "*malice,*" to "*covetousness,*" can also be explained on the basis of what he has already said about social feelings (EW 2: 288). Malice, for instance, "is the egoistic form of pride joined with antipathy" (EN 2: 288). In other words, malice is pride, understood in its degenerate form of taking a vain interest only in oneself, coupled with antipathy, or the feeling of being revolted at the other person for failing to live up to an ideal. In malice, we feel a peculiar kind of indignation at the person for failing to live up to the ideal of our narrow selves—we hold it against the person, rather perversely, for not being as we want them to be, where the "we" here is not our shared ideal self, but rather the particular, wayward conceits and desires of my individual self.

"Moral feeling" is the second type of personal feeling. This is the feeling of obligation we have towards others with whom we can identify. Grounded in sympathy, and expanded to include all human beings, moral feeling consists of the sense of "rightness" we feel about good acts, when we feel that our ideal personality could be realized in the acts (EW 2: 288).

> In moral feeling man feels his true self to be one which comprehends possible relations to all men, and all acts which are necessary to bring the actual self into harmony with this true self, to make his will, in other words, conform to a universal will, he conceives as *duties.* (EW 2: 289)

I think here of our obligations to future generations, for example. Is it right to pollute the earth to the extent that life becomes a hardship to humans who come after us? Not if they, too, are an aspect of our true self. If they are part of us, then to harm them is to harm ourselves. Moreover, as we feel an obligation to promote our own self-realization, so we feel an obligation to the self-realization of the humans who will come after us, since these others are in fact part of what we are, in Dewey's expanded conception of the self, and therefore we bear to them the same responsibilities that we bear to ourselves.

Herein lies one of the key points of Dewey's early position: the self extends beyond the individual organic body, even beyond our own egos, and even beyond the things closely associated with our own egos, such as family, friends, our neighborhood or nation (EW 2:286). We come more and more to identify ourselves with something larger than ourselves—indeed, with a "universal self" that is the ideal of humanity; perhaps even, as we will see, with an ideal self at work in the cosmos. This growth or expansion of self is felt in various ways, as we have seen throughout this chapter, as if the self were headed outside of itself toward some goal. It is a dizzying and unsettling process, to be sure, and at times there may appear to be no sure footing for this loss of self, for our past self's disintegration; and yet, at each stage we seem to be moving toward some other definite aspect of what we are. Moral feeling is no exception. In moral feeling, we lose the iron-clad protection of our own isolated ego, but this loss is accompanied by a sense that we share a bond with all others; we feel we are part of a universal self, and, feeling part of this self, we feel certain duties toward it and toward the others who also form a part of it. "The feeling that a universal self is our own true being is necessarily accompanied by the feeling of obligation and responsibility" (EW 2: 289).

Moral feeling contains two aspects, "*reverence*" and "*remorse*" (EW 2: 290). In the first case, we feel that this universal self is within our reach, and we feel an obligation toward it. We feel humbled in the presence of the self that is larger than us, and also we feel a duty to realize its nature in us, that is, through right actions that we strive to realize. In the case of remorse, we feel that our acts fall short of realizing this larger self—as when we feel that we have let ourselves down by behaving badly (EW 2:290).

The third and last type of personal feeling is "religious feeling" (EW 2: 290–291). There is a serious defect in moral feeling, namely, that in the end it fails. "There is a conflict in moral feeling as such" (EW 2: 290). We can never wholly be what we ought to be; we cannot always do what we ought to do. In Dewey's terms, there is a fundamental rift, "a gulf between the actual and the ideal or universal self" (EW 2: 290). As finite beings, we never achieve the culmination of all of our efforts; we never realize the inexhaustible, infinite self we could be, the universal self. Our actual selves never finally become ideal. Thus, in our endeavor to be moral, we will encounter an inevitable crisis. The moral self is negated; it must, therefore, press on to a new formation. Religious feeling is that new formation.

Religious feeling is the feeling that the conflict between my actual self and my ideal self is overcome, or so it seems, because I seem to lose any remaining feelings of separation from my ideal self (EW 2: 290). I feel that my actual self, which until now I had regarded as still to some extent separate from the whole, must now be regarded as essentially belonging to the idealized whole. I feel that my true self is realized in God, or the Absolute.

> Religious experience is the sphere in which this identification of one's self with the completely realized personality, or God, occurs. Religious feeling is, therefore, the completely universal feeling, and with it the progressive development of feeling ends. (EW 2: 290–91)

For Dewey, religious feeling, in other words, is the feeling that we are one with the universe. We identify with the cosmos, with the entire grand, awesome sweep of things, and we feel that our own self is at one with this grand sweep. Where it goes, we willingly follow; for we recognize that we are it, are at one with it, which we feel is the ideal state to be in, the way things ought to be, so that we accept the way things occur.

Religious feeling therefore involves two different emotions: "dependence" and "peace" (EW 2: 291). The *"feeling of dependence"* is the feeling of the complete loss of the isolated self within the universal self. "In religious feeling we recognize the worthlessness, *the nullity,* of this private separate self, and surrender ourselves wholly to the perfect personality, God" (EW 2: 291). The separate self is now negated; it has no existence apart from the whole. Hence, we feel our utter dependence on the life of the cosmos, and our inability as separate selves to be of any genuine ideal worth. Our personal meaning is now transcended by the higher, more ideal meanings that we impute to the cosmos. We feel that our private, individual meanings are not sufficient, that they can only find justification in the cosmos as a whole, upon which we are dependent.

This brings peace, as Dewey sees it. The *"feeling of peace"* is the feeling that there is no conflict anymore between our actual selves and our ideal selves. We no longer feel the tension of the self's resistance to the whole. Identifying now wholly with the ideal self upon whom we are dependent, and losing, at last, the final remainders of our separateness (but not our distinctiveness), we feel that the whole course of things will ultimately continue on and take care of itself and us with it. A person feels that "there can be no essential dualism in his life, for the only thing which is real for him is that Being in whom personality is complete. There is, therefore, the feeling of peace" (EW 2: 291–92). Since "the only thing" that seems real for a person at this point is God, a complete and perfect personality existing in the world, the person feels that there exists no actual self any longer to oppose this ideal self, so that the ideal self alone is what exists. This feeling that there is an Absolute self brings the person peace because he now feels that he can find comfort in the ideal self that underlies everything and holds it together.

If this were the end of the matter, however, then rupture as the mechanism of the loss of self, and its subsequent growth, would finally come to an end (EW 2: 290–91).There would in fact be a complete attainment of self-realization, and rupture would finally cease. Complete harmony in the eternal Absolute, as in the philosophy of Josiah Royce, would be the fundamental reality, securing the meaning of all actual events in its higher ideal meaning.

The matter does *not* end there, however, for Dewey goes on to write about "the feeling of faith"—what I have called faith in life. Faith is a peculiar emotion in the Deweyan conception, in that it is at once the completion and incompletion of all emotional progression. As we saw, morality ultimately fails, because it "constantly asserts that the final reality for man is that which cannot be made out actually to exist" (EW 2: 292). The feeling of faith "only brings this element to conscious recognition" (EW 2: 292). In other words, faith is the explicit awareness that we do not realize the ideal. But it is also the insistence that the ideal is nonetheless realized. We perceive keenly that God "cannot be immediately felt to be" (EW2: 292). But we claim that he exists nonetheless. In Dewey's view, "religious life," which embodies the feeling of faith, "asserts that this Personality [God] is not only ideal . . . but that it *is* perfectly real" (EW2: 292). But this "that it is . . . real" only emerges with the awareness of the failure of the ideal to be real at the same time. Faith is the assertion of the reality of the ideal even as we are aware of its lack of reality.

This feeling for the cosmic whole needs to be there, Dewey says, because otherwise all feeling is disruption and division until the end. "Without it feeling can be only dissatisfaction, for it must reveal discord between what is and what is felt after, its goal of happiness" (EW2: 363). Life would be nothing but constant tension, and fundamentally unfulfilling, without some ultimate sense of unity to our endeavors. But this sense of unity does not itself derive from our feelings. Nor does it come from our knowledge: we are never completely justified in holding that the universe forms a whole. Both human knowledge and feeling are finite, while the whole we long to be a part of is infinite. We can never adequately reach what we long for. The best we can do, therefore, is to assert through our wills that the whole is real, even as we know we do not possess it and feel that it is lacking in our experience (EW 2: 361–362).

Dewey explains this crucial part of his argument as follows: "There cannot be knowledge that the true reality for the individual self is the universal self, for knowledge has not in the individual compassed the universal" (EW 2: 361). We wish to grasp all things as a whole, but "in knowledge there is no ultimate justification for this belief. It finds its validity and the revelation of its meaning only in the will" (EW 2: 361). In fact, we understand that we should seek for complete knowledge only because it is lacking. It is our assertion that the whole must exist, even when we do not grasp it, that compels us to search for the whole in the first place and so perhaps to get closer to it. The will, the assertion of belief, takes priority over knowledge. "The motive to knowledge and the energy of its realization is the *belief* that there is truth, and that every act of intellect, legitimately performed, leads to truth" (EW 2: 361).

Nor do our feelings reveal the cosmic whole to us. "This will or faith," as Dewey calls it, "this act of faith also precedes and transcends *feeling.* There is, in the feeling of *harmony,* the feeling of unity, but this feeling accompanies will. It is the internal side of the universal or objective unity realized through the will. Without this act of will, all feeling is that of discord, of incongruence" (EW 2: 361–362). We must assert that there is a cosmic whole to which we belong before we can feel the harmony of so belonging. Our lack of the feeling, in other words, compels us to assert that there are grounds for having the feeling, and then we have the feeling, because of our assertion, which we understand, however, is based on a lack.

We can reconstruct Dewey's account of faith as follows:

1. There must be a cosmic whole to which we belong, or else everything is ultimately division and conflict.
2. We do not know for certain that the cosmic whole to which we belong exists (the last feeling we have before faith is of division and lack; it is the always-failed moral experience, and our inability to know the whole).
3. The only thing we can do is to have faith that the cosmic whole exists (we negate the *lack* of it).
4. That is, we can only assert that all division and conflict is reconciled in the cosmic whole and let this assertion influence our feeling and guide our lives.

The upshot, then, is that division and disruption always remain, but with the faith and the feeling that they are amounting to something in the whole. Faith is the feeling that there is an ideal out there that is realized, but in truth the ideal is not realized but merely asserted to exist in order to fill its absence. Faith is a feeling that is useful: it enables us to work through disruption and conflict to greater harmonies. But it can occur only with the explicit acknowledgement of our inability to realize the ideal, with the awareness, that is, of the lack of the reality of the ideal. The point of faith, in other words, is not to bring all tension to a close, but to ensure that through the tension we achieve a "progressive appropriation" of an ideal self and state of things (EW 2: 363). Faith gives us an ideal to aim for and to progressively realize.

Faith, then, relates to religious experience in a very specific manner. In faith, we understand instead that we can only ever *assert* that we can realize the ideal. Religious feeling then follows; but this means that religious feeling depends on faith, on an ungrounded assertion. We can never know that the religious feeling is validated, that its object is real.[10] We can only ever fall back on *the assertion* that it is, that the completed self can be realized. We reach out to the cosmic whole and hope for the best; and in reaching out, we are able to function and to create meanings.

Let us take an example—say, the case of the ancient Egyptians and their pyramids. Some basic stuff is given to them—rocks and mortar (or ultimately "motions," which they turn into sensations, which are then transformed into the perception of rocks and mortar as objects of knowledge)—and they transform these objects into an ideal formation, the pyramids. The ancient Egyptians make these new objects (the pyramids) to symbolize many things, including eternity. Eternity becomes the ideal meaning for these objects and for the Egyptians' selves as well, for the human lives that interact with these objects; their ideal selves are found in relation to these objects. But ultimately, we do not know that these objects with their ideal meanings mirror the actual world behind our knowledge. The ancient Egyptians had no guarantee, despite all of the ways these objects (the pyramids) bespoke to them eternity, that they were in any real and true way connected to eternity. Yet the faith that they were connected to eternity was precisely what enabled the Egyptians to build these objects, produce these ideal meanings, and so render the world as they experienced it more and more ideal and filled with meanings they could recognize.

We build castles on sand, and the sand lets us build them. So we build castles and live in them; and what else, indeed, is a human being supposed to do? Dewey's early philosophy is an honest attempt to describe the human condition, and to show us why, despite our precarious position as finite beings, we can nonetheless affirm our condition due to the power of ideals to transform the world and make it more meaningful. With the assertion of faith comes the feeling of peace, therefore; but this feeling is peace amidst the struggles of human life, not the peace of the assurance of final victory. And the feeling of dependence is the feeling that our efforts are permitted, that the world is allowing our idealizations, so that we can pursue them without fear.

If we now try to sum up personal feelings as the early Dewey understands them—that is, our feelings in relation to others, including God, who exist or could exist—then we can say that these feelings ultimately compel us to *love*. For in all forms of personal feeling—in our social, moral, and religious feelings—we extend ourselves to include others; that is, we identify with them and their interests, and this is love. Love "is active interest" in the other person, our care and concern for him beyond our narrow, isolated self and its interests (EW 2: 292). Hate, of course, is always still possible, but according to Dewey, we only hate in the person what prevents him from realizing his better or more ideal self. In fact, it is impossible to hate the person as such without hating some part of ourselves at the same time, since "personality is a universal characteristic" (EW 2: 293). Likewise, social laws, although they are grounded in a kind of hate, in that they involve force against individuals, are *ideally* an act of love; that is, they express the obligations that we all owe to one another (to "personality") in the forms of laws and norms we are compelled to obey (EW 2: 294–95). And, of course, as there is with so many other feelings, there is an abnormal version of love; it is the feeling we bear toward another only insofar as he means something for us, rather than what he means for himself and for ever-more-ideal versions of himself. The abnormal form of love is love turned inward, rather than outward toward the other person (EW 2: 293).

Love, then, as the ultimate meaning of personal feeling, bears an interesting connection to the other ultimate forms of qualitative feeling we have seen—namely, to the wonder that comes with intellectual feeling and to the admiration that comes with aesthetic feeling. In each case, but in a slightly different way in each, we lose our isolated self and expand to include as part of it something outside of it. "As wonder and admiration are forgetfulness of self in the presence of the universe of [known] objects and [aesthetic] ideals, so love is forgetfulness of self in the presence of persons" (EW 2: 293). Each feeling is a different occasion for us to go away from our actual selves and try to realize our ideal selves, the ideal meanings of which we are capable, which are to be found out there beyond our actual selves.

Lastly, we can say about personal feelings—about social, moral, and religious feelings—that they shift from a feeling to a norm, that is, to a judgment we can make about the feelings. This judgment about the feeling is what Dewey means by *conscience* (EW 2: 296). Our conscience presumes to tell us whether "a given act of ours is in harmony or in discord with a truly realized personality" (EW 2: 296). Dewey insists, however, that there is no law for this; only the life of the individual is the source of the feelings of rightness, and conscience only comes after the fact in order to help us by formulating handy guidelines for our behavior (EW 2: 296–97). In truth, the feeling self is always in "development," always "in process of realization," and it is the feeling process that is the actual reality, not the laws of perfection that we may try to prescribe to it (EW 2: 296). Dewey centers (or rather de-centers) meaning in the finite life of the actual self struggling to find the Absolute, not in the Absolute considered as an eternal entity outside of time whose perfection is guaranteed. This is precisely why, as the culmination of his account of feelings, he ends with faith, which is something finite beings might need, but not the Absolute.

This is also why Dewey insists that feelings in general, feelings taken as a whole, are actually infinite in content and meaning, with as many feelings existing as there are people to feel them (EW 2: 217). His account is only a general framework in terms of which we can understand feeling, but the feelings themselves, in all of their infinite variety and movement, are the actual reality. The self, for Dewey, is engaged in an infinite process of development, endlessly undergoing new feelings and their richness of meanings as the self grows and changes. And its feelings tend to become more universal as the self adjusts to more and more circumstances. "With every new realization of personality comes a higher ideal of what constitutes a true man, and a keener response to relations of harmony and discord" (EW 2: 296). The feelings are capable of this growth, as Dewey's account of feelings intends to make plausible. The feelings themselves are able to develop this way; there is no form imposed upon them.

We are drawn forward and outward in and through our feelings. We are drawn out of our actual self and its individual meanings into meanings beyond us that we nonetheless recognize as our own (that is, as the meanings of our higher self). Feelings, then, in general, are mental states that attend our self-realization; they are essential elements of a process (its internal, emotional aspect, as it were) by which life comes more and more to embody an idealized meaning of things, even if in the end we do not know for certain that our meanings are secured at the heart of things.

One aspect of the general framework of feelings that Dewey advances is especially noteworthy. As we have seen, each form of qualitative feeling seems to reach towards higher meanings. More specifically, presentiment guides intellectual feeling in its search for total truth, which is a higher and more rational meaning than that of mere facts, or even of our own individual, partial beliefs. Likewise, dramatic poetry expresses in aesthetic feeling the inevitable drawing out of the self to a new aspect and understanding of itself. The feeling of faith, in our personal feelings, encourages us to believe in a universe that is meaningful and harmonious in the end, even if we never see this in actual fact. In several different ways—in intellectual, aesthetic, and personal feelings—we are guided by a vague but powerful sense that there must be meanings beyond the facts and beyond our actual selves that we ought to attain and to realize.

Will as Self-Realization

Our detailed consideration of the early Dewey's neglected major work, the *Psychology*, comes to a conclusion with an account of his concept of the will. The will is the last of the three powers of human beings that Dewey thinks enable us to produce meaning in the universe—the three powers being, again, knowledge, feeling, and will. Dewey's concept of will is fairly straightforward, and for this reason I do not think it demands the kind of extended analysis I have provided for the fundamental concepts of knowledge and feeling. The devil, in those two cases, was in the details. Whatever persuasive power Dewey's accounts of knowledge and feeling achieve is earned through how much they explain; doing them justice required me to give a detailed description of their operation. Not so with Dewey's account of will—here his ideas are fairly general and can be related in general terms. Moreover, his concept of the will in many ways contains the other two concepts (knowledge and feeling) and is a summary of them, so that his concept of the will can be explained relatively easily once we understand these other concepts. I do want to caution the reader, however, that in taking this more limited approach, I will have to overlook many details of Dewey's account.

For Dewey, the self is not "a passive vessel" but an active agent (EW 3:356; EW 2:216; 318). As selves, we act; we go forth and do something. When we act we are not simply acting at random but are actually trying to realize ourselves—that is, we are trying to make the world fit our ideals, or, what is the same thing, we are trying to become a definite self in the external, objective world, a world that admits us, that harbors some of our ideals and allows for us to be selves of a certain sort. How exactly do we try to make the world fit our ideals? We do so, for one thing, in the case of knowledge. In one stage of knowledge, for example, we go out to sensations and actively seek in them a recognizable form (as in Dewey's camel in the clouds example, LW 8: 117). What we do, in other words, is actively transform our sensations into ideal forms, and we do this more and more in an ordered and reliable way, and this ever-increasing idealization is objective knowledge. In knowledge, we put ourselves into the world; we put our sense of order into it, and as a result we find an ordered universe of known objects. Feeling is the personal side of this process—we feel the extent to which we are realizing or losing ourselves in the external world through our activities, with pleasure and pain resulting accordingly. Accompanied by pleasure, our feelings progress toward more universal aspects, whether in our intellectual, aesthetic, or personal feelings. As our feelings progress, we realize our true nature more and more (e.g., we move from an isolated, egoistic self to a social self). In addition, the self acts in several

ways to control itself, and it seeks to control itself in these ways precisely in order to realize itself. "*Physical control*" and "*prudential control*" are good examples of this (see Dewey's account, EW 2: 321–41).
We seek to control our impulses (in the one case physically, in the
other in terms of what our impulses seek out) in order to achieve a
fuller or better sense of ourselves. In these cases, too, then, the self is
shaping the world—the world of its own actions—in order to render
it more ideal. It negates what is merely given, the actual self, and
pushes this self beyond its current state towards something that will be
better for the self in the long run (EW 2:209; 216; 358).[11]

This suggests that there is an ideal self toward which the self is
tending, and against which it is measuring itself. This ideal should
not be understood in terms of a Freudian superego, however, a concept, in any case, of which Dewey could not have been aware when
he wrote the *Psychology*. For Dewey, the will that in our active efforts
strives to realize itself is motivated by an ideal end, the completed self,
that it holds before itself, "the vague ideal of a completely universal
self, by which it measures itself and feels its own limitations" (EW 2:
358). The ideal self is a social self (one adopting inherited social
norms), but it is not only a social self; nor is it simply a part of us
that has developed during a certain stage of our psychosexual development, as is the case with the superego.[12] On the contrary, the ideal
end we feel drawn by is a completed self, a self that is thoroughly
ideal, without any limitations within it, lacking in nothing, a fully realized self. Not that this self is ever achieved or even clearly understood. Dewey makes it clear that "the self . . . cannot be realized by
some one act; it can be realized only by realizing every possible legitimate desire; that is, every desire whose realization does not preclude
the realization of some other. We realize the self only by satisfying it
in the infinite variety of concrete ways" (EW 2: 319). In other words,
we never can realize the self; but it is in the process of trying to do so
that we try out an infinite variety of possible self-realizations, and this
process itself is what is meaningful about the self's activities. It is a
process that, to be infinite in its production of meanings, requires the
vague, unspecific ideal of a completed self that we strive to become

but never can become. In short, the ideal of a completed self "must prevent the self resting in any realized attainment. It must form the spring to renewed action" in order for there to be endless new meanings in the world (EW 2: 319).

Some evidence that the completed self is the ideal self for which we strive can be found, Dewey thinks, in the cases of presentiment, dramatic poetry, and the feeling of faith, as we have seen. But it should be stressed that as Dewey sees it, at best these three aspects of feeling give us only a vague sense that we are moving toward something, we know not what. Presentiment, dramatic poetry, and the feeling of faith may provide a sense that we are moving towards an ideal, completed self, but they do not offer an account, with details of the nature of the completed self—a self that in truth cannot be manifest in any actual stage of existence. For the actual self, "what this will or self as complete is, it does not know. It only feels that there is such a goal" (EW 2: 358). Indeed, by the nature of the case (a finite self seeking an infinite one), the actual self cannot know what the completed self is (EW 2: 361). It can only feel that there is such a self, and based on this feeling, seek in various ways (some resulting in failure, others moving it closer to the ideal, based on the feelings that result and the knowledge gained) to approximate this self. And all the while, driven on by an unclear, infinite ideal, the self is creating meanings in the world in this way and partially realizing itself.

Now Dewey wants to say that although the ideal is drawing us on, we are not explicitly aware of this when we possess knowledge or feeling. We are simply knowing or feeling, and at best only groping our way, as it were, toward the understanding that at the basis of these activities is the lure of our higher ideal self. In fact, it is only in the will, and in particular the moral will, that we come to understand what is really going on, for with the moral will we have a will that explicitly understand that the actual self *ought* to be one with the ideal self. In morality, in other words, we understand that the ideal self ought to be the basis and foundation of our acts. We see that this "ought" is at work in all of our efforts, or at least that it should be, for we understand that it is right that it should be. We here grasp the actual explicitly in terms of what it should be, in terms of its better and more ideal nature. This does not mean, of course, that the ideal self is in fact at work in our activities, as their underlying basis, as it were, but only that we recognize that it ought to be; and we recognize that, in fact, the striving for this ought, for an ideal arrangement to things, is what has been going on all along in our other activities, although we had not brought this insight into our full awareness before in quite the same way (EW 2: 359–60).

With "the moral will," we realize that the ideal self ought to be the basis of our action. We come to see that we should act as if there really were one universe of interconnected events, in which each individual occupied a distinct and essential place. We understand that we should act in such a way that each person counts as an essential part of the whole. That is how our ideal self would act, as revealed by our moral feelings, and that is how we should act (EW 2:348). But of course the ideal self is not always at work in our actions. We sometimes go astray. In fact, realizing the moral will is forever a struggle, for even when we have formed the best of characters, we must still always choose between good and bad ends in each situation before us. That we must still always choose means, however, that our actual and ideal selves have not, in fact, been reconciled; they "have not been truly unified" (EW2: 360). The moral will, therefore, since it forever involves a choice, is never complete, and in it we have no guarantee of finding our complete self. We only know that we should strive for it.

Religious will is the will that simply asserts (or, in Dewey's words, "declares") that the ideal will is the basis of the actual self—asserts that *it* is what is drawing us on, and not only our individual, partial self (EW 2: 360). This assertion relies on faith, not knowledge, Dewey makes a point of saying, because knowledge never reveals a complete self; a complete self is not something we can know, and we cannot get behind knowledge and what we know to say what is there for sure. Thus, "there is always a chasm between actual knowledge and absolute truth" (EW 2: 361). Our actual state of knowledge at any given time does not demonstrate anything that Dewey has been arguing for—it does not establish that there is an absolute truth, an ideal self towards which we are tending. To believe that behind what we know there is an ideal self drawing us toward it, drawing us to leave our actual selves and realize its higher, ideal version of what we are—to believe in this requires faith. It requires an act of will to believe it and is not the result of our knowledge.

On the other hand, Dewey thinks that this is a reasonable faith, because he thinks that when our actions become more harmonious, they seem to become more ideal. Moreover, he thinks that this ideal, more harmonious self is always implied in our actual knowledge, and indeed in all of our activities insofar as they are idealizing, because, for example in the case of knowledge, our motive is to grasp everything, the whole of what is, and all the finite particulars, in a systematic arrangement. But in the end, we believe that this completed knowledge exists without knowing for sure that it does. In this case, we have faith, and our faith impels us to try to know and so to acquire at least some partial knowledge (EW 2: 361). In a similar fashion, we have faith that there is an ideal version of ourselves, one that treats everybody as equally essential to the whole, and this faith provides us with the motive to try to treat everyone in this way. We believe that what ought to be done *can* be done, and so we try to do it.

Ultimately, then, it is a matter of faith that our idealizations amount to anything complete—but this faith acts as "a spur" to idealizations of reality that, although partial and incomplete, do nonetheless occur and do give us meaning along the way (EW 2: 358). Faith is the motor that keeps meaning not simply going but progressing to richer and fuller contents. As Dewey puts it, faith in the ideal "has been a constant motive power, which has energized in bringing forth the concrete attainments in knowledge, beauty, and rightness" (EW 2: 359). Without the faith that our idealizations of life are possible, we would have to submit without reserve to the failures of actual life. Modernism would therefore win out in the end. Isolation of the self and its meanings from the actual world would be the result; and we would then look out to the world, ultimately, with the sense of a lack of any true connection with it. With the faith that the world can always be rendered more ideal, however, we are compelled to try to realize ideals in the world; and we have, moreover, an infinite reserve at our disposal, a constant source of resistance to the failures of the actual world. For it is a completed, or Absolute, self in which we have faith, a faith that provides the constant possibility of moving past the failures of finitude. Ironically, faith in this Absolute—in something that sounds as if it might be a *substance*—is actually faith in the endless power of rupture, or in that which disrupts all substances and final stages. To believe in ideals *means* to believe that we do not have to submit to the dictates of actual life, that these can be negated in order for us to move past them and toward something more freely developed and meaningful for human beings. To believe in the Absolute (or the ideal of the infinite) is to believe that this power of resistance to actual fact is endless, and that the world can always become more ideal.

I should stress here, then, that it is essential to Dewey's position that the whole process of rendering reality more ideal (based on the ideal of a complete self) ultimately rests on faith. As I mentioned in chapter 3, this admission is not, as Robert Westbrook has said, a confession of failure on Dewey's part.[13] It is the very point he is trying to make. The essence of Dewey's early philosophy is that we *believe* we are compelled by higher ideals to reshape the world and make it more meaningful for us. It is a belief that absolutely cannot be grounded in fact, or in any kind of knowledge (EW 2: 361). By not being grounded in fact, we are able, precisely, to move the facts toward the ideal rather than becoming submerged and lost in the facts. Rupture from facts produces idealized meanings such as we have seen throughout this study, meanings like those that are present in science, art, social life, and morality; and we have faith that these meanings are always able to move toward better and better versions of themselves, and hence are capable of taking the facts with them and literally making the world more fully ideal. But in the end we only have faith that this is so. And this is as it should be, in Dewey's view. For were we ever to think we positively had reached the completed self, we would cease to move toward it; we would only think we had arrived when we had not, for an infinite self can never be realized; and we would then have only the supposed realization of what cannot be so. We would be sunk wholly within some present facts and not the complete ideal. It is precisely by having faith that the complete ideal is possible, but not yet realized, that we keep trying to realize it, and it is precisely by our efforts to realize it that actual events in the world can become more ideal.

SEVEN

BEYOND MODERNIST CULTURE

The Modernist Self Overcome

Now that we have examined Dewey's early philosophy in detail, we are in a position to understand its promise. The main thrust of this philosophy lies in its attempt to move us beyond the whole problematic culture of Dewey's time (and perhaps of our own), namely, modernist culture itself. In this chapter, I first show how Dewey's philosophy challenges the modernist conception of the self, a conception that for Dewey entailed deep pessimism about human life and its prospects. I then show how Dewey's early philosophy challenges pessimism as such and allows us to have faith in life. I conclude the chapter by describing the new life-affirming form of culture that should emerge, in Dewey's view, after we move beyond modernism.

In the final chapter of this book, I will take stock of everything we have seen so far and show how Dewey's early philosophy, when taken on its own terms, in fact amounts to a new and important form of philosophical idealism, contrary to the standard interpretation of his early ideas. My aim is to persuade philosophers to study the early ideas more thoroughly, and I conclude the work by examining why Dewey's early philosophy matters.

To see how Dewey's philosophy challenges the modernist conception of the self, let us first remind ourselves of what that is. The modernist position is that there exists a radical split between the self and the world. On the one side, we have the isolated self with its human meanings, and on the other side, we have the facts themselves, the world as it really is, devoid of human meanings. The self cannot find a home in the real world, which lacks human warmth, and so it withdraws into itself and hugs its own meanings closely to itself, in absolute separation from the world. Viennese modernism was our example. We saw in chapter 2 how a whole cultural tradition was built on the belief that the self was ultimately alone, cut off from rude, indifferent nature. But in this isolation and separateness, according to the modernist, the self finds its own special resources. As we saw, artists such as Klimt and Kokoschka gave expression to deep, hidden forces within us, creative powers that made possible great, if sometimes terrifying, works of art.

We also saw in chapter 2 how Viennese modernism was grounded intellectually in the works of Kierkegaard and Schopenhauer, who were in turn influenced by Kant. Examining Kierkegaard in more depth may help us better understand the intellectual commitments involved in the modernist tradition. Kierkegaard serves as a good example of a modernist,[1] for his concepts of "inwardness" and "subjective reflection"[2] describe well what modernism means: withdrawal into one's own interior space as the only place to find meaning and value that are missing from the external, objective world of what we would now call third-person descriptions.[3] Kierkegaard shows us what modernism means: the primacy of inwardness over outwardness, of subjective over "objective reflection."[4]

Kierkegaard also helps us see how the modernist view leads to pessimism and even to despair, as Dewey himself sensed as a young philosopher. That Kierkegaard's modernism entails a deep and disturbing hopelessness is something that Kierkegaard himself stresses and emphasizes. While writing about "the dynamics of despair," Kierkegaard makes it plain that there are different kinds of anguish one can feel due to the modernist position. There is, first of all, despair in the face of the crowd, when we fear that, submerged in the midst of others, we will never become ourselves; we will never find a meaning in the crowd adequate to ourselves as distinct individuals.[5] Kierkegaard therefore counsels us to withdraw from the crowd and to go into our own selves alone. However, he immediately realizes that such a withdrawal will be not only lonely, but also the basis for a new kind of despair, namely "the despair of defiance," for we will then exist in total isolation, without any real basis for being a self, without the traction and conditions in terms of which alone a self could be a self.[6] This new despair is the result, precisely, of fleeing the external world and attending only to our inwardness. It is the very definition of modernism.

Kierkegaard proposes a remedy to the modernist despair: we should next turn to God and not simply to our own inwardness. But the faith that Kierkegaard recommends here is dependent on the prior experience of individualist despair; for it is only when we despair at being alone that we will feel, in total anguish, the need for choosing to believe in God as someone who is a true self and with whom we can finally connect as selves. With Kierkegaard, there is no escaping despair. Indeed, he thinks we always feel it insofar as we have not yet made an irrational assertion of God's existence.[7] Even when we are not fully conscious of this despair we feel it.[8] Dewey, on the contrary, wants to rid us of all grounds for despair, and he believes his account of faith is rational, because it leads to the creation of more ideal meanings in the world, and the world, at times, seems to lend itself to these creations.

Now Kierkegaard readily admits that his whole account of inwardness and despair amounts to a form of madness.[9] His defense is that too much objective reflection, which leaves out of the world human meanings and values, is also a kind of madness,[10] but this defense in no way takes away the element of madness from his own account. The madness, of course, derives from the absolute and total isolation of the self and its meanings from the world that Kierkegaard's account requires. An unmoored self, not anchored in anything substantial, clinging to its own cherished meanings alone, without criticism, without rebuke, might as well believe it is Napoleon, because nothing exists for such a self, nothing it must listen to that could contradict this belief. This is a form of madness, indeed, but also, as we have seen, a form of despair, inevitably leading to pessimism and our giving up on life. For life then appears as utterly devoid of anything resembling human meaning and value, and the most we can have along these lines is our own total, despairing isolation, clinging to our own meanings that no one else recognizes. To be sure, Kierkegaard believes that in our despair we will have faith and choose to believe in God, who will secure our meanings in the world for us.[11] But, on the other hand, he admits that such a thing is incomprehensible to him, and stresses that in no way whatsoever can he ever be, or conceive someone else who really could be, "the knight of faith."[12]

Modernism, then, leads to pessimism and despair, the despair that the early Dewey seeks to overcome. My analysis of the *Psychology* has sought to demonstrate how clearly that effort emerges in Dewey's major early work. As we saw there, Dewey emphasizes that there are abnormal and unhealthy modes of thought of which human beings are capable. There is no guaranteed progression of human meaning, and very often people get lost in abnormal forms of experience and life. I have charted the course of these abnormal and unhealthy conceptions as articulated in Dewey's early work, from the egoist to the cynic to the aesthete and beyond. The common denominator of all these unhealthy forms of human life is, precisely, what in the present work we have called modernism. In each case, the unhealthiness and abnormality consists in the isolation of the self and its meanings from the external world of objective fact. With the aesthete, for example, the meaning of beauty exists only for his private pleasure, not for what it says about human life as a whole. This withdrawn and attenuated feeling in fact prevents the aesthete from having any real experience of beauty, for the basis of beauty, the experience of the beauty of objects themselves, is cut off, and the aesthete thereby destroys "all

vitality of feeling." Without an anchor, his feeling "ends by destroying itself"; it loses its source and its standard in actual beautiful objects, and the aesthete himself degenerates into a pompous
connoisseur declaiming upon the nature of a beauty that he himself
cannot really even understand or appreciate (EW 2: 280). The egoist
similarly sees in other people only instruments to use for his own
gratification, not objects of sympathy and fellow feeling, not embodi-
ments of the social life of man, and as a result he misses the great joy
of life that can be found in human interaction and society (EW 2:
281–82). The cynic, perhaps most tellingly of all, has become old before his years and is world weary. He judges the entire vast cosmos
from his own limited perspective, contracting all of it into a simple
point within himself, and on the basis of this limited (and undeveloped) point presumes to judge the rest of the cosmos to be as limited,
undeveloped, and uninteresting as himself (EW 2: 258–59). But the
truth, of course, is not that the cosmos is uninteresting, but that the
cynic misses the world and what is exciting about it by taking his own
isolated self as the center of things and remaining lost within this limited view. The aesthete, the egoist, the cynic—these are so many manifestations of abnormal life that Dewey identifies and problematizes,
so many instances of a self that has failed to come outside of itself
and to identify itself more fully with objects in the world. In Dewey's
eyes, "the true self finds its existence in objects in the universe, not in
its own private states" (EW 2: 259).

We can well imagine, therefore, what the early Dewey may have
thought of the Viennese modernist tradition, and of the works of
such painters as Klimt and Kokoschka. Withdrawn into the private
phantasms of their own minds, without connection to larger, idealized human meanings put out there in the world to reflect back on
them and help shape and structure their private selves, artists like
these may have seemed to Dewey as if they were descending into
madness. Kokoschka fantasizes about murdering his mistress; Gerstl
depicts himself laughing in a suicidal state, and then later kills himself.[13] Art, for the early Dewey, is supposed to express an ideal for
all human beings, not someone's private fantasies. As exemplified in

dramatic poetry, "It shows us man, not in the interior recesses of his own subjective nature alone, nor man as swayed by forces beyond him to a goal of which he knows nothing, but man as irresistibly pushing on towards an inevitable end through personal desires and intentions. It shows us man's interior nature working itself out as an objective fact" (EW 2: 277). True art molds the world a certain way, a human way; it does not escape into inner, isolated meaning. The true artist has something to say about *us*, not just about himself; about the world as experienced by humans, not just the inner mind of a single person. "The great artists are, after all, only the interpreters of the common feelings of humanity; they set before us, as in concrete forms of self-revealing clearness, the dim and vague feelings . . . in every human being" (EW 2: 278). They reveal "some of those mysteries of our own nature which we had always felt but could not express" (EW 2: 278). Art goes wrong when, in it, "feeling . . . is shut up within itself, instead of being made the key to the unlocking of the beauty, grace, and loveliness of the universe" (EW 2: 280). This is not to say that there are not canons of taste, only that individual feeling must be trusted to get beyond itself (EW 2: 279); only that creative artists must give us meanings beyond their narrow private selves. "The epic of Homer, the tragedy of Sophocles, the statue of Phidias, the symphony of Beethoven are *creations* . . . virtual additions to the world's riches" (EW 2: 77)—they are not simply the expression of the artist's private inner life. Such works mean something for all of us, something about ourselves and our world. They teach us and enlighten us about some real, objective meanings out there in the world that we can apprehend and that apply to us all.

We can see, then, that Dewey is keen to overcome what he regards as the abnormalities of the isolated self, as they occur, for example, in the aesthete and the cynic; he is keen to refute modernism and its unhealthy states. Above all, Dewey is keen to overcome modernism's underlying pessimism and despair. For as Dewey reminds us in the conclusion of the *Psychology*, the work as a whole seeks to show that without faith that our meanings are working in the world, our knowledge "remains a blind postulate" and our feeling "can be only dissatisfaction" (EW 2: 363). As long as our meanings are separated from the world, they cannot be enough for us; life itself will then be devoid of meaning. To be able to affirm life, and to reach some measure of satisfaction within it, we must be able to realize ourselves; we must be able to find meanings conducive to ourselves in the actual world, not simply in our own minds.

And in fact, for Dewey, this is exactly what we do in our normal and healthy interactions with things. The entire, normal process of meaning-making that he has advanced consists of the self inserting its meanings into facts, and the facts then reflecting back the meanings of the self; meaning-making is about "the putting of self into fact" (EW 2: 270). The result is that facts then contain the self's attributes; the facts give back to us ourselves, for we have put ourselves into the facts from the beginning. And the normal self keeps on doing this, endlessly. It renders some facts meaningful, and the facts then come back to the self in a seemingly external, independent form as meaningful. The self grows as a result (since it has now expanded to include the world outside of itself as part of what it is); the expanded self (which may have grown into new and better formations) is able then to render facts meaningful in new and better ways, which in turn lead the facts to come back to the self as meaningful in new and better ways, and so on continuously. The normal run of things is the progressive realization of idealized meanings, a process that goes on and on with ever-increased meaningfulness, both for the self and for the facts (EW 2:363).

This position, if true, would mean that the modernist position is refuted, for then *there would be no given fact without human meaning attached to it.* Every fact would already be idealized (rendered meaningful) in some recognizable way; hence, there would be no separation between the self with its meanings on one side and the meaningless facts on the other. The facts would already contain meanings, and the self would already find itself in the facts. And so there would be no call for withdrawing from the facts in order to seek out and cultivate the meanings of the self. The meanings of the self would already be there, out in the world. The modernist self, therefore, would be overcome.

That this would actually be the case, we can see by considering once more the nature of feelings. In a key passage of the *Psychology* worth quoting again, Dewey reminds us that when we feel something about an object, the relationship we bear to it

> is not an external one of the feeling *with* the object, but an internal and intimate one; it is feeling *of* the object. The feeling loses itself in the object. Thus we say that food *is* agreeable, that light is pleasant; or on a higher plane, that the landscape *is* beautiful, or that the act is right. Certain feelings of value or worth we attribute spontaneously to the object. (EW 2: 239)

We naturally attribute our feelings to objects as an essential part of what they are. It would be very strange to say, for example—as a modernist might—that the "pleasant" light is not pleasant, we only experience it as such. For we do not experience objects first and then attribute our feeling states to them secondarily. On the contrary: we first and fundamentally experience objects imbued with the qualities of our feelings. Dewey explains the nature of feelings further when he writes:

> It is the same fact seen on the side of emotion, that we have already seen on the side of knowledge. An object becomes intellectually significant to us when the self reads its past experience into it. But as this past experience is not colorlessly intellectual, but is dyed through and through with interests, with feelings of worth, the emotional element is also read into the object, and made a constituent element of it. The object becomes saturated with the value for the self which the self puts into it . . . The world thus comes to be a collection of objects possessing emotional worth as well as intellectual. (EW 2: 239–40)

The object as it is given to us is constructed both by our past experiences and the emotional qualities of our experiences with it. Hence, we always understand the given object as ordered and arranged, as "intellectually significant," and, at the same time, we always feel the object's meaning as the meaning of the object, as part of what the object really is. "All natural, healthy feeling is absorbed in the object or in the action" (EW 2: 250).

It is, of course, possible to convince yourself that there is no meaning in objects and to feign a total detachment from them, seemingly absorbed wholly in your own mind. You could come to believe that you bear an external and detached connection to objects, as opposed to the intimate and internal connection that Dewey describes. But such a belief, for the early Dewey, would be unhealthy and contradictory. It would be unhealthy because it would exhibit an apparent inability—like that of Mersault in *The Stranger*, who is unable to find the situation with old Salamano and his dog deplorable—to emotionally and morally connect with the world around yourself.[14] Indeed, such detachment would always be slightly deranged and abnormal, for it would be a state of mind in which you might say, for example, that oranges do not "really" taste a certain way when you taste them that way; or that the music that moves you is not really moving; or that torture is not really abhorrent, that is only your subjective view of it; or in which you could come to believe that "it didn't mean anything"—did not mean anything out there in the world, in reality—when your mother died, as is the case with Mersault.[15] "Feeling is unhealthy," Dewey says, ". . . when set free from its absorption in the object or in the end of action, and given a separate existence in consciousness" (EW 2: 250). What you normally and naturally feel is that the orange itself *really tastes* as it tastes to you, or that the music itself *really has* the qualities you experience; or you feel that it *really is bad* to torture someone, or when your mother dies. What this shows, again, is that normally there never is a given object devoid of meaning (i.e., devoid of intellectual significance and feeling). The modernist may say that there is, but this assertion, in fact, is not only unhealthy but also contradictory. It is contradictory because it denies what he or she most directly and intimately experiences, namely, that given objects always possess some meaning (if they did not, the modernist would not even be able to place them and make sense of them, and so they would not be given to him or her in the first place). Some feeling and meaning there must always be, even when, like Mersault, you force yourself to deny it.

Although Mersault is apparently unfazed by his mother's death, and feels nothing, nonetheless he cares what his boss or the caretaker thinks of his responses to them; he still participates in some social meanings.[16] In cases like these, Mersault feels "embarrassed," for example, when he says something he should not have said.[17] He also clearly cares about his physical comfort throughout the novel. This, at least, has some meaning for him. At the end of the novel, moreover, to convince himself that he is right about "the gentle indifference of the world," he needs other people to be there and to hate him.[18] "For everything to be consummated," he says, "for me to feel less alone, I had only to wish that there be a large crowd of spectators the day of my execution and that they greet me with cries of hate."[19] Mersault needs people; he needs them to confirm a meaning outside of himself, namely, that the world really is indifferent to him; that it really can be filled with a hating, jeering crowd of people whose hatred only confirms what he already believes about the world. He needs people outside of himself, and he needs to not feel alone, even if it is to confirm that he is alone and that there is no meaning outside of him. Therein lies the contradiction. The world is always meaningful even if we deny meaning. That denial still *means* something to Mersault. He has cherished it all these years and he seeks its external confirmation now. There is always still meaning.

But modernism is the position that maintains that objects are inherently devoid of meaning, and that only the isolated self, utterly detached from objects, possesses what meaning there is, all alone to itself. Seen from a Deweyan perspective, however, such a view is clearly false, for there never is an object given to us that is entirely devoid of meaning. In Dewey's view, modernism is at best an aberration of the intellect, something of which it is possible to convince oneself (as the result of too much withdrawal and self-absorption and a culture that supports these activities), but it is not a true account of things, or even an account that the modernist himself can maintain about his or her own experience. For Dewey, modernism clearly fails, and we must move past it.

But if we accept Dewey's account, for which given objects always have some kind of meaning or other, then we have to accept Dewey's overall conception of knowledge, feeling, and will, such as I have articulated them in previous chapters, for his account of objects and their meaning is deeply bound up with his overall conception of these matters. But *can* we accept Dewey's conception? Is it correct? Two features of his overall conception seem problematic in particular. Is there really a progression toward more and more idealized meanings, as he says? And even if there is, the root fact of this progression—the first term, as it were—would seem to be forever un-idealized. In the beginning there is not an idealization, but some fact that we idealize afterwards and shape according to our meanings. The first fact would seem to be free from all idealizations, as that which is given to us in order to be idealized; and perhaps it is this fact, above all, that the modernist means when he says that the facts exist un-idealized on one side, and we exist with our idealizations on the other.

In response to the first objection, it can be said that there does seem to be a progression of meanings of some sort. Insofar as there is growth from nature to culture, there would also be a progression from less idealized to more idealized. Recall that "idealized meanings" simply means connections among objects that are established by us; something is meaningful when it exist in a relationship to other things, and signifies something in relation to them; and idealization is simply the process by which relationships between things are established by us, by our negation of their mere givenness and our taking them up into novel connections based on our past experiences. Insofar as this occurs in the shift from nature to culture, I would say that there is at least one step, and probably many more, in a progression of meanings.

Moreover, the progression of meanings that Dewey recounts (say, from egoistic feelings to feelings of sympathy for all of humankind) does not seem to be inherently problematic. The account he gives does not seem to be contradictory, and strikes the reader of his philosophy as coherent. Given that Dewey endorses a coherence theory of truth, we can at least say that his philosophy meets its own criterion for being true. In addition to this, however, we must keep in mind that Dewey's account includes the idea that the self is growing all along. It makes a certain amount of sense to say that if the self grows, then it can add new and possibly better meanings to what it encounters, and can reshape the world in progressive ways. But there does seem to be a problem here, for how can the self grow in response to the world, if it is only ever finding in the world what it has puts there in the first place? The answer to this question lies in the idea, mentioned previously, that the self does not always recognize that it is putting its own meanings into the world. This occurs for the most part unconsciously and habitually, as in the case of the intelligent arrangement of facts. We just go out to facts and try to give them a familiar shape (as in Dewey's camel in the cloud example that I mentioned earlier [LW 8:117]), but we are not fully aware that we are doing this. As a result, when we look on the world, we can be startled; we can find unexpected meanings there, even though they are our own. For we have only unconsciously put them there; and in many cases the "we" is the human race, all of humankind, not simply the individual. The human race has created a world of culture, which individually we can discover. We can discover a world, therefore; and we can respond to it in various ways. These ways can build on one another, and we can grow as a result of our experiences, even though ultimately it is the human self that shaped the world a certain way in the first place.

We can say, then, that since "the self" (or the collective self of the human race) that puts meanings into facts is a growing self, it stands the chance of adding new and better meanings to the facts as it grows and learns more about the world. A progression of meanings is therefore possible. But does this actually occur in the way Dewey insists? My own sense is, again, that the pattern Dewey develops (say, in the universal progression of feelings) is coherent and plausible, especially when we consider that Dewey in no way argues for a guarantee that one's experience will not flounder in its development and become "abnormal." If there is teleology here, or at least directionality, it is because Dewey is conceiving of the self as plastic and capable of development, and so any one single moment of the self's meaningful states cannot possibly exhaust the self; the self can always move on.

Hence, I would not reject out of hand, as simply naïve, Dewey's ideas about the progress of meanings becoming more and more universal, for if the self has the capacity for development (which it almost certainly does), then I do not see why, under the right conditions, it could not develop in the ways that Dewey claims.

In response to the second objection, namely, that the root fact of all our idealized meanings cannot itself be idealized, there are at least two things one can say. First, I am not sure that there must be a primary, un-idealized fact. If we sift past all of our meanings that we have added on to facts, what do we find? Dewey believes that sensations are already a product of the self, writing that "the mind has the power of acting upon itself and of producing from within itself a new, original, and unique activity which we know as sensation" (EW 2: 43). But presumably there must be some material out of which the self creates its own unique versions of this material, that is, its sensations. To reach this original material underlying sensations, we cannot use exactly correct words, of course, because this effort is anything but precise (we are trying to talk about something prior to our categories of description). But Dewey notes that although we cannot describe this original material precisely, "by analogy, we can form some probable conception of its character" (EW 2: 45).

> Imagine, for example, our organic or general sensation as it is now; the sensation of comfort or discomfort of the whole body, a feeling having no definite spatial outline nor any distinct quality that marks it off. Or, let us imagine our various sense organs losing all their powers of giving distinct sense qualities, and being retracted into a sort of substratum of sensory stuff. Perhaps the nearest we get to such an experience is when we are falling asleep: our auditory sensations fall away; then we lose our sensations of color and of form; finally, our very feelings of contact, pressure, and temperature fade away into a dim, vague sense of nothing in particular. (EW 2: 45)

If there is a first fact, it should be found here, in our direct contact with existence itself, seemingly prior to all idealization. It must be found in something like the act of falling asleep, where all of our idealizations seem to slowly fade away. But Dewey notes that even here, with these kinds of feelings (those of falling asleep, or what an infant must feel, for example), "the sense organs are still present with their brain connections and with the inherited capacities and tendencies of generations," so that *something* is still felt *by* the organism, rather than the organism being able to directly encounter a purely given fact (EW 2: 46). It may only be the sensation of "a shapeless, vague, diffused state," like might be felt by "an oyster or a jelly-fish," but the original, vague sensation is experienced as something for the organism in any case, and to that extent "idealized," that is, not pure independent fact (EW 2: 46). Indeed, in such cases it becomes impossible to say where the organism ends and the world begins. There is a fusion of "contact sensations with muscular sensations" in a person's experience, as it must already be for the infant (EW 2: 47; 45–46). "Normally [contact sensations and muscular sensations] are inextricably united. It is only in disease that we ever have one without the other. Thus the activities of our own body and those of external bodies are indissolubly associated from the first" (EW 2: 47).

It is extremely difficult, then, to locate the first pure fact, if there is such a thing. As Dewey observes in one of his early articles, what is difficult is to show "that there was somehow, somewhere present to consciousness, a conception of what reality is by which we could measure the significance of our experience. . . . [I]f reality is itself an element in conscious experience, it must as such come under the scope of the significance, the meaning of experience, and hence cannot be used as an external standard to measure this meaning" (EW 1: 192). But perhaps the objection we have posited means to say, not that there must be a first fact that we can somehow experience, but that facts themselves as such must be first, and prior, and wholly independent in their nature, existing as what they are regardless of our experiences and idealizations. The question would then be: how can we say that we really do idealize the facts, as Dewey insists? Our idealizations would rather seem to be so many rickety buildings heaped up on an unsteady foundation. We build up our ideals of facts, let it be granted; but the facts themselves are independent of these ideals,

and so at the substratum or basis of all our ideals, there are recalci-
trant facts, and our efforts to idealize the facts could always therefore
end in failure.

This objection seems more difficult, and I am not sure that a Deweyan response will satisfy. But the response to make, I think, is this:
yes, the Deweyan idealist might say, it is correct that we cannot ever
know that the root of all facts lends itself to idealizations, meanings
conducive to the self somehow, but nonetheless we can have faith that
it is so. This is a point we discussed in the previous chapter, a point
about the nature of faith. The weakness of Dewey's possible answer
here is that faith is not knowledge, and so ultimately he is asking us
to believe something that we cannot know to be the case. The
strength of the Deweyan answer, however, is also worth considering.
It involves a threefold response, which is meant to convey that this is
a *rational* faith that Dewey points to, not an arbitrary and irrational
one. Dewey would like us to believe that there are good grounds for
saying that the root of all facts contains idealizations, even if this cannot be absolutely demonstrated to be true.

First, from a Deweyan perspective, one could argue that we are
entitled to believe that the root fact is idealized in some sense, in that
it clearly contains the possibility of being able to take on our various
idealized meanings. It offers a shape, or at least the potentiality of a
shape, amenable to our creative additions; for example, it can bear
the meanings of sympathy and social life, can be rendered intellectually significant, can be transformed into sensations, and so on. The
root fact allows these additions, and insofar as this is the case, we can
say that it is like a reservoir of potential creative meanings. Something
within things lends them the possibility of becoming meaningful; and
in this sense, they are already meaningful; they are proto-meanings,
as it were, or, even better, incipient meanings, which our later creative
additions justify as having all along been the case (EW 2:77).

Second, this faith that the root fact lends itself to idealizations is
not grounded in the total separation of fact from meaning (as maintained by Kierkegaard, for example), according to which human beings with their meaning are more or less consigned to a form of

madness—the madness of being forever isolated from the real world and its facts, of being lost totally in their own private, individual meanings. On the contrary, the faith that the early Dewey advocates is one in which there is an absolute connection between the given facts and human meanings. Its primary assumption and hope is that the world is meaningful; that our ideals are not totally foreign to the world. This view has a certain vigor. Its adherents might naturally claim for it a kind of normality—for, as we will see shortly, it allows us to shrug off pessimism and the madness of total, hopeless separation from the world and to engage in the world with more confidence. To have faith that the world really does have meanings, just as it seems to, is the faith of healthy-minded common sense, as opposed to the withdrawal and excessive introspection of the modernist.

Third, Deweyan faith has another power to offer, besides the hope of overcoming pessimism. To hold that the root fact will always suffer our idealizations is to say that it can always be transformed and improved, so that we are not ultimately dependent on this root fact. Said another way, since Deweyan faith locates the meaning of facts outside the facts themselves, in the ideals that transform the facts into their meanings, this conception of faith frees us from dependence on facts. It gives us an endless power to critique the facts and to strive to make of them something more than what they are. Surprisingly, this conception of faith has a good deal in common with more recent thinkers, such as Jean-Luc Nancy and Jacques Derrida, as we will see in the next chapter.

The upshot of these considerations, and of Dewey's early philosophy as a whole, is that we always belong to a meaningful universe, with the promise of always belonging even more. We are surrounded by significant objects and events, with emotionalized objects that we can relate to and understand and in relation to which, to some extent, we can exert our will. This is the kind of world in which we live; it is a meaningful world, and we are entitled to have faith that it really is as we find it, for reality lends itself to these meanings, and we are free to keep creating meaning, rendering the world more and more ideal through our efforts.

With these fundamental points in mind, let us now turn to the main concern of Dewey's early philosophy, overcoming pessimism. With everything that has been said so far about the kind of faith in life Dewey advocates and the way this faith enables the world to become idealized and filled with meaning, we should be in a good position to see how Dewey's philosophy responds to pessimism, and to the entire culture of modernism tied up with this pessimism. As we will see, the early Dewey ultimately seeks a new and better culture beyond modernist culture, a unique social arrangement that allows us to fully embrace life rather than encouraging us to withdraw from it.

After Pessimism

Two beliefs define modernism: 1) that the facts are devoid of human meaning and, in effect, hopeless; and 2) that we should withdraw into ourselves in order to find meaning and consolation. We have seen that the first belief is difficult to maintain, because the facts are filled with human meaning after all. It follows that there is little reason to maintain the second belief. If the facts of life are filled with human meaning, we can go out into the world and embrace life with confidence, comfortable in our understanding that the world is meaningful, that our human meanings are sustained by the world, out there in objective fact.

But how far are we able to take this position? To what extent are we willing to say that the world is filled with human meaning? Let us take the difficult case, the worst-case scenario, and consider whether the fact of death can in some way be rendered meaningful and, more importantly, a cause for hope—an occasion for finding existence to be good and worthwhile rather than an occasion for pessimism and despair. Can even this fact, the fact of death, somehow be rendered "ideal" and conducive to our human needs?

We must admit that the modernist has nothing much to offer along these lines. The modernist accepts the fact of the matter just as it is, without any idealization: that in death we are annihilated. For

the modernist, there is nothing human or comforting or even meaningful about death, if by "meaningful" we intend anything ideal.
Death is a cold, hard, merciless reality. In this sense, the modernist
has no adequate response to death. He acknowledges death; sees occasion for despair in the heart of the facts, and tell us that the most
we can do is to withdraw, to recoil, and to intensify our inner life.
The modernist cannot surmount death; the most he or she can offer
is inward flight, inner creativity. But the fact of death, conceived in
the worst case as annihilation, will of course always persist; it will
haunt us and remain always a problem. Isolation and inner creativity
may inflate our sense of individual importance and give us a feeling
of power, making us seem higher in significance than mere nature,
but these results of modernism are not a solution. The objective fact
of death remains in all of its horror. The individual self, great as it is,
will still be annihilated.

Next consider a potential Deweyan response to death. Dewey mentions "the grave" in the *Psychology* in connection with his claim that
facts by themselves are without meaning. A world of bare facts, he says,
"would be . . . a world in which the home would be four walls and a
roof to keep out cold and wet; the table a mess for animals, and the
grave a hole in the ground" (EW 2: 77). He laments: "What a meager
life were left us, were the ideal elements removed!" (EW 2: 77). And,
we might add, what a sad and tragic death—our personalities would
be forever obliterated, and our final resting place would only be "a hole
in the ground" and nothing more. The fact of death, in a Deweyan
view, should rather be idealized to help give life meaning. We need to
create ideals about death and other realities of human life so that we
may "make life rich, worthy, and dignified" (EW 2: 77).

The key to seeing how idealization is possible in the case of death
is to recall what we have seen earlier. Dewey believes that we are able
to identify ourselves with something more than ourselves, with an
idealized whole—if not with the cosmos in its entirety, or the human
race in its entirety, then at least with the social body to which we
belong and of which we are a contributing member. In Dewey's view,
the self grows to become more than the isolated, narrow, individual

self that it begins life as, and it comes more and more to identify itself with a larger, idealized whole beyond itself, even as the self acquires a sense of its own individuality in this very process. Said another way, the self recognizes that it is only in terms of a larger whole that it is enabled to become its own truly distinct self. A person realizes that he can identify with the larger whole even as he retains his own sense of self, as when, for example, the social whole is such as offers a distinct place for the individual within it, one that permits him to exercise and develop his own individual responses within a pattern of social meanings.

What the early Dewey would say about the fact of death is that it should not hinder our ability to cope with life, because even in the thought of our own death we can identify with the whole that has allowed us to play our own distinct part within it. The crucial insight here is that we are part of something larger. This is an intuition we can have, Dewey would say; mystics and poets and philosophers have had a similar intuition for ages. It is quite a significant idea, although for one who does not experience this insight, or who perhaps does not recognize it for what it is, the idea is easy to ridicule. In any case, a sense of the oneness of the cosmos (or perhaps merely of the human race, or of one's society), coupled with the realization that one forms a distinct part of this oneness, is what Dewey's early position involves. In the face of death, therefore, in this view, one can let oneself go without feeling that one is losing oneself; one can see oneself as part of something larger, woven into its very fabric, as it were. Thus, as we saw in the case of religious feeling in chapter 6, we come to believe that the continuation of this vast thing is also the continuation of oneself, the continuation of something with which one identifies, or the continuation of something in which one has played one's part. The feeling of peace then descends upon one, a feeling that occurs "so far as one gives up wholly his own particular self . . . and takes the life of the completely harmonious Personality for his own" (EW 2: 291). One is no longer the particular thing, but the larger thing, identifying with the larger thing's interests and not one's own—the larger thing, be it noted again, in terms of which alone any distinct sense of self is possible. One therefore feels peace, for one feels at one with the ongoing, whole event of the universe, even when this means one's own particular demise, and one is grateful that such an event has allowed one to become oneself in relation to its larger meaning.

This element "of identity and of difference" (EW 2: 126), of finding one's distinct self in relation to a larger whole, is not an arbitrary addition to Dewey's thoughts but is rather built into his very conception of knowledge, as we have already seen. According to the early Dewey's theory of knowledge,

> The relations which connect mental contents are those of identity and of difference. . . . The process of adjustment consists in bringing the past experiences to bear upon the present so as to unify it with those ideal elements which resemble it, and separate it from those which are unlike. These two processes necessarily accompany each other, so that, while the goal of knowledge is complete unity, or a perfectly harmonious relation of all facts and events to each other, this unity shall be one which shall contain the greatest possible amount of specification, or distinction within itself. (EW 2: 126; 130)

With the feeling of peace, Dewey has only extended into an ultimate ideal the idealization processes that are at work in all knowledge—the simultaneous achieving of unity and differentiation. The ideal of a larger whole is, like so many other things we have discussed in Dewey's philosophy, a human construction and meaning that is imaginatively added to the facts of the universe; and yet this construction takes on value and significance and vital force precisely to the extent that we have faith in its genuine existence as a reality at the root of our own being, or at least to the extent that we have faith in our ongoing ability to create more and more idealized meanings like the ideal of a larger whole, for example, a society that is more and more conducive to our needs and that will recognize us as essential elements within it.

In any event, the feeling of peace results because we recognize, when we have faith in the existence of a larger, idealized, meaningful whole of which we are a part, or which we could at least help to create and sustain, that even in our individual deaths the larger, meaningful whole continues. And since I am identified with its meaning, I identify with its continuing. Since what *it* is includes my distinct part within it, insofar as it continues, so too do I, conceived as a distinct individual whose life and meanings are made possible solely within its larger life and meanings.

This feeling of peace, it should be noted, is consistent with the one mystical experience that Dewey himself is reported to have had. As we have already seen, as Westbrook points out, Dewey once had "an experience of quiet reconciliation with the world . . . [a] blissful moment of 'oneness with the universe,'" which seems to have profoundly affected him for his entire life.[20] Something like the feeling of peace may at some point have descended on the young Dewey, and one could even surmise that this powerful feeling may have shaped Dewey's response to life from then on, allowing him, in fact, to embrace life, that is, to live with security, and hence to be so productive as a man and thinker. Certainly one who felt defeated by life could not have been as productive as was Dewey. Of course, this idea is merely speculative as applied to Dewey's own case, and yet there is logic to the general idea. And in fact the solution to the problem of death is meant to be logical, not only mystical. It is a rational working out of the mystical insight, and stands or falls with the rational explanation, not the mysticism. The idea is that identifying with a larger, meaningful whole enables one to embrace life, for even in death, with the loss of one's self, one is still in a way alive, and one's preferred meanings are still at work in the world (see MW 14:226). Under these conditions one can accept life; one can feel secure in life, no matter what happens. One can therefore live. Rather than seeing life as devoid of warmth and meaning and turning away from it, one can turn toward life as full of immense significance—the significance of a cosmic whole beyond oneself that nonetheless simultaneously includes oneself.

It should be stressed that Deweyan peace is compatible with endless process and rupture. To arrive at the feeling of peace is to feel oneself part of an endless process. A person feels that he is in the "flow" of events, contributing his small part to it. But being in the flow means being carried by it as well as contributing something to it; and what carries us is always changing too. The peace in question is not the certainty of belonging to an "accomplished result." The world will become many things after I am gone; it will keep changing (and what I amount to within the world will keep changing too). The peace comes, however, in the realization that, as the flow goes, so do I. I die knowing that I am part of something that carries me with it wherever it goes. I realize that I never was anything apart from this larger process, that I belong to it, and that I have been able to contribute my small effect, while alive, to what the process will become. This realization is what brings peace: that I am forever part of the ongoing flow, tension, and development of existence (EW 4:366–68; EW 2:358).

Moreover, in my one life, while I still live, there will always be toil, even when I have this peace. Toil and continued struggle are part of the flow itself; and so the peace I attain in my realization that I belong to the flow is not the absence of struggle, disjunction, and rupture, even in my own life. What happens, rather, is that I am able to affirm life and death—affirm the flow—by virtue of the realization that I am part of the continued struggle wherever it goes. With a calm and peaceful mind, I affirm the endless process of rupture. I am emboldened for the tireless struggle of life and I go out to meet the world courageously and well prepared for the battle (EW 4:366–68).

But does Dewey's solution to the problem of death really solve the problem? Could a modernist ever be won over to it? Let us utilize the philosophy of Friedrich Nietzsche to answer these questions. Nietzsche was the enemy of all idealisms, and in this he represents a good deal of philosophy in our day, which since Hegel has in various ways moved beyond idealism. Nietzsche was a fellow nineteenth-century thinker, of the same epoch as Dewey, and perhaps struggling with similar issues. It will help to see the contribution of Dewey's early position on these matters if we begin with the hard case, with a stringent critique of his general position and a consideration of an alternative.

However, before we turn to a Nietzschean response to Dewey's early idealism, it is important to point out that Nietzsche himself, at

least as I read him, waffles on the question of whether he is a modernist. On the one hand, he sides with modernism in accepting the fact
of death, and bidding us to creatively turn inward as the only proper
response to death. On the other hand, at times he tells us that we should
not only accept death but love it. He says that we should embrace everything without alteration. These are two very different responses to life
and to the problem of death. Let us see how this combination of views
might challenge Dewey's idealism. That way we can see how the early
Dewey might respond to the modernist, and also how he might respond
to another pessimistic but competing account of life.

Let us begin with the Nietzsche who says that we should embrace
life as it is. How would this Nietzsche respond to Dewey? No doubt
he would try to run roughshod over Dewey's philosophy, critiquing
it mercilessly, even mocking it, and commenting, perhaps, that idealisms such as Dewey's are always transparent and laughable for one
who knows how to expose their true motives. Nietzsche expresses his
opinion of all forms of idealism in a way that shows that the critique
of idealism is something like the crux of his own philosophy: "*Over-
throwing idols* (my word for 'ideals')—that comes closer to being part
of my craft. One has deprived reality of its value, its meaning, its
truthfulness, to precisely the extent to which one has mendaciously
invented an ideal world."[21] For Nietzsche, idealism is a rejection of
reality; it denies the facts, which it fears and despises, and instead of
embracing the facts creates fantasies, "ideal truths," which it clings to
in spite of the way the world really is.

To be more specific, the facts, for Nietzsche, are heartless and un-
pitying, or at best utterly indifferent to human concerns. As Nietzsche
puts it in an early essay, "And woe to that fatal curiosity which might
one day have the power to peer out and down through a crack in the
chamber of consciousness and then suspect that man is sustained . . .
by that which is pitiless, greedy, insatiable, and murderous—as if
hanging in dreams on the back of a tiger."[22] This position, moreover,
stays with Nietzsche, who in one of his last works insists not only that
life is terrible but also that we need "affirmation of life even in its
strangest and sternest problems . . . beyond pity and terror, *to realize*

in oneself the eternal joy of becoming—that joy which also encompasses *joy in destruction.*"²³ For Nietzsche, the facts about our existence are thoroughly un-idealized, and what he councils in relation to them, and to life, is that *we should affirm the facts in all of their uncertain and horrible nature.* "A pessimism of *strength*"²⁴ would enable us to do so. One who possessed this type of pessimism would be able to love life even in its "sternest problems,"²⁵ for such *"ascending life,"*²⁶ as Nietzsche calls it, "wants deep, wants deep eternity,"²⁷ wants everything just as it is no matter how it is. Such a person will not "slander" life,²⁸ but instead will accept it and affirm it, even when life goes against his deepest human desires and needs. This is perhaps why Nietzsche's hero is the *"overman,"*²⁹ the one who is willing to reject deep human needs (like the need to idealize things) and to embrace what is beyond the human.³⁰

From the perspective of one who wants no comfort, from the perspective of the pessimism of strength, Dewey's view must appear ridiculous indeed, an attempt to slander life, made by a coward. A Nietzschean might charge that at work in Dewey's position is a very deep dread of materialism: consider the earliest expression we have of Dewey's thought—his first published essay is an attack on materialism, an attempt to reject materialism at all costs (EW1: 3–8). Consider, too, the ideas at work in the *Psychology,* indeed their very basis, which is the refusal to countenance even a modicum of matter in the formation of ideals. As we saw early in this study, Dewey postulates that at the origin of our meanings lies not matter alone, but rather motions. In Dewey's words, "it is not the mere thing, but the thing with the characteristic of motion, that is the extra-organic stimulus of sensation" (EW 2: 30). Dewey will not allow "the mere thing" to be at the root of our sensations and instead holds to the belief in an original movement. Moreover, as we saw, he firmly rejects a materialist understanding of how this original motion would give rise to sensations: "there is no identity," he says, "between the sensation as a state of consciousness and the mechanical motion which precedes it," and hence the mechanical motion cannot ever account for the sensation (EW 2: 40). And so on and so forth. What is clear is that Dewey will not countenance materialism. Indeed, we have a philosophy here that explicitly amounts to the claim that there are no given facts devoid of the self's meanings. But what is this, a Nietzschean might say, but proof of Dewey's underlying dread of matter, of his subsequent retreat into ideals, and of his willingness to lie about reality—the willingness to lie that Nietzsche says is at work in all idealisms of whatever stripe?[31]

There might also be the further Nietzschean charge that Dewey's philosophy is, accordingly, "human, all too human."[32] Not only does Dewey add human meanings to facts, but insofar as he does so, he reveals thoroughly human motivations for doing so—weakness, fear, perhaps even resentment against the facts and those who can tolerate and embrace the facts. Again, what Nietzsche advises instead is that those who are capable of it should turn to and embrace the facts, even in all of their pitiless nature. We should love life no matter what, even in its brute indifference to human concerns.[33]

These would be formidable charges, coming from a formidable philosopher. One can make the case, however, that Dewey manages to evade such Nietzschean charges and offers the better response to pessimism in the end. For one thing, we must not think that Nietzsche had a monopoly on responding to pessimism. His response is a powerful one, with the seeming capacity to energize and prepare us for the battle of life; it seems at first to have what William James calls that inborn "pugnacity" that makes "life on a purely naturalistic basis seem worth living," giving us the fighting strength to go on.[34] But if we look at the matter more closely, we can see that there is a fundamental element of resignation in Nietzsche's position as well. What he ultimately asks of us is that we should *identify* ourselves with alien forces. We should give up our own human meanings and identify with the raw, merciless facts that supposedly lie at the very basis of the world and are totally indifferent to us.

Is such a thing even possible? Let us continue with our example of death and work through the possibilities. Nietzsche would say that nature is indifferent to us, that death is more than likely annihilation; and that *we should align ourselves with this*—that is, with nothing, since, after all, we are supposed to affirm all things just as they happen for all eternity. The result of Nietzsche's pessimism of strength would thus amount to a negation of what one is, and not, as Nietzsche has claimed, "how one becomes what one is."[35] In this case, we can see how Nietzsche's vaunted call for us to become what we are really amounts to a negation of what we are. But *can* we really identify ourselves with what we are not? That is, with total and absolute lack of anything? This is not a matter of growing into another self, with which we could then identify. On the contrary, the situation is one in which we would not grow into anything at all; every aspect of us would be obliterated. How can one possibly identify oneself with such a total absence? And yet this is what Nietzsche's philosophy calls upon us to do. For it calls on us not only to love the world as it is— cold and indifferent—but also to will this *same* indifferent world endlessly, for eternity. Such is the meaning of Nietzsche's concept of "*amor fati.*"[36] A Deweyan idealist might say that Nietzsche's philosophy is therefore a form of madness, for it demands that we should identify ourselves with what is not, and never can be, ourselves. It is similar to a philosophy that would ask us to consider ourselves to be Napoleon—to see ourselves, point for point, as what we are not and can never really be. In this, it seems, the Nietzschean pessimism of strength is simply out of touch. It is in fact nihilism, choosing nothingness over something, even though, at times, Nietzsche claims he is himself overcoming nihilism. But it is also definitely madness: it is a philosophy that asks the self, as a self—that is, as a something—to affirm the absolute denial of itself, without any hope of reconstituting the self in any shape or form whatsoever. More particularly, one could argue that this is a philosophy of extreme masochism. For it asks us to accept, even to love, our own annihilation, to desire it for eternity, again and again. We are to actively *want* what harms and obliterates us, and to want it repeatedly. It is a philosophy that asks one to identify with, and to love, absolute nothing, to identify with what one never could be, with that with which, in principle, one never could identify; to ask one to do so is, therefore, if not lunacy, at least the product of disturbed thinking.

Madness or peace—these are our options, if we had to choose between Nietzschean pessimism and the idealism of the early Dewey. And it seems fair to say that if we did have to so choose, peace would be the more rational option. We could not rationally choose madness.

So if we want to mount a Nietzschean critique of Dewey, Nietzsche's pessimism of strength may not be the way to go. Instead, the perspective of the more decidedly modernist Nietzsche might offer a greater challenge to Dewey's idealism. Let us turn, therefore, to the response to Dewey that would likely be made by the Nietzsche who says that our best shot in life is to invent ourselves, rather than to embrace all things.

The modernist Nietzsche's main position seems to be that, above all, we must run away from "the herd." Since life is horrible, and the crowd of others around us is mediocre, never striving for greatness, the only thing that can make life worthwhile for us is to seek solitude and work on becoming great for ourselves. But here the problem with modernism that we saw in the previous section of this chapter comes into play. Nietzsche may convince himself that in his isolation he can create himself, but such a view is contradictory. For Nietzsche still needs others in relation to whom he can invent himself. He needs the great dead philosophers to critique, and he needs his future readers, his "philosophers of the future," to confirm his greatness.[37]

An advantage of the early Dewey's view over Nietzsche's in this respect is that it openly admits and affirms our connection to others as the source and meaning of our own individuality. It avoids the contradictory stance of Nietzsche and of modernists in general on this score; and it identifies the specific context in which we can hope to seek out our own individuality, namely, in relation to a certain kind of social order that might allow for it. A further advantage is that in advocating contact with and embrace of what is external—namely, a meaningful social world outside of oneself—Dewey's view allows us manifold possibilities in what we are opened up to and the kind of selves we can become. Contrast this position of openness with the position of the world-weary cynic, contracting in upon himself and chagrined at the world, and we get a sense of the

Deweyan advantage. Indeed, in the case of Nietzsche, we can sense this advantage distinctly; for Nietzsche's position never allows that there could be genuine, meaningful relationships between the self and society. To be sure, when Nietzsche says that we should withdraw from the herd, as Lawrence Hatab makes clear, he also stresses that we can still seek others with whom to be friends, as long as they are our equals, those with whom we can bring ourselves to joust in "an agonistic interaction."[38] But what is this but an admission that Nietzsche's position misses entirely the countless different kinds of joys that are possible through our interactions with others?[39] Like a true modernist, Nietzsche constricts the self to a miniscule point within itself and its opposition to others, whereas Dewey's self relates itself to others (in sympathy, for example, as well as in antipathy), enlarges itself thereby, and grows endlessly in meaning. Nietzsche, one of the "Hyperboreans"[40]—the man who writes from icy heights above humanity—isolates the self to the point of excessive restriction. Deweyan idealism, on the other hand, although it does involve an element of faith, a faith that one's ideals may ultimately be at work in facts, produces meanings—a world of others in meaningful relation to oneself that yields richer and more significant values in one's life than can be achieved by one's own narrow self alone.[41]

But still it may be objected that Dewey's early view is simply too ideal, too implausible to be accepted by thinking people. For, after all, his view admits that meanings are ideal constructions, while at the same time it asks us to believe that these ideal constructions are somehow at work in the very structure of reality. Even when we know that ideal meanings are merely constructions of ours, we are nonetheless supposed to accept them, on faith, as holding for reality. Could there ever be a clearer instance of a position that fits Nietzsche damning remark that " 'faith' means not *wanting* to know what is true"?[42]

One thing this objection misses, however, is that on Dewey's view facts *become* ideal. They really do take on ideal meanings when we give these meanings to them—a sensation, for example, is originally an extra-organic fact (a motion) that literally becomes of a certain

quality through our activity, namely, the quality of the mental sensation we are experiencing. (In a work of art, likewise, some physical
objects, newly organized, literally become beautiful objects; in friendship our external relations really do take on a deeper significance
through our idealized additions of sympathy and fellow feeling; and
so on.) While this would not happen, of course, with religious faith
(that is, we would not expect the universe itself to suddenly form a
larger, meaningful whole solely through our idealizations), yet faith
in such a thing, as we have seen, is a way to allow our continued
idealization of facts to occur, and occur in reality—as what counts as
genuine reality through our efforts. For Dewey, idealized meanings,
let us remember, are *progressive* realizations. The lure of believing in
the ideal formation of a larger meaningful whole may be one way to
help create it in fact—that is, to idealize the facts in precisely this way.

And here, I think, we come to the heart of the matter with Dewey's
early philosophy. It encourages us to have a life-sustaining faith that
the universe is one ongoing interconnected event in which we play
our part. We come to believe that "there is no such thing as an isolated fact in the universe, but that all are connected with each other
as members of a common whole" (EW 2: 201). And while the reality
of such a thing is something we can only hope for, and struggle ourselves to create, nonetheless we have a partial realization of this hope
and faith in the very existence of our social life (EW 3: 371). This is a
point, in fact, that the later Dewey will emphasize, namely, when he
says at the conclusion of *Human Nature and Conduct* that

> within the flickering inconsequential acts of separate selves dwells
> a sense of the whole which claims and dignifies them. In its pres-
> ence we put off mortality and live in the universal. The life of the
> community in which we live and have our being is the fit symbol
> of this relationship. (MW 14: 227)

In this remarkable passage, which could easily have been written by
the early John Dewey, we have his essential idea. There is a larger
cosmic whole, and the society to which we belong is the symbol of it.
For at work in any society, and in our connection to it, is the fundamental idea that the self is not an isolated atom but extends outward

into the universe of other things, and can see itself as a part of these other things (EW 2: 259). This idea plays out socially because the self can only exist to the extent that it can identify with the members of its community. Each self must come out of itself and identify with its community to be itself, to get a definition of itself *as* itself (EW 2: 289). And so, on this view, we identify with the community; we see ourselves as one with it; and we wish for its continued success, for its success *is* our success. We sustain the community in our actions and in our memories. We remember its dead and we give them their due. And others in the community will remember me, and they will sustain their thoughts of me, for I am also one with their common life, and in this sense I shall live on after my death in the life of the community itself. I will take care of the community, and it will take care of me. I will remember each of the others, and they will each remember me.

We will each die, but we will be sustained by the common life that carries us on.[43] And this thought gives us courage. It helps us to live without fear of death; for our thoughts and our actions will not simply *disappear*. They will amount to something in the course of things. They will continue on.

Nietzsche's philosophy, on the other hand, insists that we identify, precisely, with nothing, and it sees our community as that which, above all, should be resisted as we flee into our own isolated, authentic selves. We do not wish the community well, and we do not see ourselves as forming any part of it. Death is annihilation, the total loss of everything, since, never connected to a community, we feel no sense in which we might live on in its presence. We lose everything when we die, and it is this absolute blackness and total loss that Nietzsche, in his madness, asks us to embrace as if it were our very selves.

That social life is of the essence of Dewey's early position can be seen from a fundamental feature of his *Psychology* discussed in the previous chapter. We saw that there is a crucial link for Dewey between social feeling, moral feeling, and religious feeling. Social feeling is rooted in the fact that we feel ourselves—feel who we are—in response to others. Sympathy, that complex emotion in which I feel in relation to another that I am both myself and, in some sense, the other as well—this feeling, Dewey insists, is at the basis of moral feeling also. Dewey explains that "Sympathy . . . is the reproduction of the experience of another, *accompanied by the recognition of the fact that it is his experience*" (EW 2: 285). In feeling sympathy, we possess

> [f]irst, ability to apprehend . . . the feelings of others, and to reproduce them in our minds; and, secondly, the ability to forget self, and remember that these feelings, although our own feelings, are, after all, the experience of some one else. Sympathy involves distinction as well as identification. I must not only assume into myself the experiences of a man who is suffering from poverty, in order to sympathize with him, but I must realize them as *his*; I must separate them from my own personal self, and objectify them in him. (EW 2: 285)

Or, as Dewey puts it even more succinctly, to feel sympathy, "we must not only take their life into ours, but we must put ours into them" (EW 2: 285). Once more, and as always with the early Dewey, the self expands; it becomes more than it was, and in this expansion the self not only creates new meanings in the world, but also find itself at work in the life and nature of others.

Sympathy, then, is a fundamental social feeling by which meanings are created in the world; and it is also at the basis of our morality, Dewey says. We do not feel moral obligations, at first, to strangers. We do originally feel moral obligations, however, towards those who are like us, those with whom we can sympathize. Thus, according to Dewey, "the moral feelings are based upon the social feelings, and are an outgrowth of them. We recognize moral relations to those whom we feel to be identical in nature with ourselves. The feeling of sympathy as the basis of this identification of natures is, therefore, the source of all moral feeling" (EW 2: 288). But moral feeling differs in that it can enlarge itself to cover all things, so that we can feel a moral obligation to all of humanity, for example, or even to all of nature, which exists beyond our narrow range of friends. Religious feeling, by contrast, is the assertion that this universal moral obligation we feel (rooted in sympathy) does apply to all the world: that the entire world is a single interconnected whole with which I can sympathize—meaning that I can both identify myself with it and, through this identification, learn the true meaning of my distinct self within the whole to which I belong.

We can see, therefore, that at its root Dewey's philosophy is about sympathy, in particular the sympathy we feel toward the community of which we are a part and toward its members. This element of social life is the basis, the fundament, in terms of which our later idealizations become possible—in terms of which morality and religion become possible. Community is therefore, quite fittingly, the symbol of our larger meanings. It is through our community life that we can distinguish and define ourselves, and it is through it, and through idealized extensions of its meanings, that we gain access to all that may be more universally significant and rich in human life.

It should come as no surprise, therefore, that in trying to overcome modern culture and its pessimism, Dewey should focus his energies on the problematic nature of social life that modernism engenders, and on rethinking what it would mean to have a healthier and more appropriate mode of living together. As we will see in what follows, Dewey's other major work of this period, *Outlines of a Critical Theory of Ethics*, is not really so much about ethics, as some commentators have supposed,[44] as it is a response to our cultural condition. Although Dewey never explicitly puts it this way in the book, *Outlines* is about how to conceive of both social life and of the nature of the self as we move beyond modernist culture.

Rethinking Self and Society

In my view, *Outlines of a Critical Theory of Ethics* should be situated conceptually in terms of Dewey's larger project; it is not just a work in ethical theory. On the contrary, the book's most essential feature is that it presents Dewey's alternative to the modernist conception of social life. In what remains of this chapter, I cannot hope to offer an extended analysis of this interesting text, but I do hope others might become interested in doing so. It is a rich philosophical work worthy of more sustained attention. What I can offer here is a basic sketch of what I regard as the book's central feature, that is, its powerful vision of what a culture beyond our current, pessimistic one could look like. The central idea is that by inventing a new, more idealized community and struggling to realize it, we can move closer to creating the kind of world in which each person will matter in the larger scheme of things. We would thereby help to create the conditions by which pessimism can be overcome and life can be worth living.

Modernist culture can only conceive of the self as opposed to society. As Dewey saw so well in his essay, "Poetry and Philosophy," the pessimism of his times amounted to "a twofold isolation of man—his isolation from nature, his isolation from fellow-man. No longer . . . may man believe in his oneness with the dear nature about him" and, although "man, repulsed from the intimacy of communion with Nature, may turn to man for fellowship . . . here, too, is found isolation" (EW 3: 115). Dewey quotes Matthew Arnold:

> Ah, from that silent, sacred land
> Of sun and arid stone,
> And crumbling wall and sultry sand,
> Comes now one word alone!
> From David's lips that word did roll,
> 'Tis true and living yet:
> No man can save his brother's soul,
> Nor pay his brother's debt.
> Alone, self-poised, henceforward man
> Must labor.
>
> (EW 3: 116)

On which Dewey comments: "the life of common brotherhood, struggle and destiny . . . has given way to the old isolated struggle of the individual" (EW 3: 116).

When one is isolated from other people in this way, never able to connect with them and to form a common bond, one is forced to withdraw into oneself and to find one's own law within. "Isolation is translated into self-dependence. Separation throws man farther into himself, deepens his consciousness of his own destiny and of his own

law" (EW 3: 117). It is the solitary man that modernism triumphs—
the singular individual who is his own law, who defines himself in
isolation, completely detached from his fellow human beings and his
relation to them. From everything we know about Dewey's early philosophy at this point, we can see clearly that he will resist such a
conception.

In Dewey's alternative vision of culture, the self is actually defined
in terms of its *connection* to others. More specifically, it is defined in
terms of an ideal "'moral community,'" which is "a unity of action,
made what it is by the co-operating activities of diverse individuals"
(EW 3: 326). In the moral community, each individual "forms the
unity" by "doing his specific part" in the society (EW 3: 326). There
is reciprocal interplay and mutual exchange between self and society,
not opposition. Each gives something fundamental to the other.

Society gives to the individual a function in life in terms of which
he or she may become an individual, that is, a distinct member of the
group (EW 3: 326; 339). It is hoped that the individual, in turn, will
give to the society by maintaining one of its specific social functions,
thereby giving it opportunity to forward some of its ends. Self and
society in this way grow together rather than existing in open conflict
with each other (see "reciprocal relation" in EW 2:281).

The moral community is an ideal, not a fact. But its possibility is
grounded in actual events. It seems clear, for example, that modernism is mistaken about the nature of individuality. As Dewey rightly
explains, "individuality means not separation, but defined position in
a whole" (EW 3: 326). This is the case because in point of fact "desires
are socialized" and do not exist as self-standing, independent forces
(EW 3: 387). The individual with his desires grasps the meaning of
himself (and his desires) only in relation to others, and, in particular,
in relation to the function he performs in the social body. There is a
social circumstance in which the individual, as a functioning self, always finds himself and in relation to which his desires are typically
formed. "There are environments existing prior to the activities of
any individual agent; the family, for example, is prior to the moral
activity of a child born into it" (EW 3: 313). What can happen is that

the individual adjusts to the activities of the prior group, which "means *making the environment a reality for one's self.* . . . The child takes for his own end, ends already existing for the wills of others. And, in making them his own, he creates and supports for himself an environment that already exists for others" (EW 3: 313–14). A reciprocal interplay begins to emerge between the self and society: the self adopts certain social norms as its own, a certain given function within the society, and the social norms are sustained and at times even creatively modified through the self's adoption of these norms and the performance of its social function.

The individual, in other words, does not simply adjust to the society; the society also, at times, adjusts to the individual. For it is the individual who is the carrier of the environment and its meanings, and the individual always has some idiosyncrasy or other that is present when he carries the meanings of the environment. "Adjustment," as Dewey puts it, "is not outer conformity; it is living realization of certain relations in and through the will of the agent" (EW 3: 314). Living activity is changing and messy, and sometimes creative, and so does not ever fully reproduce exactly what went before, although it does embody this and carry it on in some form.

Now in adopting the social norms of the group, making them his own, and even developing them in some ways, the individual seems, in effect, to be working for the good of the group, even when he thinks he is only satisfying his own desires. The individual performs a function, he plays a role, as defined by the society; but in doing so he sustains and develops the social environment that affects others as well.

> Since the performance of function is . . . the creation, perpetuation, and further development of an environment, of relations to the wills of others, its performance *is a common good.* It satisfies others who participate in the environment. The member of the family, of the state, etc., in exercising his function, contributes to the whole of which he is a member by realizing its spirit in himself. (EW 3: 314)

There is a secret bond that appears to exist between the individual and society. Looked at from the side of the individual, a person who performs his function is simply trying to fulfill his desires and realize himself: "in the performance of his own function the agent satisfies his own interests and gains power" (EW 3: 327). In giving a person a function to perform, in terms of which he can exercise his powers and realize himself, society grants the person the status of an individual. Looked at from the side of society, however, the individual is ideally sustaining and assisting the society of which he is a member by performing his special function within it.

This latter point is not, however, a certain result. It could be the case that in performing his specific function the individual has no impact whatsoever on others, or that perhaps he only looks out for himself. One might, as an individual, use others to one's own advantage, without contributing to them, indeed in such a way as to positively harm them. This is precisely where, once again, the concept of faith enters into Dewey's early thought. "The Ethical Postulate," as Dewey calls it, is "a faith that, in realizing his own capacity, he will satisfy the needs of society" (EW 3: 320). The individual is fully entitled to throw himself into his own work, and to gain his individual power and meaning thereby, with faith as the only guarantee that he is assisting society to realize itself through this process. Indeed, Dewey goes so far as to say that "the basis of moral strength is *limitation*, the resolve to be one's self only, and to be loyal to the actual powers and surroundings of that self" (EW 3: 321). With so much the modernist would agree. And the modernist would agree with this also: "All fruitful and sound human endeavor roots in the conviction that there is something absolutely worth while, something 'divine' in the demands imposed by one's actual situation and powers" (EW 3: 321). A person will never amount to anything if he does not trust himself as an individual.

And yet, this self-trust, while it energizes the individual and enables him to realize his possibilities and become a distinct individual, is not equivalent to withdrawn, isolated, and egoistic behavior. There is at work in the individual's behavior, when it is moral (and when his character is formed as such), a faith that by performing his specific function he is at the same time forwarding the growth of others and enabling them to realize themselves as well. The moral individual says to himself: "What is really good for me *must* turn out good for all, or else there is no good in the world at all" (EW 3: 320). The moral individual has faith, in other words, that "self and others make a true community," that the self's interests and activities are not wholly severed from its connections to others, and that it can, in fact, make a positive contribution to the well-being of others (EW 3: 320). This is, again, a faith that one has; nothing establishes it in fact. But it is a vital faith, an essential one, if there is to be any significant connection between the self and society. It is "what is vaguely called 'faith in humanity.' . . . But what is meant is just this: in the performing of such special service as each is capable of, there is to be found not only the satisfaction of self, but also the satisfaction of the entire moral order, the furthering of the community in which one lives" (EW 3: 321–22). It is a faith both in oneself and in others: a faith that each of us can attend to our own individual function and, in doing so, attend to one another.

Such faith is grounded in sympathy, for I must feel some connection to others in whom I have faith, but it builds on this sympathy and goes beyond it by affirming the other's potential to make a unique contribution to society simply by realizing his own powers (EW 3: 321). It is a faith that each counts; that each has something to contribute simply by being himself.

This faith in the moral community finds a parallel in the conclusions of science. Dewey says that "all science rests upon the conviction . . . that objects are not mere isolated and transitory appearances, but are connected together in a system by laws or relations" (EW 3: 323). It is the same with our moral faith. "Moral experience *makes for the world of practice* an assumption analogous in kind to that which intellectual experience makes for the world of knowledge" (EW 3: 323). We have faith that no individual is separate; that his activity is not withdrawn and detached, but out there in the world making an impact on others and contributing to what they become, contributing to a system of organized relations.

This means, in effect, that there is both unity and difference between the self and society—a reciprocal interplay, as I have called it, rather than an opposition. By performing a specific function, one is distinct from others; but one is also connected to them, or at least one has faith that one is so connected, because one's distinctness functions within society, making a helpful impact on it. "The exercise of function by an agent serves, then, both to define and to unite him. It makes him a *distinct* social member at the same time that it makes him a *member*" (EW 3: 326).

The contrast between Dewey's new vision of culture and that of modernism should be clear. Whereas modernism can see only separation between, say, individual freedom and social obligation, Dewey's vision makes sense of them both together. The modernist, with his isolated self, achieves his freedom only by resisting all social obligation. Or else he achieves social obligation only by sacrificing his own freedom and authentic self-expression. In Dewey's view, by contrast, the self has an obligation to the community of which it is a member, for the self is bound by the rules of the game, by the function it performs, a function that only gains its meaning and definition in relation to a social whole; and yet the self is free at the same time because by performing its function, the self realizes its own capacities and exercises its own individual power (EW 3: 327).

Indeed, in Dewey's view, far from a rift existing between freedom and obligation, both are able to constantly grow together in a "progressive development," in a constant expansive interplay (EW 3: 370). The more society supports the individual in allowing him to perform his specific function, the "richer and subtler individual activity" becomes; the situation results "in increased individualization, in wider and freer functions of life" (EW 3: 370). One becomes more and more of an individual, a unique person with distinct, individual, creative powers. On the other hand, the more the individual is supported by the society in this way, so as to become an individual, the more there is generated—according to the Ethical Postulate, at least—a greater individual desire for and contribution to the good of the whole. One chooses to support the community that enables one to really be oneself. There is "increase in number of those persons whose ideal is 'a common good,' or who have membership in the same moral community; and, further, it consists in more complex relations between them" (EW 3: 370). Adopting an idea partly from T. H. Green, Dewey even postulates a progression to the development of this belief in the moral community and how far it will extend. "The social consciousness" begins with one's limited group and then extends, ideally, to all of humanity: "There has been a period in which the community was nothing more than a man's own immediate family group, this enlarging to the clan, the city, the social class, the nation; until now, in theory, the community of interests and ends is humanity itself" (EW 3: 371). What is more, with social consciousness increasing in this way, there is also an increase in the kind and quality of moral ends one feels oneself inclined to adopt.

> When the conceived community is small, bravery may consist mainly in willingness to fight for the recognized community against other hostile groups. As these groups become themselves included in the moral community, courage must change its form, and become resoluteness and integrity of purpose in defending . . . humanity as such. . . . Let the community be truly spiritual, consisting in recognition of unity of destiny and function in co-operation toward an all-inclusive life, and the ideal of courage becomes more internal and spiritual, consisting in loyalty to the possibilities of humanity, whenever and wherever found. (EW 3: 371)

The ends of action become more and more spiritual, more and more ideal, to the extent that we conceive of them in terms of an ever-widening moral community. The ends of our action enlarge themselves to include more and more people, and the quality of our desire to assist these other members of our group accordingly grows in richness and meaning, until we might even be prepared to die, for example, for a fellow human being whom we do not even know, because we conceive of him or her after the ideal, as a member of the same human community, and hence as significant and important as any other human being.

Against modernism, then, which holds that the single human being always exists in opposition to his society, always needing to affirm his freedom in opposition to social obligations or else to lose it, Dewey shows us how it is possible to fundamentally rethink these relationships. Thanks to Dewey's vision, it is possible to think of a social arrangement in which the individual human being is enabled to be singular, and free, even as he becomes bound to his community and bears it some definite obligations. Dewey sums up his new vision with a passage not from the modernist poet Matthew Arnold, but from Shakespeare:

> To thine own self be true;
> And it must follow, as the night the day,
> Thou can'st not then be false to any man.
>   (EW 3: 322)

If one were to go against oneself, one would go against something deep and profound within oneself, against something like a principle of all humanity. Conversely, by being oneself, one also achieves something for humanity. Where society empowers the individual to be himself, the individual in turn is able to empower society; that is, he is able to create conditions that might empower other individuals in his moral community. Through belief in the Ethical Postulate, we have faith that where the individual is so empowered to act, he will also definitely empower others.

Incidentally, despite an apparent similarity, Dewey's vision is different than the Kantian principle that by giving myself the law, I also constrain myself to the obligation of respecting other rational beings as ends in themselves and never treating them as mere means.[45] True, it seems as if Kant has also found a way to unite freedom and obligation, since, on his view, I must *freely* give myself the law, which I am then *morally bound* to obey. But the difference is that, as Dewey sees it, Kant's view comes down too hard on the side of the law, that is, of the obligation one bears to the moral community. Kant downplays

desire, as that which cannot be a constitutive part of one's moral obligation. When we choose what to do, according to Kant we need to
choose the right thing even if it goes against our desires. The moral
law trumps desire. But for Dewey, contra Kant, desires *do* count in
what constitutes the moral community and our obligation to it. "The
law is not something wholly apart from the desires"; on the contrary,
the whole aim and effort of Dewey's vision is to get the individual to
eventually possess the desire to obey his or her obligation to others—to no longer see individual desires and obligations to others as
separate (EW 3: 293). With the right kind of community, the separation can be overcome; individual desire and social obligation can become one and work together in a mutual, ongoing progression of
meaning.

The modernist will object to Dewey's vision, perhaps, and insist,
not that individual desires should not count in moral life, but that
they are *all* that should count, or at least they should count far more
than Dewey will allow. The modernist may well think that as a result
of Dewey's vision, the individual would never really be able to exercise his freedom. For from the beginning of this account, it may be
noticed, Dewey has insisted that "desires are socialized" (EW 3: 387).
The individual is from the start brought into social life, even at the
level of his individual desires; and so the modernist might argue that
in this view the individual is never really enabled to develop his own
free individual self; were he truly to do so, he could only ever act in
opposition to the social norms imposing themselves on him.

But here, I think, the early Dewey would simply insist that the
modernist is wrong.

> The child finds . . . ends and actions in existence when he is born.
> More than this: he is not born as a mere spectator of the world;
> he is born *into* it. He finds himself encompassed by such relations,
> and he finds his own being and activity intermeshed with them.
> If he takes away from himself, as an agent, what he has, as sharing
> in these ends and actions, nothing remains. (EW 3: 346)

"Nothing remains"—nothing remains, in other words, if we try to
conceive of the modernist self, the self whose desires and ends are

stripped away of all social meanings and goals. This self is a pure negation, an imaginary entity; for to be a self, even to be a free, independent self, is to be embedded in a social life of some sort, in terms of which the self adopts and strives for certain ends as opposed to other ends and receives the very meaning of its own purposes. In Dewey's words, even "freedom becomes real . . . it becomes force and efficiency of action, because it does not mean some private possession of the individual, but means the whole co-operating and organized action of an institution in securing to an individual some power of self-expression" (EW 3: 349). It takes an enabling, free form of association for the individual to gain some measure of freedom. Social life is omnipresent in the individual; it is inescapable, forming the very ends and desires he possesses, but this fact is consistent with the existence of freedom. The real question is not how to access a separate self outside of society that activates our individual liberty, but rather what type of society or culture will enable us to be free and help us engender genuinely free individuals within it. We know what Dewey will say: it will be the type of society that will enable us (to paraphrase Shakespeare) to be true to our own selves, while also expecting us to be true to others and to enable them to be true to themselves as well. It is a society in which we all work together to be our own selves. This is Dewey's vision.

We have before us, then, Dewey's alternative conception of culture—a culture beyond modernism with its restricted, narrow, and antisocial self, beyond a problematic modernist culture that Dewey believes results in the proliferation of unhealthy types, of cynics and egoists, aesthetes and skeptics, and, above all, of pessimistic and despairing cases who are nauseated with the very prospect of living (EW 3: 41). The early John Dewey wants to help us to move us past all this. He wants to engender in us a potent sense of life's meanings and possibilities; he wants us to become characters who can embrace life, and one another, rather than being nauseated by everything we see around us. Dewey offers us a philosophy of health and vigor as opposed to a philosophy of cynicism and despair. And the crucial element of this philosophy is the recognition it forces upon us that we can think of ourselves as part of a moral community; we can see ourselves as part of a larger whole that gives point and purpose to our lives. In the end, Dewey's philosophy tells us to have faith in the possibility of achieving a social whole that cares for us and nurtures us as individuals, a social whole that may therefore serve as the symbol of something even larger and more significant—a community of the meaningful relationships we bear to all of reality, to what has been, what is, and what shall be. In Dewey's life-affirming view, we are entitled to think that we count in the nature of things after all; for we possess the symbol for such a conception in our social life, which lends itself to the possibility of striving toward a perfect whole in which each person counts for something significant in the whole, in which each person may realize himself in the society to the height of his capacities.

In conclusion, it must be stressed once more that Dewey's alternative conception of culture is only an ideal—but in this it is actually the culmination of all of his early efforts. Dewey nowhere claims that his conception of culture is real, or even that it ever could be made real. We know by now that for the early Dewey true meaning lies not in mere facts, but in facts that have become idealized, taken on our meanings, the meanings of our healthy, normal, socialized selves. What Dewey advances is an ideal of a better culture, beyond our current one; he explicitly advances it *as* an ideal, and in this he expresses the very essence of his early philosophy. For the essence of that philosophy, as we have seen in the present work, is that through rupture from what is given, idealization occurs, meanings are born, and the infinite movement of self-realization becomes possible. It is only by having faith in such ideals as Dewey has put forward, ideals of a different and better culture, that we can work against actual facts; and it is only by working against actual facts that we can achieve definite meanings, all along in our progress toward the ideal. The real goal, in effect, is not to attain the ideal, but to pursue it. As Dewey says, "The realizing of this ideal is not something to be sometime reached once for all, but progress is itself the ideal" (EW 3: 387).

EIGHT

A NEW IDEALISM

Dewey beyond Morris and Hegel

My main claim in this book is that Dewey's early thought amounts to an original and significant philosophy. This claim challenges the standard interpretation, which holds that aside from helping illuminate Dewey's later writings, his early work has nothing important to teach us; that taken on its own terms it is unworthy of our sustained attention. It may be objected to my thesis that Dewey's early thought is typical Hegelian idealism, reflecting the philosophy of his teacher, George Sylvester Morris, if not simply of Hegel himself, and merely reiterates pre-existing idealist claims. In this final chapter, I will demonstrate that the philosophy I have analyzed throughout this book really is a new mode of thought, specifically a new form of idealism, with sufficient merits in its own right to warrant careful study.

I begin with a summary and reminder of the fundamental logic of Dewey's early thought—the logic of rupture and movement. I then show how this underlying logic differentiates his early ideas from the philosophies of both Morris and Hegel, two of Dewey's most important influences. To underscore the continuing relevance of Dewey's early ideas, I then compare them with those of some important contemporary thinkers in Continental philosophy, most notably Theodor Adorno and Jean-Luc Nancy. Dewey's early ideas, we shall find, are still fresh and vital today, and even able to address some of our own pressing philosophical concerns. Lastly, I show that Dewey's early philosophy is important in another way: it actually poses a significant challenge to Dewey's later philosophy in important respects. This surprising discovery serves to show just how potent Dewey's early ideas really are, and it should give pause to those who unquestioningly accept the view that Dewey's later ideas are superior and alone worthy of study. In sum, I hope to show that Dewey's early philosophy is far more sophisticated than generally supposed and makes genuine contributions to philosophical inquiry, including, above all, its ability to confront philosophical pessimism.

The logic of rupture: this is how I describe the early Dewey's general mode of thinking. As we have seen, for Dewey there is no first, un-idealized fact, but rather a series of idealized and meaningful facts. The facts always rupture—break apart from themselves—and move toward something else, something potentially more ideal; for as idealizing selves, we force the facts apart in this way, seeking to render them more conducive to ourselves, more meaningful than they are in their brute givenness. This process of rupture is going on all the time, even unconsciously in our acts of knowledge, and it explains how facts become meaningful; that is, how they are put into relationships with other facts, in terms of which they become significant. Our past experiences and our creative efforts are brought to bear on each given experience; they establish novel relationships for the experience and so generate new meanings for each experience as it comes. The process of the rupture of facts and their subsequent idealization always takes place as movement, as an ongoing, continuing event that occurs precisely through the disruption of what is given before us.

Let us take an example that Dewey himself gives to further clarify the basic logic of his position. Consider, for example, "the law of justice" and what it might mean in human life (EW 3: 350). Dewey says two things about this law. First, any collection of individuals requires the ideal of justice to become a society; but, second, the ideal of justice is never reducible to the actual collection of individuals and their behavior. Dewey explains the first point:

> The law of justice states a certain relation of active wills to one another. . . . To imagine the abolition of these laws is to imagine the abolition of society. . . . A society in which the social bond we call justice does not obtain to some degree in the relations of man to man, is *not* society. (EW 3: 350)

The ideal of justice is a necessary condition of any real society.

And yet, this does not mean that justice is the same thing as how justice appears in a given society (EW 3: 350). Justice may obtain in some actual facts, but its meaning does not consist in the actual facts. On the contrary, the meaning of justice lies in the future, in the continued idealization of what justice means in the ongoing movement of the actual society. What justice means at any given point is incomplete—its complete meaning, therefore, lies forever outside the situation, as an ideal toward which the actual situation, in its incompletion, is reaching, but which it never attains. Dewey puts the point in this way:

> The very imperfection, the very badness in the present condition of things, is a part of the environment with reference to which we must act; it is, thus, an element in the *law* of future action that it shall not exactly repeat the existing condition. In other words, the "is" gives the law of the "ought," but it is a part of this law that the "ought" shall not be as the "is." (EW 3: 351)

This is precisely the concept of rupture: "the badness in the present condition" helps give us the ideal for future action: that it shall be different from the present condition. It shall be more ideal. Every society presupposes an ideal of justice, but its actual behaviors may not be just; and yet in their injustice, these behaviors point the way toward what would be just. This is just another way of saying that true meaning, for Dewey, lies not in bare facts (here, the facts of the given society), but in facts that have become idealized and that endlessly reach forward toward some future better state (the ideal of justice that emerges out of an unjust condition). The logic of rupture, then, maintains that there is an ideal source of meaning beyond imperfect existing conditions whose *absence* from these conditions drives us on to find it. With this crucial idea in place, let us turn next to a consideration of Dewey's relationship to other idealists, most notably to his teacher, George Sylvester Morris, and then to Hegel himself.

Dewey clearly had a close relationship with Morris. In a moving eulogy that he wrote, published as "The Late Professor Morris," the reader can detect Dewey's real affection for the older man and genuine appreciation of his way of thinking (EW 3: 3–13). Robert Westbrook notes that "Dewey took all of Morris's courses and quickly became the idealist's favorite student."[1] Indeed, Westbrook states that his connection with Morris more or less determined the nature of Dewey's early philosophy. In Westbrook's words, "Dewey and Morris worked together," but "Dewey's work in the mid-1880s was continuous with that he had done in graduate school, and he was clearly the junior partner in this relationship. His essays and books elaborated on and applied the organic idealism he had learned from Morris and the British neo-Hegelians."[2] As Westbrook sees it, Dewey's work was derivative of the work of other idealists, especially Morris.

Westbrook's assessment, however, does not get us deep enough into Morris's and Dewey's respective views to really note substantial similarities or differences between them. Westbrook identifies common views and sentiments—the need to overcome alienation, the search for unity between subject and object, the rejection of pantheism in favor of Hegelian absolutism, and so on—but these are general aspects of their thought; he does not provide a detailed appraisal.[3]

Certainly Dewey learned a lot from Morris. To help us understand what he learned, and also to help us understand the specific differences between the two men, I will first examine Dewey's view of his former teacher, and then I will examine Morris's philosophy itself.

The eulogy Dewey wrote for Morris deserves a closer reading than Westbrook and other commentators have provided. "The Late Professor Morris" was published in 1889, two years after the *Psychology*, by which time Dewey had fully worked out his own early position. In this important article the young philosopher makes clear what he thinks is of lasting merit in the work of Morris. But even here, in the delicate context of a eulogy, he also makes clear, although perhaps unintentionally, the differences between their viewpoints.

"The Late Professor Morris" suggests that Dewey took three important ideas from his professor. First, he took a version of Morris's concept of idealization. Dewey describes a strange experience that Morris told him about, something like a philosophical breakdown in which Morris's entire understanding of the world seemed, as Morris had said, " 'to melt away, and there remained, as the whole sum and substance of the universe, only the empty and inexplicable necessity of being' " (EW 3: 5). A Heideggerian might perceive in this strange experience a fine example of "uncanniness,"[4] or a direct encounter with the question of Being that can sometimes vaguely steal over one, "like the muffled tolling of a bell."[5] Morris himself, however, interpreted it as justifying idealism. For Morris noted that the experience seemed to consist only of " 'a chaos of shapeless elements,' " after which there immediately returned again " 'the world such as it had actually shaped itself in my imagination—the earth, with its green fields and forest-covered mountains,' " and so on (EW 3: 5). This is, to be sure, an idealist interpretation of the event: Morris could see meaning only in the world his imagination had created, not in the brute, given reality of being. Moreover, according to Dewey, Morris emphasized that his *imagination* had created this world. Morris's interpretation of his strange experience almost perfectly mirrors Dewey's idea of idealization as the basis of the very meaning of the world, and it is highly instructive that Dewey singles out this experience and Morris's interpretation of it to help delineate the late professor's thought. We can safely assume, I think, that in this case the student adopted the insights of the teacher. The parallels between their accounts of idealization are too close to ignore; and it is likely that Dewey adopted some of the

meanings of his teacher's highly interpreted account of his strange experience and the significance it could have for any concept of idealization. As a matter of fact, Morris insisted that the process of idealization
was the result of " 'a bent common to the universal mind of man,' "
which " 'more or less blindly' " seeks " 'to introduce order and permanence' " (EW 3: 5). Like Morris, Dewey, too, came to believe that what
we are is something larger than our narrow individual selves.

Second, Morris evidently saw in this direct encounter with " 'the
empty and inexplicable necessity of being' " a potential cause for pessimism, if one were not entitled to idealize being and claim for it
something more than brute existence. For in Dewey's rendering of
the event, Morris states that his attempt to interrogate existence and
find out its meaning all by itself had the immediate result of being
negative (EW 3: 5). Additionally, Dewey stresses when describing
Morris's character and concerns that his former teacher went on to
reject materialism—the granting of superior status to brute matter—
exactly for its "failure to support and inspire life" (EW 3: 6). As
Dewey describes Morris, he battled the pessimistic and paralyzing affects of materialism and won. "He was preeminently a man," Dewey
says, "in whom those internal divisions, which eat into the heart of
so much of contemporary spiritual life, and which rob . . . the will of
its belief in the value of life, had been overcome" (EW 3: 9). I think
it fair to conclude that here, too, the early Dewey adopted or at least
shared his more experienced teacher's revealing concern for the extent to which, in the face of materialism, we are entitled to find value
in life. It is almost point for point Dewey's own fundamental concern
in his early work.

Third, Dewey took from Morris the idea that social meaning is a
symbol of cosmic meaning, though the two philosophers differ in
their ways of expressing the idea. Notice this important character
trait, and its philosophical significance, that Dewey attributes to
Morris:

> He found the substance of his being in his vital connections
> with others; in the home, in his friendships, in the political orga-
> nization of society, in his church relations. It was his thorough

> realization in himself of the meaning of these relationships that
> gave substance and body to his theory of the organic unity of man
> with nature and with God. (EW 3: 10)

This idea about actual social life, when it is successful, serving as the
basis for a belief in cosmic meaning is obviously very close to Dewey's
own rethinking of the relationship between self and society. It certainly makes one wonder about the extent to which Dewey's idealism
is distinct from the idealism of Morris.

But these similarities notwithstanding, fundamental differences
between the two thinkers do exist, according to Dewey's account. The
most crucial difference is the absence of anything like the concept of
rupture in Morris's idealism; and as I have argued, this is the early
Dewey's most central concept and indeed his singular innovation.
When Morris thinks of the process of idealization, he thinks of the
mind's urge " 'to introduce order and permanence' " (EW 3: 5). But
in Dewey's account of the process of idealization, the mind seeks not
permanence but the progressive development of meanings through
continual rupture. True, the self has faith that its own meanings are
part of something larger, but this larger something (whether we think
of it as the moral community or as a meaningful universe) is the object of faith, and the function of this faith is to keep us generating
actual, finite, particular meanings in the world. This is the fundamental point that we have seen at work again and again in Dewey's early
philosophy. The early Dewey wants us to understand that "our life is
one of progressive realization, not of completed development, of
growth rather than of attained being" (EW 2: 260). The craving for
permanence that Morris desires is worlds apart from the spirit and
letter of Dewey's thought. Dewey embraces process, while Morris
wants permanence.

Even more importantly, with regard to the relationship between
the individual and the larger, meaningful reality outside of himself,
Dewey explains that Morris saw the individual as bearing a " 'direct
relation with the Absolute Mind' " (EW 3: 9). Indeed, in Dewey's
view, "the firmness with which he held this truth is the key to all of

his thinking" (EW 3: 9). Yet Dewey in his own work insists time and again that we bear no direct relationship to this larger reality; for him, the self is always thrown outside of itself, and becomes something more, and so on endlessly and forever, as it develops its infinite capacities and realizes itself in the world more and more completely. This means precisely that there is no direct relationship between the self and God or the Absolute; there is no end to the process toward which the self inevitably and demonstrably tends; there is only the whirlygig of constant movement, *along with* the faith that this movement leads somewhere. The precise point and function of this faith is to keep the whole process in motion—to keep us embracing life and the process of continual meaning-making. Any claim that this process results in a direct relationship to God is explicitly abandoned by Dewey.

I think this marks a substantial difference. There are idealisms and idealisms. Many share common features, such as the view that reality is shaped by mind, and yet we rightly distinguish between them. The same thing must be said for the idealisms of Dewey and Morris, and most particularly on this score. For Morris, again, as Dewey quotes him, " 'the very sense of philosophical idealism . . . is to put . . . man in direct relation with the Absolute Mind' " (EW 3: 9). Morris needed to have a direct connection with God. For Dewey, on the contrary, as quoted before, "the self has always presented to its actual condition the vague ideal of a completely universal self by which it measures itself and feels its own limitations. . . . [W]hat this . . . self as complete is, it does not know. It only feels that there is such a goal" (EW 2: 358). We do not bear a direct connection to the universal self, but only feel a vague, unfulfilled longing, the point and purpose of which is to function as "a constant motive power . . . bringing forth the concrete attainments in knowledge, beauty, and rightness" (EW 3: 359). Dewey did not need to know for certain that he was one with God or any higher reality whatsoever; he sought only to provide us with an explanation for the unending process of meaning-making that goes on in the world. His explanation was that as finite beings, our work is always unfinished; there is always more meaning and value for us to create in the world. There is always something more, and better, for us to strive to be. This is a fundamental difference of philosophies; it is the difference between a philosophy of vigor and nerve and a philosophy of acquiescence, between a philosophy of action, so characteristic of Dewey's late work also, and a philosophy of submission to its author's deepest metaphysical longings.

There is one more crucial difference between Dewey and Morris. As we have seen, Morris may well have been the source for Dewey's idea that social life is the symbol for cosmic life, so important to Dewey's overall early thought. And yet Morris comes down decidedly more on the religious side of this equation than on the social, whereas Dewey comes down decidedly more on the social side.[6] Dewey emphasizes Morris's "strong religious nature," while in Dewey's own work one gets the sense that religion is secondary to society (EW 3: 7). After all, in his *Outlines of a Critical Theory of Ethics*, the outgrowth and fuller working-out of the main ideas of the *Psychology*, religion is peculiarly absent, while the concept of the moral community comes to dominate the discussion. In applying his insights from the *Psychology*, Dewey chose to write about ethics and social philosophy, not religion. And even in the *Psychology*, we have seen that the crux of Dewey's position, its real motive, as it were, is to overcome pessimism by helping us rethink our social relations in such a way that life would be worth living within them. The real motive of Morris's position seems rather to achieve direct contact with the religious element itself, which alone can truly inspire us to live, while social life serves merely as a point of access to this religious element. As Dewey observes, "it was characteristic of Professor Morris that the two writings from which he most often quoted were the *Dialogues* of Plato and the Gospel of St. John. In the fundamental principle of Christianity, he found manifested the truth which he was convinced of as the fundamental truth in philosophy" (EW 3: 8).

Dewey's definition of the two positions, then, lets us say that his idealism is distinct from Morris's idealism in significant ways. Morris's unwillingness to embrace process, his inability to accept anything less than a direct connection to the Absolute, his subordination of the social ideal to religious life—these are fundamental points of differ-ence between the two thinkers. And even if we were to suppose that Dewey was simply a disciple of Morris, the fact remains that Dewey worked out his own philosophy in great, sophisticated detail. And when it comes to philosophy, the devil, we know, is in the details. The sheer comprehensiveness of Dewey's efforts, all that his philosophy purports to explain, alone renders it an interesting philosophical ex-pression. But in any case it seems clear that Morris and Dewey do differ significantly enough—they differ as to the very nature of how one should combat pessimism, which is to say, in fundamentals.

It is important, however, not to rely solely on Dewey's account of Morris to make these points, but also to turn to Morris's work itself to weigh the similarities and differences between the two thinkers. It is one thing to consider what Dewey perceived his intellectual debt to his teacher to be and another to consider what the texts themselves reveal.

Morris's most important and characteristic work is *Philosophy and Christianity* (1883).[7] This book originated as an installment of the Elias P. Ely Lectures on the Evidences of Christianity.[8] Morris's aim in the book is "to show that intelligence, as such, is the true bulwark, and not the enemy, of religion."[9] *Philosophy and Christianity* tries to show how reason, which can take religion as well as anything else as its object of investigation, does not vitiate religion, but rather con-firms and endorses it, especially the religion of Christianity. Morris's basic strategy is to present the latest insights of German idealism in terms of the nature of knowledge and reality and then show how they match, point for point, the religious doctrines of Christian thought. His book is a work of Christian apologetics, utilizing Hegelian ideal-ism as its main philosophical resource.[10]

When we come to the specific ideas advanced in the text, two points become clear. First, Morris holds, as does Dewey, that there is no real separation between subject and object, so that the objective world we find ourselves in already embodies human, subjective meanings. "We have just as much right to say," according to Morris, that the subject finds its forms in the object as that the subject puts its forms on the object. The one is just as true as the other. The individual, therefore, as a knowing agent, finds himself set in the midst of an intelligible world, of which he is a part, or to which he is akin, and not placed as a knowing machine, over against a world, which is wholly unrelated to him and refuses to have anything to do with the forms of his intelligence.[11]

This is Dewey's point as well. We find in the world the meaning that we have already put there, so that we can, in effect, feel at home in the world. So far the philosophies of Dewey and Morris are very similar.

Second, Morris holds that we are able to find this human meaning in the world "only in the *light* of self-consciousness."[12] This again sounds like Dewey, in that they both insist on a higher ideal that would unify subject and object, ensuring that the meaning of one is the meaning of the other. Morris sounds even more like Dewey when he stresses that man's attainment of this higher unity "is still always incomplete. Man finds himself, after all, only as an organic part of an intelligible world, in knowing which he assumes, with reference to it, the attitude of its organic head. This *rôle*, however, he only assumes; he does not *fill* it. . . . [H]e never completely fills it."[13] For both Morris and Dewey, the attainment of our highest ideal, the realization of the Absolute, is forever elusive. It is a goal that we never realize.

It is precisely here, however, that the crucial difference emerges between the two thinkers. When Morris explains what he means by our inability to reach the Absolute, he reveals that he means something fundamentally different from what Dewey means. Morris is driving at the idea that *we* can never *be* the Absolute; he never for a moment holds, as Dewey does, that we can never become immediately certain of its presence and that this very uncertainty drives us to search for it. Morris says only that we are not ourselves the Absolute, and that our self-conscious activity of apprehending a meaningful world is not the work of ourselves alone: "self-consciousness in man is *intrinsically* dependent upon an absolute self-consciousness."[14] About our own self-consciousness, we can say: "it is dependent."[15]

But the absolute self-consciousness is totally independent and self-sufficing. "It is the radiating or expansive center of a process which extends over the whole world of intelligence without ever losing itself."[16] For Morris, "the essential truth" of the Absolute "is guaranteed" to us through our very dependence on it.[17] This is his main point. Having argued that our intelligence helps shape the meaning of the world, he then says:

> But now, the world is not created by our intelligence. . . . It exists independently of our individual intelligence and independently of the intelligence of the whole aggregate of finite and knowing individuals in the universe. It only remains, therefore, to suppose that the individual subject's synthetic activity in intelligence is not simply or primarily creative, but the rather recreative, not productive, but reproductive.[18]

In other words, Morris holds that our finite forms of intelligence, which give form to the world, are really only forms possessed by the Absolute. Like T. H. Green, while admitting that we create the relations in nature, he nonetheless maintains that our own self-creations really only occur in the bosom of the Absolute and its self-creations.[19] But Dewey, as we have seen, centers meaning in the finite self pursuing the Absolute, not in the eternal and completed Absolute itself.

Moreover, Morris insists on our immediate connection to the Absolute in this respect, whereas, as we have seen, Dewey insists that there is no immediate connection. In a person's relation to the Absolute, Morris says,

> nought can separate him, whether principalities or powers, or things present or things to come. For to this, the everlasting and absolute and ever-present source of his being, he is immediately related. With this he is connected by the innermost springs of his being. It is in this that he immediately lives and moves and has his being. With all else his connection is indirect.[20]

We are ensconced in the Absolute, totally immersed in it, and so always connected to it at an essential level of our being. Such a connection is our most fundamental reality, everything else being secondary and "indirect." Indeed, to understand this immediate connection to the Absolute is, for Morris, to become "the true man. It is the creative-redemptive realization of the *perfect man*, in living union with the Absolute, with God."[21] In Dewey's philosophy, however, our connection to the Absolute always still eludes us. Our intuition of the Absolute, it will be recalled, is never direct or immediate.

Furthermore, the Absolute as Morris conceives of it is a perfect, timeless unity. While Morris does make a point of saying, like any good Hegelian, that "the unity in question is a *living* unity . . . an *identity*, the very condition of whose existence is *diversity*," he nonetheless also stresses, again like Green, that this unity unfolds itself in time while the Absolute itself remains outside of time in a pure, eternal state of being.[22] As Morris puts it, our "knowledge of God, is said to be eternal life,—not simply the condition of such life, but identical with it."[23] In intelligence, when we grasp the Absolute, we share in truth, in the eternal life of the Absolute.[24] And to share in this eternal life of the Absolute means to be outside of time and change. In the life of the Absolute, "the eternal is an everlasting Now; in it there is no distinction of past, present, and future; in this sense it is superior to time. Time is the emblem and the condition of mutability, of change, of impermanence. . . . [W]hatever is characteristically subject to the condition of time, is . . . unreal, insubstantial . . . without true and abiding reality."[25] Not so with the Absolute, which stands above all change and decay and gives true reality to all things, including those who grasp the Absolute in their own minds. For a human being, "it is only through his participation in an eternal life, that he has in him true substance or reality."[26] Only insofar as a human being participates in the timeless, changeless state of the Absolute does he possess full and actual reality. For Dewey, on the other hand, the finite self is the focus and the idea of the Absolute eludes us. We never have any direct evidence that the Absolute exists as a perfectly realized unity somewhere.

The differences between Morris's philosophy and Dewey's should now be clear. As we have seen, Dewey holds that the Absolute is absent; that we bear no direct connection to it; and that it nowhere forms a perfect unity, but rather that division and disruption are its most primary elements, although of course the Absolute does allow us to achieve temporary unities of meaning and experience as determined by the harmonious experiences it seems to make possible. For Dewey, the Absolute is an absent ideal, and herein lies its power. This is point for point different from the ultimate conclusions that Morris draws. Morris, as we have seen, holds that we are fully connected to the Absolute; that we bear a direct connection to it; and that it forms a perfect unity. In a word, Morris, like all traditional Hegelians, gives primacy to eternal harmony in his conception of the Absolute, while Dewey gives primacy to the finite activities of process, development, dislocation, and rupture. Even where Morris makes a point of saying that we will never fulfill the conditions of the Absolute, what he means is that we will never *be* the Absolute, that we are dependent upon it; but this point in no way takes away from his insistence that the Absolute is immediately present to us as a timeless, changeless, and perfect unity, standing like "the rock of ages, which can never be moved" above the divisions and ruptures of our merely apparent life.[27] It never occurs to Morris, as it does to Dewey, that the Absolute might itself be a force of rupture and dislocation, and that these negative processes its absence makes possible might be the crucial phases of meaning-making for us.

I think it fair to conclude, therefore, that while Dewey without question learned a great deal from Morris and shared many of his key concerns, he also went beyond Morris in the fundamental features of the idealism he developed. Dewey took what he could from Morris and created something new. He shared Morris's worry about pessimism, and he may have taken from Morris his belief in the necessity of seeing meaning in ideals, including social ideals. But he added to this mix the logic of rupture, the embrace of process, and the uncertainty of outcome, and he worked out in original detail a bold new vision of culture in which realizing oneself, as an individual, makes possible a reciprocal interplay between selves in which the coordinated community can grow in meaning and significance.

Granted, then, that Dewey's early idealism does distinguish itself from Morris's idealism—what about its relationship to the idealism of Hegel? Surely here, if anywhere, we can say that Dewey's idealism is not unique; that Dewey—to echo Westbrook's remark about Dewey's relation to Morris—has only "elaborated on and applied" the ideas of Hegel.[28]

But the question is: which Hegel? Hegel's philosophy is notoriously difficult to pin down and define. Or, rather, there are so many versions of Hegel that one must first specify which Hegel one means before asking whether someone is or is not merely reproducing Hegel. If we mean Hegel the philosopher of total unity, of accomplished ideal results, then Dewey's idealism is not Hegelian, since it posits endless progression instead of unity. If we mean Hegel the philosopher who holds that society is objective mind, then again, the early Dewey is not Hegelian, since he thinks of society as consisting of definite individuals who each pursue their own tasks of self-invention, even as they shape the society for the better; Dewey does not think of society as the literal instantiation of the mind of God. If we mean Hegel the philosopher of the dialectic, for whom a real logic runs through things and holds them together, then once again Dewey is not Hegelian, since he holds that rupture is what runs through things—a rupture made manifest above all through feeling, rupture that never once demonstrably comes to closure. It is only on the assumption of faith that Dewey's logic of rupture *may possibly* cease and give us rest somewhere, whereas Hegel, in some readings, took himself to have rationally demonstrated the logic of the dialectic and had little room for faith. If we mean by Hegel someone who believes in an Absolute Mind that knows all things, as many idealists believe has to exist, then Dewey is not Hegelian, since he believes in finite individuals yearning to realize themselves; and he believes that this yearning for the not-yet-accomplished is the very path to the progressive development of finite meanings.

We can say that Dewey shared with Hegel a deep desire to overcome the problem of alienation, and that he adopted the basic contours of Hegel's solution for overcoming it, as we saw in chapter 1. Like Hegel, Dewey understood modernism to be a negative force that painfully separated the isolated self wholly from the world. And like Hegel, he saw that the way to overcome this separation was to understand that what is outside of oneself (nature, other people) is actually part of oneself, when we enlarge the meaning of the self to include the whole fabric of society and of the cosmos. As for Hegel, this is a mystical insight backed up with rational arguments. When he was young, Dewey once felt a healing oneness with things, and sought to rationally justify and explain this feeling through his philosophy. But unlike Hegel—or at least unlike Hegel as traditionally understood—Dewey thought, first, that we can never completely justify this feeling rationally (we can get right up to the point where we nearly can, and after that we need faith), and second, he never deceived himself into thinking that our alienation would ever be perfectly overcome. For him, the effort to overcome it, and to establish human meaning in the world, was an endless process—a process that itself gave meaning to the world. Perhaps this explains why Dewey could become a pragmatist in the end; at the beginning of his career he was already an idealist who was against "the quest for certainty" (LW 4:7). This does not mean that Dewey's idealism and pragmatism are identical, nor does it mean that Dewey's pragmatism is simply a later development of his idealism. As we will see in the last section of this chapter, there are grounds for seeing two distinct philosophies here. The early Dewey developed a form of idealism that affirmed endless process; but this is not necessarily the same thing as developing a form of proto-pragmatism.

But if Dewey developed a form of idealism that affirms endless process, this throws into a new light the relationship that Dewey bore to Hegel. If we wish to understand Dewey's Hegelianism, we need to start by rethinking the traditional conception of Hegelianism, whereby Hegel seeks to bring process to an end and to hold all things together in Absolute Mind. We need to look toward more contemporary and innovative readings of Hegel for a fair sense of the kind of Hegelianism that Dewey in his youth had developed.

Contemporary Comparisons

Jim Good has done more than anyone to help us understand the relationship between Dewey and what Good calls "the non-metaphysical Hegel,"[29] which I interpret to mean a historical Hegel, a Hegel of human situatedness rather than transcendence. But I think we can press the case further and discover other connections between Dewey and Hegelian strains of thought if we turn, not to "humanistic/historicist" readings of Hegel, which ultimately privilege unity, but to readings that emphasize the acts of rupture and separation in Hegel's philosophy.[30]

Such recent Continental philosophers as Theodor Adorno, Jean-Luc Nancy, and Slavoj Žižek have shown us a new and fascinating Hegel, no longer a Hegel of the fixed and finished Absolute, where everything works towards harmony, but a Hegel of disturbance, of continual negation and differentiation. Adorno maintains that Hegel's philosophy "is incompatible with any kind of tendency to harmony. . . . His critical thought . . . is not a matter of unbroken transition but a matter of sudden change, and the process takes place not through the moments approaching one another but through *rupture.*"[31] Jean-Luc Nancy makes a similar argument, to the effect that "Hegelian thought does not begin with the assurance of a principle. It is simply identical to the restless."[32] "This world of movement," Nancy says, "of transformation, of displacement, and of restlessness" is what Hegelian philosophy is all about.[33] No fixed trajectory constitutes Hegel's Absolute, only ongoing rupture and change. Žižek gives voice to a similar idea when he emphasizes the "negative, disruptive, decomposing aspect" of Hegel's philosophy. He adds that the idea has an important political implication, namely, that the rupture of thought—its negation of things, its "absent centre"—is required for an emancipatory politics that can move beyond existing conditions.[34]

Could John Dewey in his early work have also achieved such an understanding of things? Could he really have arrived, through his studies of Hegel, at ideas similar to those of these late-twentieth-century thinkers? Let us consider once more what we have discovered about Dewey's early philosophy. And as our measure for what constitutes rupture, let us take Adorno's description of it quoted above: it "is not a matter of unbroken transition but a matter of sudden change, and the process takes place not through the moments approaching one another but through *rupture.*"[35]

The early Dewey's advocacy of a philosophy of endless process can be seen from this remark, quoted previously: "Our life," he insists, "is one of . . . growth rather than of attained being" (EW 2: 260). So there is never a final result. We are constantly making meaning in the world and growing in our own meaning as selves, without arriving at any fixed point. But how does this growth occur? Does it occur as "a matter of unbroken transition" or as "a matter of sudden change"?[36] Do the growing elements of meaning occur because one element approaches another and communicates its meaning to it directly, or does one meaning wholly *erupt* out of another, a present meaning leaping out of a past one as a new and unforeseen result?

Let us recall what we have seen so far. As we worked through Dewey's conceptions of knowledge, feeling, and will in the *Psychology*, we learned that for Dewey meaning was constituted in each case by an abrupt shift away from a given element (or fact). The first and perhaps most important instance of this is in the case of knowledge, indeed at the very beginning of all knowledge, with the first occurrence of any mental content at all. We encounter an abrupt shift when we attempt to understand "the relation between the external world, including the organized body, and the mind or self," or, what is the same thing, "the connection between sensations or psychical states and the physical and neural changes which excite them" (EW 2: 37). Dewey is emphatic on this point: "there is no identity between the sensation as a state of consciousness and the mechanical motion which precedes it" (EW 2: 40). He goes even further: "a chasm" exists between them (EW 2: 39). An external motion may precede every sensation, but "sensations are not motions. The sensation of red may have a dependence upon a certain number of etheric vibrations, but as a sensation it is a unique psychical state, having no motion, no vibrations, no spatial length nor form. . . . [O]ne exists as an objective spatial fact of movement, the other as the unique psychical fact of consciousness" (EW 2: 39; 40). Because of this fundamental difference between them, one cannot be the cause of the other; for one thing can cause another only if the two things are of an identical nature, but in this case they are of different natures (EW 2: 39).

Moreover, the physical explanation of how mental contents emerge requires that the mental contents are of a quantitative nature, so that, for example, according to the law of the conservation of energy, one quantitative, measurable event passes its energy into another definite quantitative something, and the same amount of energy at work in the physical cause is transferred to the resulting sensation. But in this case "no quantitative transformation can be made out, for the simple reason that the consciousness is not a quantity" (EW 2: 40). Hence, Dewey concludes that there is "a chasm which the law of the correlation of energy cannot bridge" (EW 2: 39).

But a chasm is more like a rupture than continuity. For the early Dewey, there is no continuous relation between an external motion and a mental content; on the contrary, the mental content "is a virtual creation"; it "cannot be in any way got out of" the physical events (EW 2: 42). Mental contents such as sensations are the product of rupture, of a sudden change. "A sensation is not the simple affection of the soul by some bodily change. . . . The sensation is the state developed out of and by the soul itself upon occasion of this affection" (EW 2: 42–43). Sensations, in other words, do not develop continuously out of physical events, in definite, explicable steps, but are rather "virtual additions" to reality, something entirely new that is brought into the world by the mind's "power of acting upon itself and of producing from within itself a new, original, and unique activity which we know as sensation"—through the mind's power, that is, of rupturing given events and moving away from them to create something new (EW 2: 77; 43). Because of this process of rupture, there is no given fact: "knowledge always consists in going out beyond the present sensation. . . . [T]he known fact is not a bare fact . . . but is idealized fact, existence upon which the constructive intelligence has been at work" (EW 2: 127; 126).

And so it goes for the whole of Dewey's early philosophy. When it comes to memory, for example—or better put, "retention" (Dewey distinguishes between these two, but the distinction need not concern us now)—we can safely say that the past is dead. And yet it lives on as a virtual creation in our minds. "Our past experiences have no

more *actual* existence. They are gone with the time in which they occurred. They have, however, *ideal* existence" (EW 2: 132). How does
this process occur? As we have seen, it occurs in much the same way
as the tree is affected by external nutrients but takes them up and
utilizes them in its own unique ways, according to its own structures.

> As the tree is not merely passively affected by the elements of its
> environment—the substances of the earth, the surrounding mois-
> ture and gasses—as it does not receive and keep them unaltered
> in itself, but reacts upon them and works them over into its living
> tissue—its wood, its leaves, etc.—and thus grows, so the mind
> deals with its experiences. (EW 2: 132–33)

Once more, the mind takes up some external element but does not
merely reproduce it. Some external event happens. The mind gives the
event an ideal meaning "by connecting it with the self, and thus putting into it significance, which as bare existence it does not have"—
something, again, which is a virtual creation, because the bare existence
simply does not possess this meaning in itself (EW 2: 122). Now, in the
case of memory or retention, the original event that occasioned the
process eventually passes, but the ideal existence of the event that
the self created for itself is "wrought into the character of the self," and
because of this the self retains its ideal meaning of past events within
itself as it continues on in its life (EW 2: 132). It has memories, or reten-
tions, which it can carry into new experiences. But note that here, too,
as with sensation, there never occurs within this process an element of
continuity. There are, in fact, two acts of rupture involved: first, the
original event is given an ideal meaning by the mind, a meaning which
the "bare existence" simply does not possess, a meaning *which is simply
not there*, and which must be created by the self out of its own resources; and second, the ideal existence (the thing remembered) continues on in the life of the self *even though* the original event no longer
has any actual existence, that is, even though it has no direct, continuous connection to the self (EW 2: 122). True, the original event did
form our habit of being able to act differently now, but this is not the
same thing as the mental image, which is a new present creation of a
past and no-longer-existent event.

Consider next the transition that occurs between perception and imagination. With this case, we begin to move into an account of how the logic of rupture is involved in feeling as well as in knowledge. In perception, the mind has taken up sensations and produced in relation to them a new object, which itself is composed of almost no sensations (this is another act of rupture): "in the perception of an object, as an apple, there are actually present, it will be remembered, only a few sensations," since the unity of the object is not something given in the sensation of red, round, sweet, and so forth. "All the rest of the perception is supplied by the mind" (EW 2: 168). More specifically, the object of perception is a product of the imagination:

> The mind supplies sensations coming from other senses besides those in use; it extends and supplements them; it adds the emphasis of its attention, and the comment of its emotions; it interprets them. Now all this supplied material may fairly be said to be the work of the imagination. The mind idealizes—that is, fills in with its own images—the vacuous and chaotic sensations present. (EW 2: 168–69)

So the imagination adds new content to our sensations, and the result is our perception of an object. How does this "growth in meaning" (EW 2:184) occur? The growth cannot come about from the imagination simply taking up material that is already present in our sensations; for none of these elements is present in the original material (say, the isolated perception of red)—rather the mind must give its own "emphasis of attention," "the comment of the emotions," and so forth. This is all the new and original work of the imagination, which it supplies to the sensations by virtue of its own powers.

But now—and here is the really important point—the mind makes a transition from the perception of an object, in which the new, added, ideal images "are swallowed up in the product, so that the object of perception appears to be a mere thing, which exists without any ideal connections," to an object that is the product of the imagination proper and is recognized as entirely ideal, such as an imaginary apple (EW 2: 169). How does this growth of meaning occur?

How can the mind move from the perception of an actual object to its imaginary stand-in, or even to an imaginary object pure and simple, an image without any direct reference to an object? Dewey's answer is that when this occurs, the image is "severed from connection with some facts actually existing" (EW 2: 169). His choice of words here, of course, is interesting—the image is "severed," or cut loose, from any actual thing. The ideal element already at work in the perception of an object "is freed from its reference to some existence, and treated freely; that is, as an image, not as tied down to some thing or event" (EW 2: 169). And this severed image "is not confined to isolation and combination of experiences already had, even when these processes occur under the influence of sensitive and lively emotion. It is virtually creative. It makes its object new by setting it in a new light" supplied by the mind itself (EW 2: 171). Once again, it is difficult to see how this process can occur through the elements of meaning making contact with one another; it seems rather to involve their separation. An image is "severed" from reality; it is "not confined to . . . combination of experiences already had"; "it makes its object new" (EW 2: 169; 171). This is the language of rupture.

It is the same with Dewey's account of our feelings. "In aesthetic feeling," for example, "we advance beyond . . . and feel the relation which some experiences of ours bear to an ideal. . . . [T]he self . . . is taken beyond its limitation to its immediate sensuously-present experience, and transferred to a realm of enduring and independent relations" (EW 2: 245). These relations do not exist in actual fact; the ideal cannot derive from them (EW 2:42). It is similar to the feeling of sympathy. This feeling is not at work in our relations to others; rather, it must be wrested out of these relations. Sympathy is "an *active* interest in others," in which we must go out to the experience of the other and allow his experience into our own life (EW 2: 285). The feeling does not exist without this active interest and projection: it is the result of something the mind does, a certain way that it breaks away from our own self-interest and creates something wholly new, a new feeling of absorption in the other and the resulting feeling of connection.

Consider next Dewey's conception of the will, and the different ways that disruption and separation are involved in willing. Physical control puts the body in check, and prudential control manages our actions in order to help us achieve results (EW 2: 320). But each of these forms of control results in actions that are incomplete, that are only arbitrary and one-sided in the demands they make upon us, while in moral control we find "the absolutely obligatory end. It alone is absolute end" (EW 2: 320). Moral will fulfills all the other acts of willing that would otherwise be merely contingent exertions. So we would expect, in this view of things, that morality would be the last word about willing. But Dewey emphasizes that the moral will never perfectly completes itself: "the moral will is incomplete or partial in its action" (EW 2: 360). "The will as ideal and the will as actual have not been truly unified" (EW 2: 360). To have any hope that they could be unified requires the religious will. It requires faith. But how does this growth of meaning occur? "Religious will declares that the perfect will is the only source of activity and reality"—it *declares* this, asserts it (EW 2: 360). This assertion comes from an act of will, a pure choice, a free self-determination to believe. Nothing in the moral will compels us to this result, for the moral will is imperfect, always constituting a division. That any unity could come out of it requires a total shift, a new assertion—in short, rupture.

And the religious will itself is not the completion of the process either, as we have seen. Having faith that our ideals are at the basis of fact does not make it so. But faith allows us to go on; it constitutes a "motive power" for us to keep creating meanings (EW 2: 359). Faith, or "the religious life," is the explicit "recognition" that "the final reality for man is that which cannot be made out actually to exist," precisely since it is an ideal, and in faith we affirm the supremacy of the ideal (EW 2: 292). The moral life itself, in any case, requires rupture to move beyond itself. And the moral life is also itself fully constituted by processes of rupture. "Man's moral nature is in process of realization," Dewey explains, "with every new realization of personality comes a higher ideal of what constitutes a true man" (EW 2: 296). This process of increased meaning goes on without any past determination, without continuity: "the heart of the moral life lies in the free personal determination of right and wrong. No set of rules can take the place of this personal determination" (EW 2: 297). This is why the "degradation of manhood" is always possible as well as its realization (EW 2: 296). But in any case the moral life is constant disruption, constant upheaval, without continuity with the past—the birth, in every instant, of new possibilities. Insofar as we must speak of a "moral law," we must recognize that it

> is thoroughly individualized. It cannot be duplicated; it cannot be for one act just what it is for another. The ethical world is too rich in capacity and circumstance to permit of monotony; it is too swift in its movement to allow of bare repetition. It will not hold still; it moves on, and moral law is the law of action required from individuals by this movement. (EW 3: 352)

I take this passage to mean that the process of rupture is constantly going on in the ethical world—in other words, no event is simply repeated and "duplicated" in our lives, but rather every event counts as a wholly new addition—and that any "moral law" that might be applicable to this process of rupture *is itself* a product of this process of rupture.

This is similar to what we saw about justice at the beginning of this chapter. In the case of the law of justice, "the 'is' gives the law of the 'ought,' but it is a part of this law that the 'ought' shall not be as the 'is'" (EW 3: 351). Said another way, any ideal of justice can emerge only in reference to some actual, moving, imperfect, and unsettled ethical world, just as any sensation can emerge only on the occasion of an external motion; but the ideal of justice *is not* identical to the actual ethical world in reference to which it emerges, just as the sensation is not caused by the external motion that is the occasion for the sensation to occur. There is an upheaval in the heart of the ethical world; justice is not given there; the ideal of justice is born. It is the ideal of justice toward which the actual world should tend, but the ideal is not present there within it.

We can sum up these results in a few words. In Dewey's view, the ideal makes itself present negatively, that is, by leading "to discontent with every accomplished result," which "urges on to new and more complete action" (EW 2: 358). There are "dim and vague feelings which surge for expression in every human being" (EW 2: 278). We do not know what the ideal is; we do not know what it demands of us; we do not know toward what we should be striving. "What this will or self as complete is, it does not know. It only feels that there is such a goal" (EW 2: 358). All this is just to say that everything is always unsettled. Every "this is it here," one might say, turns out not to be "it." The ideal functions as an inexhaustible resource preventing any actual fact from summing up reality. Every fact that presents itself as summing up reality will always be split up; it will always exist in a divided state between what it is and what the ideal version of it is, or what it should be. Rupture will always occur in the very heart of existence.

This does not mean that there is no progress of meaning—that we should despair of ever attaining meaning. All along the way meaning is being attained; with every leaving off of some past, incomplete meaning, we progress toward a new and possibly better meaning, and sometimes partially achieve it, a meaning that we feel approximates, through its harmony, the ideal we yearn for. As we partially realize the ideal, we inch closer to it. Faith is the embrace of this process, the affirmation of life, defined as forever capable of growing in meaning.

The logic of rupture and the meanings it makes possible can be summed up in the following passage:

> The will is in itself universal, and this presence of the universal element must prevent the self resting in any realized attainment. It must form the spring to renewed action. . . . This real self . . . holds before itself . . . an empty ideal without content. . . . *What it is* . . . this we do not know. But this empty form is constantly assuming to itself a filling; as realized it gets a content. Through this content we know *what* the true self is. (EW 2: 319)

The present fact always comes up short of the ideal. The fact is therefore disrupted and must give up its claims to supremacy. A new meaning emerges, and to the extent that it approximates the ideal we yearn for, there is meaning. But this approximation, though meaningful, will never be the complete ideal, and so there will be rupture again, and so on and on.

But if this is the case, and the logic of rupture defines the early Dewey's position, then we have reached a surprising result. For the logic of rupture is also the defining element of much cutting-edge Continental philosophy that also draws on Hegel. As we saw with Adorno, Nancy, and Žižek in their uses of Hegel, disruption is the driving force, pointing to an unrealized ideal to which we should aspire—and so it is also with the early John Dewey. Adorno, for example, insists that we should "attempt to contemplate all things . . . from the standpoint of redemption," and this sounds a lot like Dewey's insistence that we must always judge our present experience to be inadequate as measured by its absent ideal.[37] In any case, these thinkers have taught us that Hegelianism ought to imply the logic of rupture, and we have just seen that Dewey employs this logic—and that he may even have developed it on his own from his reading of Hegel. But let us be more specific and see whether any definite links can be made between the philosophy of the early John Dewey and the philosophies of some of these more recent thinkers.

When Adorno offers his interpretation of Hegel as a philosopher of rupture, he does so in order to make the larger point that Hegelianism after Hegel "is all a regression." "His system," Adorno explains, "is not an overarching scientific system any more than it is an agglomeration of witty observations." But nonetheless this is how most people have understood Hegel's work. They have either reduced it to "clear methodology and iron-clad empiricism" or have seen it as an overarching scientific system and "missed the concrete content on which Hegel's thought first proved itself." What Adorno wants people to realize is that empiricism and speculation go together for Hegel; they cannot be separated. More specifically, Hegel insists on totality, on the reality of the whole, but this totality is not something that exists ready-made outside of events; it is rather a result and product of finite, particular events as they unfold. "If Hegel's whole exists at all it is only as the quintessence of the partial moments, which always point beyond themselves and are generated from one another; it does not exist as something beyond them. This is what his category of totality is intended to convey. It is incompatible with any kind of tendency to harmony." The idea, in short, is that the rich, unfolding nature of actual experience yields ideals; it blossoms into them, as finite particular moments somehow manage to "point beyond themselves"; and the Absolute whole, then, is nothing else but the jagged, unsteady way in which all of these moments together unfold in the real, messy world of everyday life. Speaking of Hegel, Adorno says, "he knows that the whole realizes itself only in and through the parts, only through discontinuity, alienation, and reflection." This is identical to Dewey's idea that "facts" could themselves be consistent with "thought," with a more human and orderly universe, if we take them as they occur in their various patterns of emergence.[38]

That is to say that for Hegel, the Absolute does not impose forms on reality, but instead, forms emerge from it. Due to its absence, the perfect ideal makes itself felt in each finite particular, and the process is driven on beyond itself toward something better and more. Events in their "immanence" move unsteadily toward the Absolute. Hegelian idealism "permits nothing to remain outside the subject, now expanded to become infinite, but instead sweeps everything along with it into the current of immanence." "Hegel's much-admired material richness is itself a function of his speculative thought," and yet, the speculative moment, of belief in the infinite subject, the Absolute, is derived solely from the particular moments as they unfold in their disharmonious, unsteady way, as in life. "Hegel," as Adorno puts it, "is driven by the idea that knowledge, if there is such a thing, is by its very idea total knowledge, that every one-sided judgment intends, by its very form, the absolute, and does not rest until it has been sublated in it." And again: "Hegel everywhere yields to the object's own nature . . . but it is precisely this kind of subordination to the discipline of the thing itself that requires the most intense efforts on the part of the concept."[39] From within events themselves, as we follow their various connections, which are never seamless and steady, but rather discontinuous and sudden in their change, we can nonetheless discern an emerging whole, a progression of the ideal, which makes itself more real. Facts, in all of their messiness, nonetheless go beyond facts and become ideal.

Such a position is crucial to much Continental philosophy. The worry is that, in being reduced to facts, to what actually is, we lose any resource for resistance to what is. The strategy here, in Adorno's rendering of Hegel, is to employ the facts themselves as disruptive, as unstable and so capable of "sudden change,"[40] so that their necessity is loosened, and they provide within themselves the resource for idealizing the world and working toward progress, toward something better than what the facts themselves, if fixed in their nature, would allow. Continuity would seem to imply necessity, the acceptance of the causal chain and what must come next from the facts, while rupture from within the facts permits, on the other hand, a weakness in necessity itself, a gap in which new, unforeseen events and free decisions can occur. Hegel's Absolute is the ideal of freedom making sure to be present in every otherwise determined series of facts. It is the precondition of distinctly human meaning in the universe and the precondition of the progression of meanings toward something better than the present state of things. But again, the crucial phase of this conception is that the facts themselves erupt into freedom. Freedom is unassailable, precisely because it is not imposed top-down upon events in the world (a world which in that case would offer resistance to it), but rather emerges from the world itself in its own development.[41]

The crucial moment of this Hegelian strain in Continental thought, the moment of the immanent ideal as the point of access to freedom from how things actually are, freedom from the necessity of facts, is expressed well in the work of Jean-Luc Nancy and his appropriation of Hegel. Nancy, too, insists that Hegel is a philosopher of rupture. For Hegel, as Nancy sees it,

> this world, the realm of the finite, shelters and reveals in itself the
> infinite work of negativity, that is, the restlessness of sense. . . . It
> is in this way, in the restlessness of immanence, that the spirit of
> the world becomes. It neither seeks itself (as if it were for itself an

exterior end) nor finds itself (as if it were a thing here or there), but it effectuates itself: it is the living restlessness of its own concrete effectivity.[42]

The Absolute is immanent; it is the working through of the facts themselves. And this working through involves a dissolution of facts, of the finite world. It is destroyed and remade. There is a negativity involved, in which things are undone and then put back together in new ways.

To characterize this process as a form of "restlessness," moreover, is to say "that there will therefore be no foundation." We are always in the midst of an unsettled world. There is no first point to return to, as in Descartes; "everything has already begun. . . . [T]he course of the world will not be stopped in order to be recommenced. . . . [I]f the thread of history is broken, this happens of itself, because its very continuity is only division and distension." To speak of the Absolute's restlessness is also to say that there will be no end state; there is an "absence of completion." For Hegel, according to Nancy, "the infinite or the absolute will be presented in no determinate figure. There will be other figures, but they will now be known for what they are: successive forms in passage, forms of passage itself, and forms born away by passage. The finite figure thus presents, each time, only itself—itself and its infinite restlessness." There is one dynamic process, forever unsettling itself. For what reason? So that meaning can be made; so that freedom from facts, from getting lost in any static substance, and a subsequent movement toward greater meanings, can occur.[43]

Thus, for Nancy in his appropriation of Hegel, the static element in life is removed, and only in this way is freedom possible. Restlessness is required for this result, undoing every given. Meaning, or "sense,"[44] is made in this way: "it is an upsurge in the course of the given, a rupture, nothing that could be posited as such. . . . Which means: negativity, hollow, gap, the difference of being that relates to itself through this very difference."[45] This is what Hegel means by the Absolute, according to Nancy. It is not an accomplished result, not a ground he presupposes, but rather the lack of ground of an ever-developing free process. "Hegel, if one likes, presupposes the absolute. But this presupposition is made precisely in order to ruin all presupposition or pre-givenness."[46] What exists is a process that disrupts every given: a "power of the negative that inhabits the gap where relations open, and that hollows out the passage from presence to presence: the infinite negativity of the present."[47] Not the final unity of separate moments, not guaranteed harmony, but inevitable disruption characterizes Nancy's conception of the Hegelian Absolute, the undoing of every given in its due time.

And this negative process, this inevitable upheaval and unsettling work of the Absolute, is one with the ideal of freedom. But it is also the very process by which meaning is made. The reason why this is possible, why negation can give rise to positive meanings, is because of what Nancy identifies in Hegel as the " 'negation of the negation.' " The first negation is negation of the given. Negating the given, I become free from it. "If I penetrate this first truth, that neither the stone nor the ego has the value of simple being-there or of an identity . . . this penetration is already liberation." I become free from having to be this or that, or having to submit to this or that. We realize that "being is in itself nothing," but this realization by itself must also be negated, or else we have not attained real freedom, but only perhaps "an abyss or lack," a total negation. Thus,

> the second negation denies that the first is valid on its own: it negates pure nothingness, the abyss or lack. It is the positive liberation of becoming, of manifestation, and of desire. It is therefore self-affirmation. But as this liberating affirmation is not a return to the point of departure—to the stone or to me, which in turn was already only a derived given, a provisional deposit along the way and the fleeting instant of a presentation—it is also not a new, simple position.

What Nancy means here is that the given is first negated; and then this negation is negated, so that something definite and positive emerges. But what emerges is not simply a repetition. Having been the result of no given, it has been freed. It is a positive free thing, as, for example, are any of the things I have made (or that have made me), through my own free self-creations: "the stone in my slingshot, in the wall that I have built, or in the statue that a sculptor exhibits to us, indefinitely liberates itself from its exteriority, enters into a history and into multiple senses, and brings us along with it. The result is again a liberation—and that is what negativity means." When we negate the given, for example the stone in our midst, we do not, however, remain in the realm of pure negation, but rather, negating our first negation as well, move to the point where the negated given takes on positive content and allows us to create ideal meanings of our own out of the pure negation. We create a positive meaning for the stone.[48]

And here is the crucial point: in reaching positive, ideal constructions through double negation, we do not rely on any foundation to our constructions, nor do we ground them in given facts; and so we attain freedom from the given, while at the same time coming to possess meanings. This liberates us from reduction to mere physical nature, or to any alien necessity, while also making meaning in the world possible for us. It allows us, in the end, to feel at home in the world we inhabit. Nancy expresses this point by saying that "truth comes back to us. It finds or happens upon itself *as us*, and it is *to us* that it is entrusted."[49] "To us: to the upsurge of our existences, together, as the surging up of sense. To the upsurge of this, that the world is precisely what does not remain an inert weight, but what manifests itself as a restlessness. This restlessness is not only ours, it is itself 'us'—that is, it is the singularity of singularities as such."[50] In a word, there is no foundation to the world, but only the actual events of the world, such as they are, *and also* the free, developing possibility of their becoming more ideal, more meaningful to us as time goes on. There is only the world; but the world, in its freedom, in its "restlessness," in its tearing away from every given, enables meanings to emerge, which we can, at times, come to possess and to enjoy as "sense," as that which is significant and makes sense.

I submit that Dewey's early philosophy closely resembles such reflections as these, and for this reason it goes beyond traditional versions of Hegelian philosophy, such as were offered, for example, by the British idealists. We have already seen how there is no foundation to meaning-making for the early Dewey. Each time the given is negated, but there is no first something that anchors the process. We have seen, too, how for the early Dewey ideal meanings are nonetheless made beyond the given, meanings which then take on positive sense and substance in actual, harmonious states of experience that we (temporarily) attain. We have also seen that the Absolute is not a timeless unity or eternal substance for Dewey, but an ongoing process, a kind of unsettling "restlessness," as Nancy has put it. Lastly, it must be stressed that Dewey, too, saw that freedom and feeling at home were essential to this process. Our knowledge, for Dewey, is never simply a matter of conforming to what is. On the contrary, "we know the world because we idealize it" (EW 2: 211). But in idealizing it, we put the self into it, and when we realize that we are doing this, that "more and more of the activity of the self" is "implied" in our knowledge of things, then we "form the *conception* of *freedom*, as we recognize that the process is one which goes on through self alone" (EW 2: 211). We come to understand that the world is a free creation of selves. A free world, moreover, is one in which we can feel at home as human beings. Unlike an alien and determined world, it is one in which "personality . . . shall itself be a moving force counting for something in the universe" (EW 3: 42), and it is for this reason that Dewey wishes to emphasize the free, idealizing aspect of our knowledge of the world and its events.

The early Dewey, immersed in Hegel, was, in effect, a Continental philosopher. He shares the same fundamental impulse: to create a space for resistance to the given, a space for human beings to count in the course of the world, a space that prevents us from being "the playground of natural forces" (EW 3: 42). Moreover, he had an advanced understanding of the Continental tradition, anticipating a way of reading Hegel that has only recently been advanced by such thinkers as Adorno and Nancy. He went beyond his contemporaries in the nineteenth century, beyond his teacher, Morris, and beyond the British idealists, who themselves could envision only a fixed, static, and atemporal Absolute, a more pristine Absolute, which acted like a metaphysical foundation securing with necessity the world's development.

The key to Dewey's advance, I believe, is his early antifoundationalism, which has emerged clearly in the course of this study. It is this insight that brings his early philosophy closer to our times. There must have been something in Dewey that freed him from requiring the fixed and firm basis to things that those around him required as the way to overcome pessimism. He could live with a greater amount of fluidity and uncertainty, although he shared with his contemporaries (and recent thinkers too) the need to surpass pessimism and to demonstrate the existence of a meaningful world.

To see this antifoundationalism at work and to further confirm the reading of Dewey presented here, consider one more example—an example pertaining to the social and political realm, a realm to which, as I have noted in previous chapters, some of the early Dewey's most important insights are directed. We will return to the case of justice that introduces this chapter and consider how a recent Continental philosopher, also influenced by Hegel, handles this conception. I choose Jacques Derrida as a fitting, if surprising, example of a contemporary whose thoughts on justice bear comparison with the early Dewey's conception of justice.[51]

To understand Derrida, we must understand his concept of "iterability." As Niall Lucy makes clear, Derrida believes that ideals exist, such as justice, morality, truth, and so on, but he thinks that in order for them to exist they cannot be reducible to any of their present instantiations.[52] Each instance of an ideal is repeatable, and when it is repeated it is always different from its previous instance. Any realized ideal is therefore both what it is and not what it is. The ideal can be at work in the situation, but there is always something more to what it is than any actual instance of it. When the ideal repeats itself, it will be different, and when it is different of course it will not be the same. "Iterablity refers to this structure of repetition-as-difference, which both enables and limits the idealization of every single thing's singularity, purity, presence."[53] Because of iterability, deconstruction can take place; that is, there can be no given, purely present, and strictly identifiable object or event that we could privilege above all others for its secure, foundational certainty. Every instance of an ideal ruptures and splits into what it is not.

And yet, of course, ideals still do exist and can guide our lives. Lucy is again instructive: he reminds us that "the concept of iterability doesn't commit Derrida or deconstruction to nihilism, relativism, obscurantism," and so on. "Since Derrida admits to ideality . . . how could he ever be against values and beliefs, as if to say anything goes? Rather than seeing iterability in opposition to ideality and identity, then, we should see that, as the precondition of ideality and identity, iterability is opposed to the *certitude* of ideals, the *dogma* of beliefs, the *self-assurance* of identities and the *constancy* of values."[54] Ideals exist, but any one instance of an ideal is not the ideal, although the ideal must grow out of such instances. What follows is that we have ideals, we function according to them and use them, but we never have the certainty that we own or possess the ideal.

An important example that helps bring out this feature of all ideals, for Derrida, is the ideal of justice. For Derrida, justice is employed in the law courts, and so on, and does not exist outside of them, and yet we would be wrong to mistake the court's decision for justice. In Lucy's words,

> a verdict seen as arbitrary or whimsical would never be seen as just; and so there is no question (on Derrida's account) that justice is not outside the law in a transcendental sense. But while justice is never absolutely outside the law, neither could we say there must be justice once 'the law has run its course.' We cannot think that justice remains to come until the court settles on a verdict, at which time there is justice. Out of respect for its radical undeconstructibility we cannot afford to think of justice as something that happens in the present—as something belonging to presence. We could never say that, at this very moment, there is justice.[55]

We approximate justice, but we never reach it. The instances of being-close-to-justice are where anything like justice must occur; anything like justice occurring must grow out of these instances and

meet their specific needs. But no instance of an approximation to justice adequately defines a just situation, or perfectly meets the ideal,
which always still exists to unsettle our present efforts and make us
move forward to try to realize ever more instances of justice and
come closer to the ideal.

It is the same with Dewey's concept of justice, where, as we saw,
"the 'is' gives the law of the 'ought,' but it is a part of this law that
the 'ought' shall not be as the 'is'" (EW 3: 351). Actual instances of
justice exist in some situations; the ideal is partially realized in what
a Hegelian would call a harmonious experience. But the justice we
approximate in the situation does not exhaust the ideal of justice,
which keeps its distance, as it were, and therefore functions for us as
an important resource for creating more and better instances of justice in every future situation. Justice exists, but it is never fully realized. We never have the certainty, therefore, that we have reached
justice in the present case, only the need to unsettle that case as it is,
and to move forward to approximate the ideal as best we can in the
case at hand. Derrida himself, like Dewey, even speaks of such ideals
as justice as really being about the future, about meanings that could
still be possible (EW 3:351).[56]

One might continue with this comparison between the two thinkers and find other surprising similarities. Derrida's concept of democracy, for instance, resembles to some extent Dewey's vision of culture
beyond modernism. All existing political systems, including demo-
cratic systems, imply identity, the categorization of the other person—so that we can say who this person is and who that (for
example, is he for us or against us?). But a political system in which
this occurs would never be democracy, because in it people would
not be left to stand as who they are and be enabled to help shape the
society as real individuals, beyond our categorization of them. So, we
must not confuse our current democracy or, indeed, any democracy
whatsoever, with "democracy-to-come," the ideal of democracy that
we should keep striving to reach.[57] "But of course even to imagine the
impossibility" of this new democracy "one has to be in some place
that is other than purely imaginary in itself. And that place . . . is the

place of democracy today."[58] So, again, as in Dewey's philosophy, here too the instance of a better society must grow out of a present society, but it cannot be wholly identified with the features of that society—it would be *that* society perfected. Moreover, it would be a society (for Dewey as for Derrida) in which each self is not cut off from its relationship to others (each self is not fixed in its identity and its identity exhausted), but each self would be enabled to become itself, to be an individual, and yet at the same time would be helping to constitute the very fabric of the society as a democracy.

What it comes down to, for both thinkers, is that there exists an ideal community that brings us together, but we must not mistake any actual community for this ideal. A space needs to be set apart, even as the condition of any real community, from which the real community may draw its inspiration and meaning, but the real community can never come to occupy fully this space. The ideal works in and through actual events as they develop, but these actual events never exhaust it. It retains its separateness, its meaning "out there," beyond, as the necessary precondition of the meaning of the actual community, which always lacks the full ideal, but drives towards it precisely because of this lack.

I would not push the comparison too far, but there appear to be surprising similarities between Dewey's early philosophy and the philosophy of Jacques Derrida. And the main basis for these similarities seems to be, if not a shared new reading and development of Hegelian idealism,[59] then at least the logic of rupture. Deconstruction, as I understand it, reveals the lack of identity between the actual and the ideal, the gap between them, which keeps us striving to render the actual more ideal, even as we realize that the ideal is never the actual. And this is what philosophy means for the early Dewey, for whom the given fact is always idealized, but imperfectly so; and this imperfection "serves as a spur to the actual self to realize itself" and to try to move closer to an ideal version of itself, which it nonetheless does not yet know and cannot yet attain (EW 2: 358).

But there would seem to be this important difference between the early Dewey and these Continental philosophers: Dewey offers a more comprehensive and constructive account of the processes of rupture than do these recent thinkers. For he tries to explain almost every feature of human life in terms of these processes—sensation, perception, memory, imagination, judgment, reasoning; feelings in all their different grades and meanings (including feelings of triumph, defeat, brooding, drudgery, play, envy, cheerfulness, melancholy, malice, beauty, ugliness, hatred, and love); physical, prudential, and moral control; the religious will. It is a monumental effort, and none of the more recent thinkers I have mentioned has tried to accomplish anything nearly so vast in scope. Moreover, this effort is constructive, not merely deconstructive, in the sense that it offers positive (if always imperfect) recommendations for intellectual, emotional, moral, religious, and social ideals to strive for; for example, ideals of sympathy or health.

This does not mean that Dewey's early philosophy is better than these other philosophies. Many of the recent thinkers I have mentioned refuse to be system-builders, or refuse to state positive ideals, and for very definite reasons; and they might critique Dewey's early effort for its pretensions along these lines. But what the greater comprehensiveness and constructiveness of Dewey's early philosophy of rupture does reveal is that, again, Dewey is working with the same basic logic, the logic of rupture, as are these thinkers; and that there is more work to be done to explore these lines of comparison more fully, and to determine which type of employment of the logic of rupture, systematic or nonsystematic, possesses greater philosophical merit.

That we can make such comparisons, in any case, indicates that Dewey's early philosophy is far from naïve and unsophisticated. This is a philosophy that invites comparison with some of the most important and interesting philosophical theories today.

Dewey versus Dewey

That the early Dewey was an antifoundationalist, as are the recent Continental philosophers with whom he favorably compares, may tempt us to see direct links between Dewey's early and later thought on this point, since the later Dewey is also very much antifoundationalist in orientation. Perhaps throughout this study the reader has seen in the early Dewey's philosophy crucial, even formative, connections with his later philosophy, whether in the area of his antifoundationalism, or in his view of us as active beings, or with respect to the concept of growth or some other concept. While there are important threads that run through both philosophies, we must not suppose that the sole significance of Dewey's early position lies in its anticipation of his later thinking, or, noting that Dewey's later position retains key idealist elements, view his idealism as significant only for the way it lives on in his pragmatism. For there are fundamental differences between Dewey's earlier and later philosophies that cannot be easily reconciled; and each period of the philosopher's work needs to be taken on its own terms.

The two Deweys differ, for one thing, on the status of the Absolute. For the early Dewey, the Absolute is the crucial resource that enables us to negate every given and move on to create better meanings. The later Dewey seems to reject the concept of the Absolute, or at least ignore it, as when he criticizes Hegelians for putting too much stock in it (see, for example, LW 4: 51–52). A second major difference concerns the theory of truth. The early Dewey offers a coherence theory of truth, while the later Dewey insists upon an instrumentalist or pragmatic theory of truth. A third major difference is that the later Dewey does not seek for the good life, but only the better one.[60]

The most fundamental and unavoidable difference between the two philosophies, however, is this: the early Dewey explains meaning-making primarily in terms of rupture, while the later Dewey explains it entirely in terms of continuity, at least in his naturalism.[61] The later Dewey maintains that there is continuous development from the biological to the cultural, a claim that is crucial to his whole position, according to which there is no split between mind and matter, and we are fully natural creatures, even in our spiritual and cultural products. Indeed, the later Dewey explicitly defines "the idea of continuity," which he embraces, as an idea that "excludes complete rupture . . .

the appearance upon the scene of a totally new outside force as a cause of changes that occur" (LW 12: 30–31). The idea of continuity, according to the later Dewey, "precludes complete breaks and gaps" (LW 12: 30). But breaks and gaps, as we have seen, are just what the early Dewey insists upon.

To better appreciate this crucial difference between the two Deweys, one might pit them against one another. Let us suppose, for example, that one looks at the idea of continuity from the perspective of the logic of rupture. Instead of assuming the later Dewey's superiority, as many Dewey scholars might, let us speculate whether the early Dewey could mount a critique of the later.

It is conceivable that the early Dewey's emphasis on rupture could explain more than the later Dewey's emphasis on continuity. As Slavoj Žižek has argued, drawing on the works of Freud and Lacan, it takes a violent pulling away from our immediate life and the consequent repression of its desires (and their deepening inward focus) to generate the cultural norms (or what the early Dewey might call the ideals) by which we can live. Our repression of natural desires focuses them inward, where they intensify, and an eruption of new cultural creations occurs as their new outlet and manifestation. Žižek puts the point in an interesting way, which is worth quoting at length. Referring to his own original interpretation of Hegel's concept of the subject, he writes:

> The subject . . . his very core, the gesture that opens up the space for the Light of *Logos,* is absolute negativity, the "night of the world." . . . [T]here is no subjectivity without this gesture of withdrawal; that is why Hegel is fully justified in inverting the standard question of how the fall-regression into madness is possible: the real question is, rather, how the subject is able to climb out of madness and reach "normality." That is to say: the withdrawal-into-self, the cutting-off of the links to the environs, is followed by the construction of a symbolic universe which the subject projects on to reality as a kind of substitute-formation, destined to recompense us for the loss of the immediate, pre-symbolic Real. However, as Freud himself asserted . . . is not the manufacturing of a substitute-formation, which recompenses the subject for the

loss of reality, the most succinct definition of . . . the subject's attempt to cure himself of the disintegration of his universe?[62]

All the basic elements of Dewey's early philosophy are here. The self negates what is given, moves on from it into its own activities and powers, and creates a substitute world for itself in which it can find the meaning that is absent from the missing facts themselves. In creating these virtual worlds, the self becomes "normal," that is, cultured, as opposed to a mere animal immersed in immediate experiences that have a far less developed meaning—no complex emotions, no morality, no religion. At stake here is precisely the emergence of culture, as Žižek well realizes: "the key point is thus that the passage from 'nature' to 'culture' is not direct, that one cannot account for it within a continuous evolutionary narrative: something has to intervene between the two, a kind of 'vanishing mediator,' which is neither Nature nor Culture."[63] And the creation of culture, of these ideal virtual worlds, and our absorption in them is a way for a person to be healthy or normal, to "cure" himself, as Žižek says, of "the disintegration of his universe," that is, of "the loss of the immediate . . . Real"—or as the early Dewey might suggest, of the absence of the given.[64] Surprisingly, therefore, the early Dewey and Slavoj Žižek have much in common, having both drawn significantly from Hegel.[65]

Now the important thing about rupture as an explanation of culture, as Žižek's analysis reveals, is that this explanation shows how cultural products can be free and novel products of human activity. Rupture as a process takes us beyond nature and allows, for the first time, distinctly human productions, such as works of art, music, science, and so on. "Something has to intervene"[66] and break up the natural desire and send it into new and more meaningful directions; there must be rupture, break, discontinuity, a negation of the desire as it is and its push into new avenues. A philosophy of rupture can account for how unique cultural productions occur, namely, as "negated" desires that are stopped, repressed, brought into the mind and intensified in light of its own idiosyncratic tendencies, and then transformed into totally new, external, symbolic substitutes for our desires. The natural desire, unable to find expression anywhere, implodes and mutates into a new kind of force, a symbolic substitute for that destroyed part of us, which gets to live on in a new form. This is how we might explain culture-formation for a philosophy of rupture. But can a philosophy of continuity account for novel cultural productions?

Relying on the idea of continuity, the later Dewey has to account for culture in a seamless way, as something that emerges continuously from out of our natural interactions. There can be no sudden eruption of new cultural products into existence. Somehow a symbolic substitute for a natural impulse must arise from the continuous flow of experience. A cultural product has to emerge as does "the growth and development of any living organism from seed to maturity," that is, continuously (LW 12: 30). How does this occur?

The later Dewey says that culture in any given individual emerges when his or her raw impulses are shaped into a coherent set of habits through the customs of society. The individual finds it easy to adopt his society's way of doing things; it is something he does as a matter of course. Dewey puts the point this way in *Human Nature and Conduct:* "Few persons have either the energy or the wealth to build private roads to travel upon. They find it convenient, 'natural,' to use roads that are already there; while unless their private roads connect at some point with the high-way they cannot build them even if they would" (MW 14: 43–44). Social habits are transmitted through the individual's natural and easy adjustment to custom; the adjustment takes place when the individual's own native impulses are reorganized along the pathways of the society, which occurs in a convenient and natural way for most people.

Dewey elaborates on this point and stresses that we do not actually have much choice in the matter. "If we would live," he says, we must "take some account" of social customs. "Social pressure," he explains, "is but a name for the interactions which are always going on and in which we participate, living so far as we partake and dying so far as we do not" (MW 14: 224). This account of social adjustment basically means that one either adjusts to the social customs or one does not; one either adopts the available cultural meanings or one does not. If a person adjusts, he or she gets to live and becomes a functioning member of the society; if a person does not adjust, then he or she dies, is rejected from the group, violence befalls him or her, and so on. We simply *do* adopt our social norms, "our culture," and that is how culture emerges for us. It is one with our environment, with who we are (insofar as we live), and we quite naturally adopt its ways.

But can this process really give rise to cultural meanings in the individual? People clearly have impulses, at times, that go against their culture, and it may not always be convenient and natural for people to squelch these impulses and redirect them into socially acceptable channels. These impulses, as repressed, would then persist; they would get redirected and find other, new outlets (sometimes creative outlets) in our behavior. There is something too simple and easy in the later Dewey's account of adjustment to society as an either-or, life or death, occurrence. This account seems to preclude repression and its psychic affects—the hidden rifts at work in one's mental life.

The later Dewey does stress, however, that there is something like repression or "suppression" going on, despite the passages quoted above where he suggests otherwise (MW 14: 108ff.). He clearly sees the need for this concept to help explain our behavior, for he offers it as one of three options "in the career of any impulse activity" (MW 14: 108). Along with the direct expression of the impulse without thought, there is the sublimation of the impulse, and there is its suppression (MW 14: 108). Suppression, he says, is problematic because the impulse "is neither exploded nor converted, it is turned inwards, to lead a surreptitious, subterranean life," and this will result in "all kinds of intellectual and moral pathology" (MW 14: 109). The proper result to hope for is sublimation, where the impulse will "become a factor coordinated intelligently with others in a continuing course of action" (MW 14: 108).

But the question is, how are suppression and sublimation possible in a philosophy of continuity? If we first consider suppression, in which an impulse is "driven into a concealed, hidden activity" (MW 14: 114), we will want to know whether it is realistic to say that every impulse finds an outlet somewhere, even if in "hidden activity." Are there not some impulses that can never get expressed, that is, whose objects can never be attained? The later Dewey's examples of suppression are relatively benign. For instance, he says that "the imperative demand for companionship not satisfied in ordinary activity is met by convivial indulgence" (MW 14: 109). Examples like this make it easy to see how suppression can occur in a naturalistic philosophy, guided by "the idea of continuity" (LW 12: 30). But notice that Dewey is maintaining here that in suppression, impulses "demand and secure a special manifestation" (MW 14: 109). They always "secure" an outlet in some activity. They always find some comparable object that will satisfy them. An impulse for companionship, for example, will always achieve a social connection somehow, even if in a perverse or dangerous form. But is that correct? Do impulses always "secure" their expression? Do they always attain their objects one way or another? If we imagine less benign examples, in which the object aimed for is never permitted, as Freud, for example, might discuss, then we should probably say instead that not all impulses secure a "manifestation." What then happens to these impulses? Where do they go? What do they become?

The later Dewey wants to say, to be sure, that such impulses can be sublimated, becoming "coordinated intelligently with others in a continuing course of action" (MW 14: 108). Consider the case of art, for example. For the later Dewey, art is definitely the result of sublimation. As he says, "without inhibition there is no instigation of imagination" (MW 14: 114). He believes that "any imagination is a sign that impulse is impeded and is groping for utterance. Sometimes the outcome is . . . an articulation in creative art" (MW 14: 113). And his example is that "an excitation of sexual attraction may reappear in art" (MW 14: 108). Some impulse arises, it is thwarted, and it gets intelligently redirected along with other impulses into an accepted channel of activity. Imagination is the creative searching for a new and more acceptable place for the thwarted impulse. A new artwork would then arise when intelligence helps the imagination to find a proper outlet for the impulse.

But how exactly doe this process occur? For example, how does "an excitation of sexual attraction . . . reappear in art"? The only way it could, given the idea of continuity, is for it to get redirected (it could never get extinguished and be created as something new),[67] as when social forces, for example, push the impulse into already given, accepted patterns of activity, namely art; or when intelligence and imagination work together to coordinate the impulse with other, pre-existing activities similar to art.

Once again, all is smooth and easy in the later Dewey's account of the psyche. Everything stays on the surface, and the re-coordination of a renegade impulse is achieved by its assimilation with accepted cultural forms. The later Dewey, relying on continuity, would say that every impulse gets expressed somewhere, even when it is suppressed or sublimated. For an impulse to be suppressed or sublimated means, for him, that the impulse finds some other area of culture in which to be expressed. There is, in a sense, no real suppression, only redirection. So any "new" production is really only the result of an impulse that finds expression in some existing course of action, modifying that course to some extent, but also getting assimilated by it in a natural and easy way. Something new can therefore emerge, but it will be new in a restricted sense. It is only ever possible to express the impulse in already prescribed channels of activity, to create a meaning in an already prescribed cultural form. As a result, nothing totally sudden and unforeseen is possible.

But then the question arises as to how culture could have arisen from nature in the first place through this mechanism. If continuity is the overriding consideration, and the old merely gets reshuffled in new ways, how can we account for the existence of something like a symbolic substitute for our desires—for new cultural formations in which we find ourselves involved, but which are not simply the expression of some previous desire, but are instead that desire transformed into a new meaning for us? The later Dewey wants to be able to say that such a thing is possible, for he will not reduce the cultural product to the natural impulse. But how can he make good this account of things? In our previous example of art, how did the art that could serve as a substitute for sexual attraction arise in the first place? Or more generally, how did the cultural part of that to which I easily assimilate when I assimilate to culture arise in the first place? Every impulse must be either simply acted on or taken up into the existing cultural meanings, but how does any cultural meaning, which would assimilate the impulse, occur at all through this procedure? How does it occur, specifically, when the sublimated impulse itself is not supposed to generate any wholly new cultural meanings, but only, at best, redirect the old ones? How could a natural impulse originally create culture, when culture is required to redirect and assimilate the natural impulse?

As if to solve this problem, the later Dewey is compelled, at one point, to say that we have an impulse for creativity. "In short, among the native activities of the young are some that work towards accommodation, assimilation, reproduction, and others that work toward exploration, discovery and creation" (MW 14: 70). So the native impulse for creation would have to be the one that compels culture to arise. When the creative impulse is allowed to express itself it will lead to cultural meanings, it seems. But how does an impulse know, so to speak, that it is creative? What makes impulses, which are themselves "blind, unintelligent," creative in their nature? (MW 14: 108).[68] In the view of the later Dewey, an impulse receives meaning and direction from already available cultural meanings. But what defines a creative impulse as creative before there is a culture relative to which the impulse is creative? Sticking with the idea of continuity, which restricts the imagination to finding an appropriate cultural outlet for an impulse, would seem to make it impossible for the imagination to create at any point the cultural meanings in relation to which it would then be a serviceable tool. Cultural meanings, in turn, would seem to be products totally devoid of imagination, nothing truly creative; and creativity would be restricted to those acts in which a renegade impulse was intelligently assimilated into the culture.

Here there is a fundamental difference between the earlier and the later Dewey.[69] They would explain the emergence of culture differently, and the earlier Dewey would do so potentially better, with fewer problems, than the later Dewey. Rejecting the idea of continuity, and relying on the logic of rupture, the earlier Dewey might say, as does Žižek a century later, that cultural meaning is always the creation of something totally new, totally other than nature, which occurs through the repression and transformation of our natural desires, through the negation of the given. "Absolute negativity" is involved, in the sense that the natural impulse must die an unnatural death; it must *cease to be* itself as a natural impulse. The natural impulse must be totally denied, and this denial must lead to a positive new meaning; nature must become antinature, which Žižek explains by saying that "this . . . of course, is the death drive."[70] Only a radical break in continuity, something that is "no longer nature" but "not yet *logos*," something like the death drive, or the negation of the given, the logic of rupture, can account for the passage to culture.[71] For nature would only continue its drive; it would not turn against itself and destroy itself. Nature cannot of its own accord develop into antinature and become something new. Through negation and rupture, on the other hand, or the desire of the self to destroy a part of itself, something new is possible. A new meaning can appear when we fight against our impulse, lose a part of ourselves, and encounter a "fall-regression into madness," but then recompense ourselves "by the construction of a symbolic universe," which "the subject projects on to reality as a kind of substitute-formation."[72] There is a void and I seek to fill it. The creative process can occur because cultural products are the result of my own destruction of my nature, brought on by the impermissibility of my impulse. Since the impulse is impermissible, I turn against the impulse and myself in a kind of madness of self-destruction; but the destruction is made good through the creation of culture, the creation of a "symbolic universe" in which I can pursue new impulses and a new version of myself in a different and higher form, or in a better-adjusted state.[73] There is a return to " 'normality' " in the new figure of the better-adjusted self.[74] Moreover, in this view, the creative process is endless, always promising something new, because an impulse that never attains its object can never be satisfied; it will continue to yearn for its object and keep searching for it,[75] turning from one object to the next, repeatedly creating symbolic substitutes in the process.

As a naturalist relying on the idea of continuity, the later Dewey seems to be at a loss in explaining the origins of culture. There would seem to be nothing in his account to explain those cases in which, to pass from nature to culture, individual desire to social norm, we have to negate a desire and create a symbolic substitute—when we have to create culture. For him, culture is already assumed, and it works on individual desire. He believes there are acts of assimilation, brought to bear on us as a matter of course by the actions of those in the group to which we belong, and we either adjust to these actions or not (and normally, he thinks, we easily adjust). But such a view does not seem able to account for the emergence of culture in the first place. Moreover, it could be construed as somewhat naïve. Very often we have to *force ourselves* to adjust and give up all hope of fulfilling our desire. We have to negate our own desires in order to adopt the culture's norms. There must be a sudden break from our natural inclinations. It is not always easy to belong to a group. There must be moments of rupture, in which we compel ourselves to belong, but with this consolation: that we can *transform* the thwarted desire into a symbolic substitute in which a totally new meaning—in which culture—occurs, and we can find and fulfill our new, unique selves, *with new desires*, there. Participating in culture is a loss for us; some part of us must die; we must enter the " 'night of the world.' "[76] That is, some natural desires are not manifested in other activities, but must be obliterated; but we are compensated for this loss by some new cultural meaning, "the Light of *Logos*,"[77] and a new persona in relation to it, in which our new selves can partly find themselves, even if they never fully satisfy themselves in the end.

But if this account of human adjustment is correct, then it is the earlier and not the later Dewey who is better able to account for it. For the later Dewey's philosophy does not have available the concept of rupture that is required to explain how we could divide ourselves from ourselves in this way and create new meanings. The philosophy of the earlier Dewey, on the other hand, lends itself readily to the idea that we break from our given desires. His work implies that we are not continuous with ourselves, but are time and again detached and disrupted from ourselves. We become more social in the process, yes, but only by resisting what we have been and pressing forward to new determinations of ourselves, even at the cost of the total submission and denial of these former selves. And the early Dewey recommends that we engage in such breaking away, above all, from the various types of modernist selves that we might have adopted, not to mention from our given and natural egoistic selves.

The later Dewey, by contrast, is hard put to explain how something truly new can occur, specifically culture, which he implies must exist first to assimilate our natural impulses, but which, presumably, as a new and creative product appearing in the world, must have been the result, somehow, of our creative impulses. The problem exists for any naturalist relying on continuity: namely, explaining how the imagination can create anything that is truly new. If the imagination is always continuous with past creations, and its results destined for intelligent assimilation, how can it *be* imaginative and create something that is *new*? Mark Johnson notes that accounting for the imagination "may be one of the most difficult problems in all of philosophy."[78] There are no easy answers. But while the early Dewey shows at length in the *Psychology* how the creative power of rupture produces the actual meanings and values of culture, the later Dewey appears unable to show how the imagination can ever produce anything new, ruled as he is by the idea of continuity and the eternally smooth and easy transference of previous meanings. If we presuppose continuity, it is difficult to see, indeed, "how the new can emerge from the old, yet without merely replicating what has gone before."[79]

This whole issue remains an open question, for we certainly cannot decide in these few sentences whether continuity or rupture better explains the shift from nature to culture. This is surely a matter for continued dispute and debate. But the discussion so far should at least be enough to give us pause. Perhaps the early Dewey is not correct in maintaining that rupture is the fundamental process of meaning-making. But in stressing that rupture is involved in the transition from nature to culture, he clearly can be said to have advanced insights worthy of consideration, even to the point of posing a challenge to the later Dewey, despite the later Dewey's many great innovations in philosophy.

I conclude, therefore, that Dewey's early philosophy is more significant than many people have realized. The early philosophy marks out new territory in the idealist terrain, as I have shown by demonstrating how it departs from the idealism of Dewey's teacher, Morris, and from traditional readings of Hegel. It anticipates vital movements of contemporary thought in very surprising ways, putting it in league with fascinating new Hegelian thinkers such as Adorno, Derrida, and Žižek. The early philosophy also challenges a prominent form of naturalism today, namely Dewey's own later philosophy. And perhaps most importantly of all, Dewey's early philosophy gives us a way to respond to philosophical pessimism in our own day, and to critique our modern pessimistic culture. It offers us a way to have faith in life. The way pointed by the early Dewey may or may not prove correct in the end, but it certainly merits our consideration insofar as we are concerned at all with fundamental issues—issues of how to live, where to find meaning, and what kind of society we should struggle to create.

Notes

1. Good and Shook seek to demonstrate the continuities that exist between Dewey's earlier and later ideas. Good believes that "a clearer understanding of Dewey's continuing debt to Hegel clarifies important elements of his thought." He wants to show that a "'permanent Hegelian deposit'" remains in Dewey's later philosophy. Shook, for his part, wants to provide "a comprehensive account of the reasons for the emergence of Dewey's empiricist pragmatism from his early idealistic philosophy." He believes that "a satisfactory account of the progress of Dewey's thought . . . is essential to a full understanding of his mature philosophy." Both authors want to understand Dewey's early philosophy in order to understand his later philosophy, and they subordinate their discussion of the early philosophy to that end. Said another way, neither author makes it his goal to provide a full-length, systematic study of Dewey's early philosophy itself, that is, a comprehensive study that examines the manifold nuances of Dewey's early thought independently of its impact on his later thought. See James A. Good, *A Search for Unity in Diversity: The 'Permanent Hegelian Deposit' in the Philosophy of John Dewey* (Lanham, Md.: Lexington Books, 2006), xxiv (and note the book's subtitle); John R. Shook, *Dewey's Empirical Theory of Knowledge and Reality* (Nashville: Vanderbilt University Press, 2000), 1. The same point holds for their joint project in which the authors draw connections between Dewey's earlier and later philosophies in order to advance the thesis that "Dewey's mature philosophy can be seen to be a non-Marxist and nonmetaphysical type of left Hegelianism." See John R. Shook and James A. Good, *John Dewey's Philosophy of Spirit, with the 1897 Lecture on Hegel* (New York: Fordham University Press, 2010), ix. Shook's dissertation presents an interesting account of some key elements of Dewey's early thought, especially his epistemology. But here again the perspective is that of trying to understand,

as Shook puts it, "the story of John Dewey's philosophical travels through Hegelianism to instrumentalism," not his Hegelianism by itself on its own terms. See John Robert Shook, "John Dewey's Early Philosophy: The Foundations of Instrumentalism" (PhD diss., State University of New York at Buffalo, 1994), 1. Morton White's study, while it covers important aspects of Dewey's early philosophy, still focuses primarily on Dewey's "development." See Morton G. White, *The Origin of Dewey's Instrumentalism* (New York: Columbia University Press, 1943), xv.

2. Neil Coughlan's *Young John Dewey: An Essay in American Intellectual History* (Chicago: University of Chicago Press, 1975) comes close to what I am doing, but as the subtitle indicates, Coughlan's book is a study in intellectual history, not philosophy. The book offers short sketches of Dewey's early works, in the context of his biography and the work of his colleagues, and in relation to his later philosophy, but it does not offer a comprehensive study of Dewey's early philosophy as such. Victor Kestenbaum's *The Grace and the Severity of the Ideal: John Dewey and the Transcendent* (Chicago: University of Chicago Press, 2002) covers some aspects of Dewey's early idealism, but Kestenbaum makes it his "central aim . . . to propose that at least one version of pragmatism, John Dewey's, has an important place for the ideal" (1). Kestenbaum is still primarily concerned with Dewey's pragmatism. Robert J. Roth's *John Dewey and Self-Realization* (Westport, Conn.: Greenwood Press, 1962), although dealing with an idea important in the early work, focuses exclusively on Dewey's middle and later works. Once more, the primary concern is with Dewey's mature efforts.

3. See Shook's view of "The Standard Account" in John Robert Shook, "John Dewey's Early Philosophy," 12–16. Shook's "standard account" is an account of Dewey's transition from idealism to instrumentalism. The "standard view," as I employ it here, is a view of the estimation of Dewey's early philosophy as a whole, an estimation of its overall significance and value as a philosophy.

4. Both scholars show that Dewey's pragmatism owes a significant debt to his idealism. This means that his idealism is much more interesting than many people suppose, for it contains, at least in germ, some of his best insights, including his overcoming of dualisms and his emphasis on social life. See James A. Good, *A Search for Unity in Diversity*, xxv–xxvi. See also John R. Shook, *Dewey's Empirical Theory of Knowledge and Reality*, 5–6.

5. Coughlan, *Young John Dewey*. For a view of the young Dewey's basic goal that is similar to my own, although I argue for his greater importance and a fundamentally different method to his position, see Robert West-

brook's discussion of the early Dewey's attempt to feel at home in the world in Robert B. Westbrook, *John Dewey and American Democracy*. 2d printing (Ithaca, N.Y.: Cornell University Press, 1992), 30.

6. I borrow the term *rupture*, which I use throughout the present work, from Adorno. I also borrow the term *harmony*. See Theodor W. Adorno, *Hegel: Three Studies*, trans. Shierry Weber Nicholson (Cambridge, Mass.: MIT Press, 1999), 4–5. Key words by Dewey and others are italicized throughout the present work.

7. This position takes Dewey even beyond Good's "humanistic/historicist Hegel." See James A. Good, *A Search for Unity in Diversity*, chapter 1. The differences between my own account of Dewey's Hegelianism and Good's will become clearer as the work progresses, but they can be summed up by saying that my account emphasizes the concept of rupture over the union of rupture and reconciliation. The focus on rupture also distinguishes my account from Shook's account, which holds that "Dewey's entire philosophy" is one that insists upon "the hypothesis of continuity." See John R. Shook, *Dewey's Empirical Theory of Knowledge and Reality*, 146.

8. See, for example, Adorno, *Hegel: Three Studies*, 4–5;. Jean-Luc Nancy, *Hegel: The Restlessness of the Negative*, trans. Jason Smith and Steven Miller (Minneapolis: University of Minnesota Press, 2002), 8; and Slavoj Žižek, *The Ticklish Subject: The Absent Centre of Political Ontology* (London/New York: Verso, 2000), 29–32. I follow Good in comparing Dewey's version of Hegel to more contemporary versions, but I focus on readings of Hegel coming from the Continental tradition. See Good, *A Search for Unity in Diversity*, xxii; 231; and also note Good's references in chapter 1, 43–54. Good focuses mainly on recent Anglo-American interpretations of Hegel.

9. I sidestep the question of whether there are actually three different periods of Dewey's development, the early, middle, and late. Since my focus is exclusively on Dewey's early work, for the sake of convenience, I divide his entire efforts into the earlier work and what comes later, or simply "the later work."

10. John Dewey, "The Lesson of Contemporary French Literature," in *John Dewey: The Early Works* (Carbondale: Southern Illinois University Press, 1975), 3: 36–42. Hereafter all Dewey citations, unless otherwise indicated, are from *The Collected Works of John Dewey, 1882–1953*, edited by Jo Ann Boydston (Carbondale: Southern Illinois University Press, 1967–91). The citations will occur in text according to the following format: EW (*Early Works*), MW (*Middle Works*), LW (*Later Works*), followed by the volume number and page number, with the whole enclosed in parentheses. Hence the above citation, for example, would read (EW 3: 36–42).

11. For more on the Hegelian terms *negative* and *negation* as I will employ them throughout this book, see Richard Schacht, *Hegel and After: Studies in Continental Philosophy Between Kant and Sartre* (Pittsburgh: University of Pittsburgh Press, 1975), 47–48. See also Slavoj Žižek, *The Ticklish Subject*, 30–32.

12. This is similar to the idea of "transcendence" that Kestenbaum discusses, in that on both readings there is the search for the ideal. See Kestenbaum, *The Grace and the Severity of the Ideal*, 24ff.; 224ff. Note once more the difference between Kestenbaum's view and my own, however, in that I develop a comprehensive account of Dewey's early philosophy in relation to this and other ideas, whereas Kestenbaum is primarily interested in showing how this idea plays out in Dewey's later pragmatism.

13. George Sylvester Morris as quoted by Dewey (EW 3: 9).

14. G. W. F. Hegel, *Logic*, trans. William Wallace (Oxford: Oxford University Press, 1975), 35–36.

15. Žižek, *The Ticklish Subject*, 36.

1. DEWEY'S PROJECT

1. Jim Good notes that "at times, Dewey scholars . . . view Hegel as an embarrassment to Dewey." See James A. Good, *A Search for Unity in Diversity: The 'Permanent Hegelian Deposit' in the Philosophy of John Dewey* (Lanham, Md.: Lexington Books, 2006), xxi.

2. "Dewey began as a kind of Christian/Hegelian idealist. He then (thankfully) moved on. . . ." This sentiment characterizes well the nature of the standard view. See Peter Godfrey-Smith, "Dewey on Naturalism, Realism, and Science," in *Philosophy of Science* 69 (September 2002), S2. Accessed online on July 2, 2008, at http://www.people.fas.harvard.edu/~pgs/PGSonDeweyPSA2000.pdf.

3. For a similar reading of Dewey, see Matthew Sanderson, "Pessimism in the Thought of John Dewey," unpublished abstract, accessed May 5, 2009, third item at http://www.philosophy.uncc.edu/mleldrid/SAAP/MSU/PD04.html. Sanderson and I agree that Dewey confronted pessimism, and that his response to pessimism makes for an interesting contrast with Schopenhauer's response. Our positions differ, however, in that Sanderson focuses exclusively on the later Dewey, while I focus exclusively on the early Dewey. Moreover, Sanderson sees Dewey as a pessimist who shares Nietzsche's attitude toward life. In my view, the *early* Dewey, at any rate, is not a pessimist, and I see major differences between Dewey's attitude toward life and that of Nietzsche, as I explore in chapter 7. For a discussion of Dewey's later philos-

ophy as an alternative to something like pessimism and to modernity in general, see Melvin Rogers, *The Undiscovered Dewey: Religion, Morality, and the Ethos of Democracy* (New York: Columbia University Press, 2009), 28ff; 47–57.

4. Theodor W. Adorno, *Hegel: Three Studies*, trans. Shierry Weber Nicholson (Cambridge, Mass.: MIT Press, 1999), 4–5.

5. Ibid., 4–5.

6. I will explain the meaning of these different terms and their function in Dewey's thought as my examination of his philosophy progresses (see EW 2:259; 282; 251; 279).

7. For a previous use of the phrase "logic of rupture," emphasizing "conflicts and tensions" and "outcomes" that are "deferred," see Mike Gane, *Auguste Comte* (London and New York: Routledge, 2006), 30. Good and Shook also discuss Dewey's relation to the other idealists. Good sees Dewey as part of "the American Hegelian tradition." Shook says that "Dewey's early philosophy should be categorized as belonging to the Cairdian phase of idealism." I understand Dewey's early philosophy to be a new version of idealism, which comes closest to contemporary Continental readings of Hegel. See Good, *A Search for Unity in Diversity*, xxii; John R. Shook, *Dewey's Empirical Theory of Knowledge and Reality* (Nashville: Vanderbilt University Press, 2000), 66.

8. Anthony Quinton, "T. H. Green's 'Metaphysics of Knowledge,' " in *Anglo-American Idealism, 1865–1927*, ed. W. J. Mander (Westport, Conn.: Greenwood Press, 2000), 22.

9. Ibid., 22.

10. Ibid., 28.

11. W. J. Mander, "Introduction," in *Anglo-American Idealism, 1865–1927*, 9.

12. Ibid., 9.

13. Ibid., 9.

14. F. H. Bradley, *Appearance and Reality: A Metaphysical Essay*. 9th impression (Oxford: Oxford University Press, 1968), 473.

15. W. J. Mander, "Caird's Developmental Absolutism," in *Anglo-American Idealism, 1865–1927*, 51.

16. Ibid., 56.

17. I discuss Dewey's relation to Royce in this regard in chapter 3.

18. "John Dewey to Alice Chipman Dewey," 1894.10.10 (00206), in *The Correspondence of John Dewey, 1871–1952*, vol. 1, *1871–1918*, Past Masters series CD-ROM (Charlottesville, Va.: InteLex, 2002). I am indebted to Martin Coleman for making me aware of this letter.

19. Ibid.

20. Ibid.

21. Ibid.

22. Ibid.

23. Ibid.

24. Ibid.

25. Ibid.

26. Ibid.

27. See, for example, Raymond D. Boisvert, "The Nemesis of Necessity: Tragedy's Challenge to Deweyan Pragmatism," in *Dewey Reconfigured: Essays on Deweyan Pragmatism,* ed. Casey Haskins and David I. Seiple (Albany: State University of New York Press, 1999), 151–68.

28. See Michael A. Principe, "Danto and Baruchello: From Art to the Aesthetics of the Everyday," in *The Aesthetics of Everyday Life,* ed. Andrew Light and Jonathan M. Smith (New York: Columbia University Press, 2005), 58.

29. Neil Coughlan, *Young John Dewey: An Essay in American Intellectual History* (Chicago: University of Chicago Press, 1975), 156.

30. William James, quoted in Robert D. Robertson, *William James: In the Maelstrom of American Modernism* (Boston/New York: Houghton Mifflin Company, 2006), 306.

31. Robert Westbrook, *John Dewey and American Democracy,* 2d printing (Ithaca, N.Y.: Cornell University Press, 1992), 16.

32. Ibid., 8.

33. G. W. F. Hegel, *Logic,* trans. William Wallace (Oxford: Clarendon Press, 1975), 261.

34. "It is clear that Spirit has now got beyond the substantial life it formerly led . . . that it is beyond the immediacy of faith, beyond the satisfaction and security of the certainty that consciousness then had, of its reconciliation with the essential being . . . and now demands from philosophy . . . recovery through its agency of that lost sense of solid and substantial being." G. W. F. Hegel, *Phenomenology of Spirit,* trans. A. V. Miller (Oxford: Oxford University Press, 1977), 4.

35. Robert Stern, *Hegel and the Phenomenology of Spirit* (London: Routledge, 2002), 193. The Hegel text that Stern cites is *Phenomenology of Spirit,* 468.

36. See Robert Solomon, *From Hegel to Existentialism* (Oxford: Oxford University Press, 1987), 58.

37. Matthew Festenstein, "Dewey's Political Philosophy," section 1, in *Stanford Encyclopedia of Philosophy,* http://plato.stanford.edu/entries/dewey-political/; accessed December 12, 2010.

38. Richard Schacht, *Hegel and After: Studies in Continental Philosophy Between Kant and Sartre* (Pittsburgh: University of Pittsburgh Press, 1975), 46–47.

2. CULTURAL AND INTELLECTUAL BACKGROUND

The first two sections of chapter 2 are revisions of my article "Situating Dewey" published in *Americana: The E-Journal of American Studies in Hungary* 3, no. 2 (Fall 2007). The article can be accessed at: http://americana ejournal.hu/vol3no2/morse. My revision of this article is included here with kind permission from the publishers of the journal.

1. Allan Janik and Stephen Toulmin, *Wittgenstein's Vienna* (New York: Simon and Schuster, 1973; rpt., Chicago: Elephant Paperbacks, Ivan R. Dee, 1996), 67–91.

2. Ibid., 74ff.

3. Ibid., 74.

4. Ibid., 75.

5. Ibid., 74.

6. Ibid., 98–100.

7. Ibid., 94–96; 101–02.

8. Carl E. Schorscke, *Fin-de-Siècle Vienna: Politics and Culture* (New York: Knopf, 1985), 213–15; 221–25.

9. Ibid., 224–25. See plate II and figure 43.

10. Ibid., 225.

11. Janik and Toulmin, *Wittgenstein's Vienna*, 101.

12. As Schorske puts it, "here eros becomes pure aggression." See Carl E. Schorscke, *Fin-de-Siècle Vienna*, 335. See also figure 60 on p. 336.

13. Käthe Springer, "A 'Romanticism of the Nerves': The Literary Fin-de-Siècle," in Christian Brandstätter, ed., *Vienna 1900: Art, Life, and Culture* (New York: Vendome Press, 2006), 321.

14. Ibid., 323; 321.

15. Janik and Toulmin, *Wittgenstein's Vienna*, 108; emphasis in the original.

16. Ibid., 110.

17. Ibid., 110–11.

18. Ibid., 111.

19. Ibid., 197–98.

20. Ibid., 197–98.

21. Newton Garver, "The 'Silence' of Wittgenstein and Kraus," in *Writing the Austrian Tradition: Relations Between Philosophy and Literature*, ed. Wolf-

gang Huemer and Marc-Oliver Schuster (Edmonton: Wirth-Institute for Austrian and Central European Studies, University of Alberta Press, 2003), 67.

22. Janek and Toulmin, *Wittgenstein's Vienna*, 197–98.

23. Schorscke, *Fin-de-Siècle Vienna*, 221.

24. Ibid., 4.

25. Matthew Arnold, "Introduction," in *The English Poets*, vol. 1, xvii–xlvii, ed. Thomas Humphrey Ward (London and New York: Macmillan, 1881), as quoted by Dewey (EW 3: 110). (For more details, see "Checklist of References," EW 3: xxix.)

26. Matthew Arnold, *Poems*, vol. 2 (London: Macmillan., 1869), as quoted by Dewey (EW 3: 115). Hereafter all passages from poems by Arnold are as quoted by Dewey from this source (see "Checklist of References," EW 3: xxix).

27. Janik and Toulmin, *Wittgenstein's Vienna*, 146.

28. Ibid., 124. The point immediately following this about the different "spheres" of human activity comes from the same source, Ibid., 149.

29. Kant, as quoted by Janik and Toulmin, *Wittgenstein's Vienna*, 146.

30. Ibid., 146.

31. Ibid., 147–48. Note a subtle but key difference that will emerge on this point between Kantianism and Deweyan Hegelianism. Dewey will argue that these fundamental ideas are not merely regulatory, but are actually and literally true in the world to the extent that they get expressed in our experience, an expression that faith in these ideas assists and allows.

32. Ibid., 149.

33. Ibid., 149.

34. Ibid., 150.

35. Ibid., 124; see also Arthur Schopenhauer, *The World as Will and Representation*, vol. 1, trans. E. F. J. Payne (New York: Dover Publications, 1969), 416–17.

36. Janik and Toulmin, *Wittgenstein's Vienna*, 150–57.

37. Ibid., 164.

38. Schopenhauer, *The World as Will and Representation*, 99–110.

39. Ibid., 99–110; 162–65. See especially this passage: "The will itself has no ground; the principle of sufficient reason . . . extends only to the representations, to the phenomenon" (107). The will has no basis in anything solid, has no reason behind it, and is always unsatisfied, "an endless striving" (164).

40. Ibid., 408–12. These are surely some of the most sad and moving pages in all of philosophy.

41. On Kraus's debt to Schopenhauer, see again Janik and Toulmin, *Wittgenstein's Vienna*, 74ff. On Klimt's relation to Schopenhauer, see Schorske, *Fin-de-Siècle Vienna*, 228–31.

42. Janik and Toulmin, *Wittgenstein's Vienna*, 161.

43. Ibid., 155–57.

44. Ibid., 158–61; see especially 160.

45. Neil Coughlan, in *Young John Dewey*, implies that "The Present Position of Logical Theory" is an unimportant text, serving primarily as an advance notice of the work Dewey was engaged in with one Franklin Ford. Ford was "an eccentric" journalist who, with Dewey, planned to publish an ill-conceived newspaper called "Thought News," whose goal was to be a warehouse for all the facts in the world, to help people think them through better. In fact, Coughlan does not establish the connection between "The Present Position of Logical Theory" and "Thought News"; he establishes only their simultaneous or near-simultaneous publication. See Neil Coughlan, *Young John Dewey*, 93–95; 98–100.

46. Richard Gale attributes to the early Dewey and to Hegel the position that unities of meaning are "imposed on us by some behind-the-scenes machinations by the Absolute or God." But, as "The Present Position of Logical Theory" shows, Dewey understood the opposite position to be the case, and to have been the real strength of Hegel—namely, the position that the unities of meaning are not "imposed" but rather develop out of actual life. Gale does not discuss Dewey's early thought at length, but he seems to share the standard view that unity is the central concept and not rupture, as I am claiming. See Richard M. Gale, *John Dewey's Quest for Unity: The Journey of a Promethean Mystic* (Amherst, N.Y.: Prometheus Books, 2010), 11.

47. Alison Stone, *Petrified Intelligence: Nature in Hegel's Philosophy* (Albany: State University of New York Press, 2005), 29.

48. Ibid., xi.

49. Schorscke, *Fin-de-Siècle Vienna*, 225–26.

3. REHABILITATING DEWEY'S *PSYCHOLOGY*

I presented a previous version of this chapter at the tenth annual meeting of the Midwest Pragmatist Study Group in Indianapolis, Indiana, in September 2008.

1. Tom Alexander, Jim Good, and John Shook, for example, have each discussed the *Psychology* in their books on Dewey. However, even where their discussions are favorable, none of them ascribes to the book any great and lasting merit as a philosophical work in its own right. Alexander points

out that "no one denied it was an impressive first book," but then he gives an account of the *Psychology* that points out its big flaws relative to Dewey's more mature works. See Thomas M. Alexander, *John Dewey's Theory of Art, Experience, and Nature: The Horizons of Feeling* (Albany: State University of New York, Press, 1987), 25–34. While Good and Shook take the *Psychology* more seriously than Alexander, their treatments of the text subordinate it to a discussion of its relation to Dewey's overall philosophical development, albeit in a fascinating and important discussion. See James A. Good, *A Search for Unity in Diversity: The "Permanent Hegelian Deposit" in the Philosophy of John Dewey* (Lanham, Md.: Lexington Books, 2006), 139–47, and John R. Shook, *Dewey's Empirical Theory of Knowledge and Reality* (Nashville: Vanderbilt University Press, 2000), 88–106; 123–33.

2. Throughout my analysis of the text, I will rely on the edition of the *Psychology* contained in John Dewey's *Collected Works* (EW 2: 1–363). This edition contains some of Dewey's revisions and, as a result, shows some indebtedness to William James and other later thinkers, as Dewey notes (EW 2: 5). However, as Herbert Schneider makes clear, in this edition "the main lines of [Dewey's] system are maintained" as he originally presented them (EW 2: xxvi). Most of his changes are minor. As Dewey puts it, "the only change involving an alteration of standpoint is in the general treatment of sensation" (EW 2: 5), a treatment, in fact, which still finds Dewey retaining his idealistic position, as we will see in chapter 4 of the present work. For additional confirmation that Dewey's idealism remains fundamentally intact, see John R. Shook, *Dewey's Empirical Theory of Knowledge and Reality* (Nashville: Vanderbilt University Press, 2000), 102–06.

3. Robert Westbrook, *John Dewey and American Democracy*, 2d printing (Ithaca: Cornell University Press, 1992), 27–29.

4. Ibid., 27.

5. Ibid., 28.

6. Ibid., 28.

7. G. Stanley Hall, in *American Journal of Psychology* 1 (1887): 154–59, as quoted by Westbrook in *John Dewey and American Democracy*, 28.

8. William James, in a letter to Croom Robertson in 1886, as quoted by Westbrook in *John Dewey and American Democracy*, 28.

9. Westbrook, *John Dewey and American Democracy*, 28–29.

10. Reproduced by George Dykhuizen, *The Life and Mind of John Dewey* (Carbondale: Southern Illinois University Press, 1978), 55–56; reprinted by Westbrook, *John Dewey and American Democracy*, 29 n. 28.

11. Westbrook, *John Dewey and American Democracy*, 28. Thanks to Ann Miller for the observation that James was then writing his *Psychology*.

NOTES TO PAGES 75–80

12. Good, *A Search for Unity in Diversity*, 147.

13. Westbrook, *John Dewey and American Democracy*, 26–27.

14. Ibid., 27.

15. This statement should not be taken to mean that just because we believe something to be true, the facts will oblige us. The statement means rather that facts are not facts independent of relations of meaning.

16. Jennifer Welchman, *Dewey's Ethical Thought* (Ithaca: Cornell University Press, 1995), 57.

17. The remainder of this quote (which is not actually from the *Psychology*) says that reason also seeks unity, which shows again that disunity and unity must work together. But in my account of Dewey, the unity is never fully complete, because the concept of faith that seeks unity is only a "spur" that drives us on to make meanings, not something that demonstrates that unity has been achieved (EW 2: 358). I will explain this point more fully as we proceed.

18. A previous version of this account of the self is presented in my article, "Pragmatism and Personal Identity," in *Identity and Social Transformation: Central European Pragmatist Forum*, vol. 5, ed. John Ryder and Radim Sip (Amsterdam: Rodopi Press, forthcoming).

19. Dewey may have taken to heart this passage from Hegel, and developed it in his own way: "All work is directed only to the aim or end; and when it is attained, people are surprised to find nothing else but just the very thing which they had wished for. The interest lies in the whole movement." G. W. F. Hegel, *Logic*, trans. William Wallace (Oxford: Oxford University Press, 1975), 293.

20. Good, *A Search for Unity in Diversity*, xix; 25.

21. This core concept informs the subtitle of Žižek's book *The Ticklish Subject: The Absent Centre of Political Ontology* (London and New York: Verso, 2000).

22. Westbrook, *John Dewey and American Democracy*, 28.

23. Since Dewey's account of meaning making in the *Psychology* depends on the self's striving for the Absolute, I disagree with Jim Good when he says that Dewey's "'perfect Personality'" or Absolute "is utterly inessential to the theories presented in the book." The early Dewey needs the concept of the Absolute to give him an ultimate ideal to strive for, an ideal which, as ultimate, is always lacking in real life, and therefore creates an experience of need in us that forever drives us on to create human meanings at a higher level. See Good, *A Search for Unity in Diversity*, 144–145.

24. Josiah Royce, *The Religious Aspect of Philosophy: A Critique of the Bases of Conduct and of Faith* (Cambridge, Mass.: Riverside Press, 1913).

25. Royce, *The Religious Aspect of Philosophy*, 433.

26. Ibid. 348.

27. Ibid., 334.

28. Ibid., 335.

29. *Idealized* and *idealization* are terms that Dewey uses throughout the *Psychology* and that I will use throughout this book. In general, these terms mean that the mind "goes beyond the sensuous *existence*, which is actually *present*, and gives this present datum meaning by connecting it with the self, and thus putting into it significance, which as bare existence it does not have" (EW 2: 122). The terms are related to *negation*, a term Dewey does not use, as far as I can tell, although the concept of negation is certainly at work in the *Psychology* (see my introduction for a discussion of negation). The relationship between negation and idealization would seem to be as follows: negation is the separating of "the sensuous existence" from its own "bare existence," while idealization is the process by which the sensuous existence, once separated from itself, is taken "beyond" what it was to become something significant.

30. G. W. F. Hegel, *Logic*, 293.

4. THE NATURE OF KNOWLEDGE

1. In effect, the early Dewey is advancing the idea that, in the words of Richard Rorty, "there is nothing which is vital to the self-identity of a being, independent of the descriptions we give of it." See Richard Rorty, *Philosophy and Social Hope* (London: Penguin Books, 1999), 235.

2. It is at this point that Dewey parts from Rorty's conception of things. The early Dewey will see great merit in holding that, precisely because there is no given identity to things, we are entitled to believe that things have been given to us to allow room, as it were, for the endless development of perfection, the endless development of a world that ought to be rather than merely the one that is.

3. This view is not really as odd as it may at first appear. In some ways it is similar to Richard Rorty's sensible view that "the world is out there, but descriptions of the world are not," by which he means that there is something there that affects us, but there is no one best way of describing what that is. The truth and meaning of what is there depend on our various descriptions of it. So, to put this point in the early Dewey's terms, brain activities (something out there in the world) may be the occasion for the occurrence of sensations, but sensations are not the same thing as brain activities; sensations depend on what we do with our brain activities, how we

invest them with our meanings, and so on, not on what is given in those brain activities as such. See Richard Rorty, *Contingency, Irony, and Solidarity* (Cambridge: Cambridge University Press, 1993), 5.

4. Although it must be stressed again that the facts allow this virtual addition to hold for them, even if the virtual addition cannot be derived from the facts. This is precisely what it means for meaning to be produced by rupture—it must be rupture out of something, and yet a new creation from out of it.

5. I continue to use Dewey's example of the orange in my analysis and throughout the book.

6. These interests, and hence the resulting knowledge, may accordingly be different for different knowers. As Dewey puts it, "the hog reads into the apple simply that it is good to eat; Sir Isaac Newton that it exemplifies the law of all falling bodies. Each puts self into the same sensation, and the result is a world-wide difference" (EW 2: 125).

7. In his introduction to the *Psychology*, Herbert Schneider notes that introducing this point is the main change that Dewey made in his revisions of the *Psychology*. Schneider suggests that this change brings Dewey a little closer to pragmatism than idealism, since now the interaction with things seems to play a more important role in knowledge. However, Schneider also notes that Dewey's idealism "continued through the revisions of *Psychology*." This is correct, because, for Dewey, even when we absorb something from "things," we are still only absorbing what we have already put into them. Said another way, there is still never a first fact that we interact with in a direct and unmediated fashion. Instead, motions suddenly become a sensuous continuum, which suddenly becomes a series of distinct sensations, which then suddenly get unified into a single field of sensations, that is, into perceived objects or things, with which we interact, learn from, and grow, and so on. See Herbert W. Schneider, "Introduction to Dewey's *Psychology*," in John Dewey, *The Early Works, 1882–1898*, vol. 2, *1887*, edited by Jo Ann Boydston (Carbondale: Southern Illinois University Press, 1967), xxiv.

5. WHAT WE KNOW

1. As Dewey sees it, science and philosophy "find their function in enriching" this basic intuition (EW 2: 212). But as Dewey explains, "the final reality for man is that which cannot be made out actually to exist. The religious life only brings this element to conscious recognition" (EW 2: 292). At most, we can only assert that God, or a complete understanding of every-

thing, exists, and this assertion is the basis of our trying to construct the kind of world in which we could understand everything. For Dewey, what prevents this intellectual search from being a vain striving is, I suspect, the persistence of the intuition, or something like hope, as well as the actual attainment of knowledge that science and philosophy do make possible.

6. FEELING, WILL, AND SELF-REALIZATION

1. I also very briefly discuss the early Dewey's account of the self and its possibilities for growth in my article "Pragmatism and Personal Identity," in *Identity and Social Transformation: Central European Pragmatist Forum*, vol. 5, ed. John Ryder and Radim Sip (Amsterdam: Rodopi Press, forthcoming).

2. See Slavoj Žižek, *The Ticklish Subject: The Absent Centre of Political Ontology* (London and New York: Verso, 2000).

3. "Knowledge," Dewey insists, "is an affair not only of objective relations, but of value for me. It bears an indescribable, absolutely personal relation to me," at least in part because I am constructing that knowledge myself (EW 2: 257).

4. I continue with Dewey's previous orange example throughout the book.

5. Note that Dewey references a book on pessimism in this discussion (EW 2: 255).

6. Albert Camus, *The Stranger*, trans. Matthew Ward (New York: Vintage Books, 1989).

7. For a reconstruction of the early Dewey's possible response to death, see chapter 7. In chapter 8, I discuss how losing our sense of self is essential for the realization of culture, or the higher meaning of our self.

8. See G. W. F. Hegel, *Introductory Lectures on Aesthetics*, trans. Bernard Bosanquet, ed. Michael Inwood (London: Penguin Books, 1993), 90–96.

9. Dewey notes that we can have sympathy for the joy of others in addition to the grief of others. But he adds that "the community of sorrow seems wider than that of gladness" (EW 2: 284).

10. I differ from John Shook on this key point. Shook holds that, for Dewey, "the attainment of union with God is the experience of faith," or more simply, "this ideal can be realized." My position is that the union with God, for Dewey, is never attained; we only ever approximate it. Faith gives us the feeling of its attainment, but only with the explicit recognition that we do not attain it. That is to say, faith enables us to carry on and to think that our efforts, which always come up short, are nonetheless amounting to

something. See John R. Shook, *Dewey's Empirical Theory of Knowledge and Reality* (Nashville: Vanderbilt University Press, 2000), 142–43.

11. I give a fuller description of this process in chapter 8.

12. There are some interesting similarities between the early Dewey and Freud, which I discuss in chapter 8, specifically with regard to the act of repression.

13. Robert Westbrook, *John Dewey and American Democracy,* 2d printing (Ithaca, N.Y.: Cornell University Press, 1992), 28.

7. BEYOND MODERNIST CULTURE

1. Allan Janik and Stephen Toulmin, *Wittgenstein's Vienna* (New York: Simon and Schuster, 1973; rpt. Chicago: Elephant Paperbacks, Ivan R. Dee, 1906), 157–61.

2. Søren Kierkegaard, *Provocations: Spiritual Writings of Kierkegaard,* ed. Charles Moore (Maryknoll, N.Y.: Orbis Books, 2007), 62–64; 58.

3. Ibid., 58–61.

4. Ibid., 58.

5. Ibid., 136–137.

6. Ibid., 139.

7. Ibid., 89–90. Here Kierkegaard uses the example of Abraham to exemplify this irrational assertion.

8. Ibid., 133–35.

9. Ibid., 58. From the side of objective reflection, he admits, "a solely subjective definition of truth make lunacy and truth indistinguishable."

10. Ibid., 58. "However, is not the absence of inwardness also lunacy?" he asks.

11. Ibid., 136.

12. Søren Kierkegaard, *Fear and Trembling,* trans. Alastair Hannay (London: Penguin Books, 1985), 67ff.; 80ff.

13. For the Kokoschka work, see Carl Schorske, *Fin-de-Siècle Vienna: Politics and Culture* (New York: Knopf, 1985), 336; Schorske mentions Gerstl's suicide on p. 354. The Gerstl painting I am referring to is *Self-Portrait, Laughing,* which is reproduced in Patrick Werkner, *Austrian Expressionism: The Formative Years,* trans. Nicholas T. Parsons (Palo Alto: Society for the Promotion of Science and Scholarship, 1993), 43.

14. Albert Camus, *The Stranger,* trans. Matthew Ward (New York: Vintage Books, 1989), 26–28.

15. Ibid., 20. See also p. 8.

16. Ibid., 3; 6.

17. Ibid., 6.

18. Ibid., 122.

19. Ibid., 123.

20. Robert Westbrook, *John Dewey and American Democracy*, 2d printing (Ithaca, N.Y.: Cornell University Press, 1992), 8.

21. Friedrich Nietzsche, *The Genealogy of Morals and Ecce Homo*, trans. Walter Kaufmann (New York: Vintage Books, 1989), 218.

22. Friedrich Nietzsche, "On Truth and Lies in a Nonmoral Sense," in *Philosophy and Truth: Selections from Nietzsche's Notebooks of the Early 1870's*, ed. and trans. Daniel Breazeale (Amherst, N. Y.: Humanity Books, 1979), 80.

23. Friedrich Nietzsche, *Twilight of the Idols and The Anti-Christ*, trans. R. J. Hollingdale (London: Penguin Books, 1990), 121.

24. Friedrich Nietzsche, "Attempt at a Self-Criticism," in *The Birth of Tragedy and The Case of Wagner*, trans. Walter Kaufmann (New York: Vintage Books, 1967), 17.

25. Friedrich Nietzsche, *Twilight of the Idols and The Anti-Christ*, 121.

26. Friedrich Nietzsche, "Epilogue," in *The Birth of Tragedy and The Case of Wagner*, 190.

27. Friedrich Nietzsche, *Thus Spoke Zarathustra: A Book for None and All*, trans. Walter Kaufmann (London: Penguin Books, 1978), 324.

28. Friedrich Nietzsche, "Attempt at a Self-Criticism," in *The Birth of Tragedy and The Case of Wagner*, 23.

29. Friedrich Nietzsche, *Thus Spoke Zarathustra*, 12.

30. And the overman will do so even though "there is little prudence in it, least of all the reason of all men." Ibid., 36.

31. Nietzsche, *The Genealogy of Morals and Ecce Homo*, 218.

32. "What's that? *Everything* is only—human, all too human?" See Friedrich Nietzsche, *Human, All Too Human: A Book for Free Spirits*, trans. Marion Faber, with Stephen Lehmann (Lincoln: University of Nebraska Press, 1996), 4.

33. See, for example, Nietzsche, *The Genealogy of Morals and Ecce Homo*, 95–96. See also Nietzsche, *Twilight of the Idols and The Anti-Christ*, 121, and Nietzsche, "Epilogue," in *The Birth of Tragedy and The Case of Wagner*, 190–92.

34. William James, "Is Life Worth Living?" in *Essays on Faith and Morals*, ed, Ralph Barton Perry (Cleveland and New York: Meridian Books, 1962), 20.

35. The subtitle of *Ecce Homo* is *How One Becomes What One Is*.

36. Friedrich Nietzsche, *The Gay Science*, trans. Walter Kaufmann (New York: Vintage Books, 1974), 223.

37. Friedrich Nietzsche, *Thus Spoke Zarathustra*, 62–65; Nietzsche, *Beyond Good and Evil: Prelude to a Philosophy of the Future*, trans. Walter Kaufmann (New York: Vintage Books, 1966), 53.

38. Lawrence J. Hatab, *A Nietzschean Defense of Democracy: An Experiment in Postmodern Politics* (Chicago and Lasalle: Open Court, 1995), 186.

39. See Hatab's response to this objection in *A Neitzschean Defense of Democracy*, 187–91. He seems to agree with my assessment of the consequences of Nietzsche's position, although he does not think it is a problem.

40. Friedrich Nietzsche, *Twilight of the Idols and The Anti-Christ*, 127.

41. I am assuming that not all people are divided into the herd and the free thinkers, and that lots of different kinds of people exist from whom we might learn. I do not argue this point, because I take it that everyday experience establishes it sufficiently, although I must admit that stifling conformity also exists in contemporary life.

42. Nietzsche, *Twilight of the Idols and The Anti-Christ*, 181.

43. As Dewey will later put the same point, "even in the midst of conflict, struggle, and defeat a consciousness is possible of the enduring and comprehending whole" (MW 14: 226). Through recognition of this fact, he says, "we put off mortality and live in the universal" (MW 14: 227). One might perhaps think here of a poem by Dylan Thomas for a poetic equivalent of Dewey's idea. See Dylan Thomas, "And Death Shall Have No Dominion," in *Collected Poems, 1934–1952* (London: Dent, 1954), 68.

44. For an example of this kind of reading, see Jennifer Welchman, *Dewey's Ethical Thought* (Ithaca, N.Y.: Cornell University Press, 1995), 63–88.

45. As Kant puts it, "this principle of humanity . . . is the supreme limiting condition on the freedom of action of each man. . . . By this principle all maxims are rejected which are not consistent with the will's giving universal law. The will is not only subject to the law, but subject in such a way that it must be conceived also as itself prescribing the law." Immanuel Kant, *Foundations of the Metaphysics of Morals*, 2d ed., trans. Lewis White Beck (Upper Saddle River, N.J.: Prentice Hall, 1997), 47–48.

8. A NEW IDEALISM

1. Robert Westbrook, *John Dewey and American Democracy*, 2d printing (Ithaca, N.Y.: Cornell University Press, 1992), 20.

2. Ibid., 21.

3. Ibid., 16–21.

4. Martin Heidegger, *Being and Time: A Translation of* Sein und Zeit, trans. Joan Stambaugh (Albany: State University of New York Press, 1996), 176.

5. Martin Heidegger, *Introduction to Metaphysics,* trans. Gregory Fried and Richard Polt (New Haven: Yale University Press, 2000), 1–2.

6. This point is confirmed by Shook. However, Shook goes on to say that Dewey's concern with God "seems to be an add-on without justification or need," whereas I would say that his concern with religion per se is de-emphasized, although his adherence to the concept of the Absolute as the source of rupture is retained, even to make social meaning and experience possible. See John Robert Shook, "John Dewey's Early Philosophy: The Foundation of Instrumentalism" (PhD diss., State University of New York at Buffalo, 1994), 76.

7. George S. Morris, *Philosophy and Christianity*, reprint ed. (Hicksville, N.Y.: Regina Press, 1975).

8. Ibid., v.

9. Ibid., vii.

10. Ibid., 1–19.

11. Ibid., 51.

12. Ibid., 51.

13. Ibid., 52.

14. Ibid., 52.

15. Ibid., 52.

16. Ibid., 52.

17. Ibid., 53.

18. Ibid., 54.

19. See chapter 1 for a discussion of Green's philosophy.

20. Morris, *Philosophy and Christianity*, 241.

21. Ibid., 251.

22. Ibid., 73;103.

23. Ibid., 103.

24. Ibid., 102.

25. Ibid., 103.

26. Ibid., 103.

27. Ibid., 1. Though Morris uses "the rock of ages" metaphor to talk about "intelligence" and "religion" in general, what he later goes on to say about these things, especially religion, would seem to be identical with what he wants to say about the eternal nature of the Absolute as well. See also *Philosophy and Christianity*, 103.

28. Robert Westbrook, *John Dewey and American Democracy*, 21.

29. James A. Good, "John Dewey's 'Permanent Hegelian Deposit' and the Exigencies of War," in *Journal of the History of Philosophy* 44, no. 2 (April 2006): 293–313.

30. James A. Good, *A Search for Unity in Diversity: The 'Permanent Hegelian Deposit' in the Philosophy of John Dewey* (Lanham, Md.: Lexington Books, 2006), 1ff. For Good's interpretation that Hegel privileged unity, see Good, *A Search for Unity in Diversity*, 3.

31. Theodor W. Adorno, *Hegel: Three Studies*, trans. Shierry Weber Nicholson (Cambridge, Mass.: MIT Press, 1999), 4–5; emphasis added.

32. Jean-Luc Nancy, *Hegel: The Restlessness of the Negative*, trans. Jason Smith and Steven Miller (Minneapolis: University of Minnesota Press, 2002), 8.

33. Ibid., 6.

34. Slavoj Žižek, *The Ticklish Subject: The Absent Centre of Political Ontology* (London and New York: Verso, 2000), 30; 377ff.

35. Adorno, *Hegel: Three Studies*, 4–5

36. Ibid., 4–5.

37. Theodor Adorno, *Minima Moralia: Reflections from Damaged Life*, trans. E. F. N. Jephcott (New York and London: Verso, 1997), 247.

38. Adorno, *Hegel: Three Studies*, 4.

39. Ibid., 5–7.

40. Ibid., 4.

41. This is why some commentators insist on Hegel's realism, as opposed to seeing him solely as an idealist. As Adorno puts it, "To the extent to which one can speak of realism in Hegel, it is to be found in the path followed by his idealism; it is not something heterogeneous to it. In Hegel the tendency of idealism is to move beyond itself" (*Hegel: Three Studies*, 5).

42. Nancy, *Hegel: The Restlessness of the Negative*, 5.

43. Ibid., 8.

44. Ibid., 7.

45. Ibid., 9.

46. Ibid., 10.

47. Ibid., 9.

48. Ibid., 70–71.

49. Ibid., 76.

50. Ibid., 78.

51. In my view, it should not surprise us that Dewey's late-nineteenth-century position could resemble postmodernism. For, as Lyotard reminds us, postmodernism always occurs within modernism. "The postmodern," he says, "would be that which, in the modern . . . searches for new presentations." See Jean-Francois Lyotard, *The Postmodern Condition: A Report on Knowledge,* trans. Geoff Bennington and Brian Massumi (Minneapolis: University of Minnesota Press, 1999), 81.

52. Niall Lucy, *A Derrida Dictionary* (Oxford: Blackwell Publishing, 2004), 61.

53. Ibid., 59.

54. Ibid., 61.

55. Ibid., 63–64.

56. "1. The Future/L'Avenir," in *Derrida: A Film by Kirby Dick and Amy Ziering Kofman*, DVD (Los Angeles: Jane Doe Films, 2002).

57. Niall Lucy, *A Derrida Dictionary*, 24–25.

58. Ibid., 25.

59. For Derrida's relation to Hegel, see Jacques Derrida, "Tympan," in *Margins of Philosophy*, trans. Alan Bass (Chicago: University of Chicago Press, 1982), ix–xxix.

60. See this comment in particular: "Instruction in what to do next can never come from an infinite goal, which for us is bound to be empty. It can be derived only from study of the deficiencies, irregularities, and possibilities of the actual situation" (MW 14: 199). This view is fundamentally different from the early Dewey's idea that an infinite goal is precisely the end of our actions, although we do not know what it is; we know it only by the harmonies it produces. The whole discussion surrounding this passage could, in fact, be read as the later Dewey's critique of his former position. This discussion would then contain a good deal of insight into why Dewey ultimately shifted his position—namely, his early philosophy eventually made him feel "discouragement and despair" because it meant "every attained satisfaction is only forever bound to be only a disappointment." In the end, he craved unity in a way that his earlier self, with his philosophy of rupture, would not endorse. See MW 14: 199. Kestenbaum also discusses this passage and the division it represents in Dewey's work. See Victor Kestenbaum, *The Grace and the Severity of the Ideal: John Dewey and the Transcendent* (Chicago: University of Chicago Press, 2002), 25.

61. He also retains continuity in his theory of inquiry, I would argue, because inquiry involves the reorganization of existing elements in the indeterminate situation, never an outright negation of any element and a leap away from it toward a new formation.

62. Žižek, *The Ticklish Subject*, 34–35.

63. Ibid., 36.

64. Ibid., 35.

65. I do not mean to imply that the early Dewey anticipated the distinct views of Freud or Lacan. The point to take away is rather that certain elements may have already been in place for such conceptions in the idealist tradition, especially the concept of negation.

66. Žižek, *The Ticklish Subject*, 36.

67. As the later Dewey says, "suppression is not annihilation" (MW 14: 109). Given his whole approach, it seems safe to assume he believes the same thing about sublimation.

68. Dewey reiterates this point about impulses when he insists that their meaning is "not native" and that by themselves they are "as meaningless as a gust of wind on a mudpuddle" (MW14: 65).

69. For a similar account of the two different roles that imagination can play, but an account with different consequences and implications than I draw out here, especially since the account attributes both roles to the later Dewey, whereas I would not, see Kestenbaum, *The Grace and the Severity of the Ideal*, 223–25. I also draw out the larger cultural implications of both roles and emphasize the latent Freudian elements involved in the one role, while Kestenbaum focuses on the different functions of the imagination as such.

70. Žižek, *The Ticklish Subject*, 34; 36.

71. Ibid., 36.

72. Ibid., 34–35.

73. Ibid., 35.

74. Ibid., 35.

75. I am grateful to Britt-Marie Schiller for this insight.

76. Žižek, *The Ticklish Subject*, 34.

77. Ibid., 34.

78. Mark Johnson, *The Meaning of the Body: Aesthetics of the Human Understanding* (Chicago: University of Chicago Press, 2007), 13.

79. Ibid., 13. Johnson believes such a thing can be achieved; and I agree with him. But the position does present a certain difficulty, as Johnson notes.

Bibliography

Adorno, Theodor. *Minima Moralia: Reflections from Damaged Life.* Translated by E. F. N. Jephcott. London and New York: Verso, 1997.

———. *Hegel: Three Studies.* Translated by Shierry Weber Nicholson. Cambridge, Mass.: MIT Press, 1999.

Alexander, Thomas M. *John Dewey's Theory of Art, Experience, and Nature: The Horizons of Feeling.* Albany: State University of New York, Press, 1987.

Bradley, F. H. *Appearance and Reality: A Metaphysical Essay.* 9th impression. Oxford: Oxford University Press, 1968.

Boisvert, Raymond D. "The Nemesis of Necessity: Tragedy's Challenge to Deweyan Pragmatism." In *Dewey Reconfigured: Essays on Deweyan Pragmatism,* edited by Casey Haskins and David I. Seiple. Albany: State University of New York Press, 1999.

Camus, Albert. *The Stranger.* Translated by Matthew Ward. New York: Vintage Books, 1989.

Coughlan, Neil. *Young John Dewey: An Essay in American Intellectual History.* Chicago: University of Chicago Press, 1975.

Dick, Kirby and Amy Ziering Kofman. "1. The Future/L'Avenir." In *Derrida: A Film by Kirby Dick and Amy Ziering Kofman.* DVD. Los Angeles: Jane Doe Films, 2002.

Derrida, Jacques. *Margins of Philosophy.* Translated by Alan Bass. Chicago: University of Chicago Press, 1982.

Dewey, John. *The Collected Works of John Dewey, 1882–1953.* Edited by Jo Ann Boydston. Carbondale: Southern Illinois University Press, 1967–91.

———. "John Dewey to Alice Chipman Dewey," 1894.10.10 (00206). In *The Correspondence of John Dewey, 1871–1952.* Vol. 1, *1871–1918.* Edited by Larry Hickman. Past Masters series. CD-ROM. Charlottesville, Va.: InteLex Corporation, 2002.

Dykhuizen, George. *The Life and Mind of John Dewey.* Carbondale: Southern Illinois University Press, 1978.

Festenstein, Matthew. "Dewey's Political Philosophy," section 1. In *Stanford Encyclopedia of Philosophy*. http://plato.stanford.edu/entries/dewey-political/ (accessed December 12, 2010).

Gale, M. Richard. *John Dewey's Quest for Unity: The Journey of a Promethean Mystic*. Amherst, N.Y.: Prometheus Books, 2010.

Gane, Mike. *Auguste Comte*. London and New York: Routledge, 2006.

Garver, Newton. "The 'Silence' of Wittgenstein and Kraus." In *Writing the Austrian Tradition: Relations Between Philosophy and Literature*, edited by Wolfgang Huemer and Marc-Oliver Schuster. Edmonton: Wirth-Institute for Austrian and Central European Studies, University of Alberta, 2003.

Godfrey-Smith, Peter. "Dewey on Naturalism, Realism, and Science." *Philosophy of Science* 69 (September 2002). http://www.people.fas .harvard.edu/~pgs/PGSonDeweyPSA2000.pdf (accessed July 2, 2008).

Good, James A. *A Search for Unity in Diversity: The 'Permanent Hegelian Deposit' in the Philosophy of John Dewey*. Lanham, Md.: Lexington Books, 2006.

———"John Dewey's 'Permanent Hegelian Deposit' and the Exigencies of War." *Journal of the History of Philosophy* 44, no. 2 (April 2006): 293–313.

Hatab, Lawrence J. *A Nietzschean Defense of Democracy: An Experiment in Postmodern Politics*. Chicago: Open Court, 1995.

Heidegger, Martin. *Being and Time: A Translation of* Sein und Zeit. Translated by Joan Stambaugh. Albany: State University of New York Press, 1996.

———. *Introduction to Metaphysics*. Translated by Gregory Fried and Richard Polt. New Haven: Yale University Press, 2000.

Hegel, Georg Wilhelm Friedrich. *Logic*. Translated by William Wallace. Oxford: Oxford University Press, 1975.

———. *Phenomenology of Spirit*. Translated by A. V. Miller. Oxford: Oxford University Press, 1977.

———. *Introductory Lectures on Aesthetics*. Translated by Bernard Bosanquet. Edited by Michael Inwood. London: Penguin Books, 1993.

James, William. "Is Life Worth Living?" In *Essays on Faith and Morals*, edited by Ralph Barton Perry. Cleveland: Meridian Books, 1962.

Janik, Allan and Stephen Toulmin. *Wittgenstein's Vienna*. New York: Simon and Schuster, 1973. Reprint, Chicago: Elephant Paperbacks, Ivan R. Dee, 1996.

Johnson, Mark. *The Meaning of the Body: Aesthetics of Human Understanding*. Chicago: University of Chicago Press, 2008.

Kant, Immanuel. *Foundations of the Metaphysics of Morals*. Translated by Lewis White Beck. Upper Saddle River, N.J.: Prentice Hall, 1997.

Kestenbaum, Victor. *The Grace and the Severity of the Ideal: John Dewey and the Transcendent.* Chicago: University of Chicago Press, 2002.

Kierkegaard, Søren. *Fear and Trembling.* Translated by Alastair Hannay. London: Penguin Books, 1985.

———. *Provocations: Spiritual Writings of Kierkegaard.* Edited by Charles Moore. Maryknoll, N.Y.: Orbis Books, 2007.

Lucy, Niall. *A Derrida Dictionary.* Oxford: Blackwell Publishing, 2004.

Lyotard, Jean-Francois. *The Postmodern Condition: A Report on Knowledge.* Translated by Geoff Bennington and Brian Massumi. Minneapolis: University of Minnesota Press, 1999.

Mander, W. J. *Anglo-American Idealism, 1865–1927.* Westport, Conn.: Greenwood Press, 2000.

Morris, George S. *Philosophy and Christianity.* Reprint edition. Hicksville, N.Y.: Regina Press, 1975.

Morse, Don. "Pragmatism and Personal Identity." In *Identity and Social Transformation: Central European Pragmatist Forum, Volume 5,* edited by John Ryder and Radim Sip. Amsterdam: Rodopi Press, forthcoming.

———. "Situating Dewey." *Americana: The E-Journal of American Studies in Hungary* 3, no. 2 (Fall 2007). http://americanaejournal.hu/vol3no2/morse.

Nancy, Jean-Luc. *Hegel: The Restlessness of the Negative.* Translated by Jason Smith and Steven Miller. Minneapolis: University of Minnesota Press, 2002.

Nietzsche, Friedrich. *Beyond Good and Evil: Prelude to a Philosophy of the Future.* Translated by Walter Kaufmann. New York: Vintage Books, 1966.

———. *The Birth of Tragedy and The Case of Wagner.* Translated by Walter Kaufmann. New York: Vintage Books, 1967.

———. *The Gay Science.* Translated by Walter Kaufmann. New York: Vintage Books, 1974.

———. *Thus Spoke Zarathustra: A Book for All and None.* Translated by Walter Kaufmann. London: Penguin Books, 1978.

———. "On Truth and Lies in a Nonmoral Sense." In *Philosophy and Truth: Selections from Nietzsche's Notebooks of the Early 1870's,* edited and translated by Daniel Breazeale. Amherst, N.Y.: Humanity Books, 1979.

———. *The Genealogy of Morals and Ecce Homo.* Translated by Walter Kaufmann. New York: Vintage Books, 1989.

———. *Twilight of the Idols and The Anti-Christ.* Translated by R. J. Hollingdale. London: Penguin Books, 1990.

———. *Human, All Too Human: A Book for Free Spirits.* Translated by Marion Faber, with Stephen Lehman. Lincoln: University of Nebraska Press, 1996.

Principe, Michael A. "Danto and Baruchello: From Art to the Aesthetics of the Everyday." In *The Aesthetics of Everyday Life*, edited by Andrew Light and Jonathan M. Smith. New York: Columbia University Press, 2005.

Rice, Daniel F. *Reinhold Niebuhr and John Dewey: An American Odyssey*. Albany: State University of New York Press, 1993.

Robertson, Robert D. *William James: In the Maelstrom of American Modernism*. Boston/New York: Houghton Mifflin Company, 2006.

Rogers, Melvin. *The Undiscovered Dewey: Religion, Morality, and the Ethos of Democracy*. New York: Columbia University Press, 2009.

Rorty, Richard. *Contingency, Irony, and Solidarity*. Cambridge: Cambridge University Press, 1993.

———. *Philosophy and Social Hope*. London: Penguin Books, 1999.

Roth, Robert J. *John Dewey and Self-Realization*. Westport, Conn.: Greenwood Press, 1962.

Royce, Josiah. *The Religious Aspect of Philosophy: A Critique of the Bases of Conduct and of Faith*. Cambridge, Mass.: Riverside Press, 1913.

———. *The Philosophy of Loyalty*. Nashville: Vanderbilt University Press, 1995.

Sallis, John. *Spacings—of Reason and Imagination in Texts of Kant, Fichte, and Hegel*. Chicago: University of Chicago Press, 1987.

Sanderson, Matthew. "Pessimism in the Thought of John Dewey." Unpublished abstract; third item at http://www.philosophy.uncc.edu/mleldrid/SAAP/MSU/PD04.html (accessed May 5, 2009).

Schacht, Richard. *Hegel and After: Studies in Continental Philosophy Between Kant and Sartre*. Pittsburgh: University of Pittsburgh Press, 1975.

Schneider, Herbert W. "Introduction to Dewey's *Psychology*." In John Dewey, *The Early Works, 1882–1898*. Vol. 2, *1887*. Edited by Jo Ann Boydston. Carbondale: Southern Illinois University Press, 1967.

Schopenhauer, Arthur. *The World as Will and Representation*. Vol. 1. Translated by E. F. J. Payne. New York: Dover Publications, 1969.

Schorscke, Carl. *Fin-de-Siècle Vienna: Politics and Culture*. New York: Alfred A. Knopf, 1985.

Shook, John R. "John Dewey's Early Philosophy: The Foundations of Instrumentalism." Ph.D. diss., State University of New York at Buffalo, 1994.

———. *Dewey's Empirical Theory of Knowledge and Reality*. Nashville: Vanderbilt University Press, 2000

Shook, John R., and James A. Good. *John Dewey's Philosophy of Spirit, with the 1897 Lecture on Hegel*. New York: Fordham University Press, 2010.

Solomon, Robert. *From Hegel to Existentialism*. Oxford: Oxford University Press, 1989.

Springer, Käthe. "A 'Romanticism of the Nerves': The Literary Fin-de-Siècle." In *Vienna 1900: Art, Life, and Culture,* edited by Christian Brandstätter. New York: Vendome Press, 2006.

Stern, Robert. *Hegel and the Phenomenology of Spirit.* London: Routledge, 2002.

Stone, Allison. *Petrified Intelligence: Nature in Hegel's Philosophy.* Albany: State University of New York Press, 2005.

Thomas, Dylan. "And Death Shall Have No Dominion." In *Collected Poems, 1934–1952.* London: Dent, 1954.

Welchman, Jennifer. *Dewey's Ethical Thought.* Ithaca, N.Y.: Cornell University Press, 1995.

Werkner, Patrick. *Austrian Expressionism: The Formative Years.* Translated by Nicholas T. Parsons. Palo Alto: Society for the Promotion of Science and Scholarship, 1993.

Westbrook, Robert. *John Dewey and American Democracy.* 2d printing. Ithaca, N.Y.: Cornell University Press, 1992.

Weston, Richard. *Modernism.* New York and London: Phaidon Press, 2002.

White, Morton. *The Origin of Dewey's Instrumentalism.* New York: Columbia University Press, 1943.

Žižek, Slavoj. *The Ticklish Subject: The Absent Centre of Political Ontology.* London and New York: Verso, 2000.

Index

absolute, 3, 7, 9, 18–21, 63, 65, 70, 73, 75–
    80, 86, 141, 142, 150, 170, 175, 176, 181,
    186, 188, 239–41, 243–49, 259–64, 270
Addams, Jane, 21–23
Adorno, Theodor, 3, 10, 16, 84, 234, 249,
    258–60, 264, 281
aestheticism, 17, 151, 167
alienation, 23, 29, 30, 34, 48, 109, 163,
    236, 247, 248, 259
American Philosophy, 4, 24
animals, 14, 28, 68, 207
anti-foundationalism, 265, 270
antipathy, 169, 172, 217
apperception, 6, 81, 85, 98, 100, 101, 109–
    11, 148
a priori, 58
Arnold, Matthew, 42–48, 51, 54, 55, 60,
    222, 229

beauty, 20, 21, 39, 43, 45, 165, 167, 187,
    193–95, 240, 269
Being, the Question of, 237
Berkeley, George, 116
body, 48, 68, 74, 82, 86, 87, 117, 149, 153,
    159, 166, 173, 202, 203, 223, 239, 250,
    255
Bradley, Francis Herbert, 15, 18, 19
Browning, Robert, 47–48, 126
Caird, Edward, 19
chaos, 57, 97, 237
compassion, 52–53, 55
conscience, 181
consciousness, 18, 20–22, 26, 63, 65, 68,
    70–72, 77–79, 88, 91, 104, 114, 149,
    158–59, 198, 203, 212, 213, 228, 250–51

construction, 18, 112, 119–20, 149, 209,
    217, 263, 271, 278
Continental Philosophy, 24, 234, 249,
    258, 260, 264–65, 268–69
continuity, xi, 4, 10, 88, 90, 251, 252, 256,
    260–61, 270–71, 273–80
continuum, 89, 95–97
cosmos, 81, 85, 97, 113, 139, 143, 171, 173,
    175, 194, 207–8, 248
courage, 26, 157, 211, 219, 228
critique, 14, 17, 205, 211, 212, 216, 269,
    271, 281
cynicism, 17, 151, 231

death, 27–29, 40, 134, 138, 159–60, 199,
    206–8, 210–12, 214, 216, 219, 274, 278
deconstruction, 265–66, 268
democracy, 267–68
dependence, 136, 138, 139, 175, 180, 205,
    244
Derrida, Jacques, 205, 265–68, 281
desire, 38, 52, 55, 75, 82, 113, 146, 157, 162,
    166, 173, 184, 195, 213, 215, 223–25, 228,
    230–31, 262, 271–73, 276, 278–80
despair, 14, 15, 17, 23, 29–31, 34, 44, 47,
    53–56, 191–93, 195, 206–7, 231, 257
discontinuity, 10, 259, 272
disgust, 61, 169
divine, 30, 225
dread, 29, 30, 59, 213, 214
dualism, 73, 94, 176

education, 25, 75, 131
egoism, 17, 52, 168

emptiness, 25–26, 28–29, 31
essence, 38, 41, 43, 51, 98, 150, 188, 219, 232
Ethical Postulate, The, 225, 227, 229
evil, 38

faith, 7, 30, 43, 73, 75, 83, 85, 136, 143, 144, 155, 177, 179, 181–82, 185–93, 195, 204–5, 209, 227, 232, 239–40, 247–48, 255; and ethics, 225–26, 229; Kierkegaard on, 53, 192, 193; in life, 2, 13, 14, 31, 35, 60, 190, 206, 257, 281; and Nietzsche, 217; and religion, 28, 178, 218; and science, 44
formal logic, 56–57, 105, 131
foundationalism, 6
freedom, 39, 50, 141, 227, 229–31, 261–64
Freud, Sigmund, 41, 184, 271, 275

God, 3, 13, 22, 29, 50, 74, 97, 139, 141, 143, 175–76, 180, 192–93, 239–40, 245, 247
goodness, 27
Green, T. H. 18, 228, 244–45
growth, 6, 21–22, 33, 75, 110–11, 145, 150, 163, 174, 176, 181, 200, 226, 239, 250, 253, 255, 270, 273

habit, 102, 161, 252, 273
happiness, 146, 160, 177
harmony, 2, 3, 13, 15–16, 18, 19–20, 73, 77–78, 80, 97, 98, 154–55, 157, 173, 176–78, 181, 246, 249, 257, 259, 262
hate, 180, 199
health, 17, 27, 39, 125–26, 151, 153, 158, 161, 167, 172, 196–97, 205, 221, 232, 269, 272
Hegel, G. W. F., 2, 3, 8–9, 11–16, 24, 33–36, 57–59, 62–63, 78–80, 166, 211, 233, 236, 246–49, 264–65, 271–72, 281
Heideggerian, 237
humility, 169, 171–72

idealism, 2–4, 8–11, 14–15, 17, 35, 59, 63–65, 75, 80, 83, 114, 128, 190, 211–12, 214, 216–217, 233, 236–37, 239–40, 24, 246–47, 259, 268, 270, 281; British, 236, 264; and pragmatism, 248

idealization, 16, 82, 97, 105–7, 111, 114, 120, 147–49, 155, 180, 183, 187, 200, 202–7, 209, 218, 221, 232, 234–35, 237–39, 265
imagination, 40–41, 60, 81, 114, 123, 130, 135, 142, 237, 253, 269, 275–77, 280; creative, 124–25, 127; mechanical, 124
individual, the, 8, 14, 17, 18, 40, 44, 45, 54, 63, 65, 69, 76, 79–80, 114, 116, 124–26, 136–38, 147, 158, 173, 177, 181, 201, 207–8, 222–27, 229–31, 239, 243–44, 273–74
intuition, 48, 81, 113–14, 127, 137–43, 164, 208, 245

James, William, 29–30, 64–65, 214
joy, 3, 43–44, 47, 126, 156, 194, 213, 217
judgment, 85, 96, 128–34, 142, 168, 181, 259, 269; analytic, 130–31; synthetic, 130–31
justice, 94, 97, 183, 235–36, 256, 265–67

Kant, Immanuel, 36, 49–51, 53–57, 191, 229–30, 288
Kierkegaard, Søren, 38, 53–54, 191–93, 204
Klimt, Gustav, 39, 60, 191, 194
Kokoschka, Oskar, 39, 191, 194
Kraus, Karl, 37–38, 51

language, 69, 70, 129, 153
law, 8, 40, 45, 50, 57, 68–69, 90–91, 129, 134, 159, 172, 180–81, 222–23, 226, 266–67; of conservation of energy, 251; and facts, 135; of justice, 234–35; and Kant, 229; moral, 230, 256
"Lessons of Contemporary French Literature, The," 5, 25, 29, 31
Loos, Adolph, 39
love, 27, 32, 53, 94, 97, 180, 213–15, 269

madness, 192–94, 205, 215–16, 219, 271, 278
materialism, 5, 30, 85, 89, 92–94, 116, 213–14, 238
memory, 81, 114, 119–24, 127, 130, 135, 142, 251–52, 269

Mersault, 159, 198–99
metaphysics, 64, 77
modernism, 5, 7, 37–39, 41–43, 45–46, 48–49, 51, 53–56, 59–60, 73–74, 81–83, 112, 126, 135, 147, 151, 158, 187, 190–93, 195, 199, 206–7, 212, 216, 221, 223, 227, 229, 231, 247, 267
morality, 20, 31, 54, 176, 185, 188, 220–21, 255, 265, 272
Morris, George Sylvester, 8–9, 14, 233–34, 236–47, 264, 281
mystical experience, 14, 30, 210, 248

Nancy, Jean-Luc, 3, 10, 205, 234, 249, 258, 260–64
naturalism, 3, 11, 31–32, 35, 50, 270, 281
necessity, 140–41, 237–38, 260, 263, 265
negation, 7–8, 14, 147, 163, 200, 249, 262–63, 272, 278
Nietzsche, Friedrich, 2, 9, 13, 15, 41, 211–17, 219
nihilism, 5, 26, 215, 266

Outlines of a Critical Theory of Ethics, 59, 221, 241

pain, xiii, 82, 146, 153, 157, 159–60, 183
peace, 175–76, 179, 208–11, 216
perception, 3, 49–51, 72, 81, 101, 114–16, 118–27, 130, 133, 135, 138, 142, 149, 179, 253–54, 269
personality, 27–28, 31–34, 55, 166, 170–73, 175–76, 180–81, 208, 255, 266
pessimism, 2, 5, 7–9, 13–15, 17, 23–37, 54–56, 59–61, 190–191, 193, 195, 205–6, 213–15, 221–22, 234, 238, 241–42, 246, 265, 281
Phenomenology of Spirit, the, 33
Philosophy of Nature, the, 58
pleasure, 82, 146, 153, 157, 159–60, 183, 193
poetry, 5, 42–47, 54, 126, 166, 182, 185, 195, 222
Pragmatism, 10, 14, 270; and idealism, 248
"Present Position of Logical Theory, The," 5, 31, 34, 55–57, 127

pride, 21, 167, 169, 171–72
Process Philosophy, 94
Psychology, the, 3, 5–6, 14, 20, 24, 35, 59, 61–66, 68, 70–71, 73–74, 76–81, 83, 84, 125–27, 137, 182, 184, 193, 195, 197, 207, 213, 219, 237, 241, 250, 280

reasoning, 85, 129, 133–38, 269; instrumental, 40
reconstruction, 8, 32
relations, 6, 18, 19, 66, 68, 72, 79, 81, 82, 90, 105–7, 118, 122–23, 128–29, 132–33, 137, 140, 142, 148, 150, 155, 158, 168, 173, 209, 224, 226, 228, 230, 235, 241, 254; moral, 220; spatial, 115–16; temporal, 120; universal, 128, 135–36, 139
religion, 31, 42, 69, 221, 241–42, 272
retention, 6, 81, 85, 98, 100, 109–11, 148, 251, 252
rhythm, 121
Royce, Josiah, 15, 77–78, 176
rupture, 2–4, 9–10, 13–17, 19, 22, 23, 35, 72–76, 78, 81, 84, 85, 87, 90, 112, 147–50, 155, 158, 176, 188, 210–11, 232–35, 239, 246–49, 251–58, 260–61, 266, 269–73, 278, 280–81; logic of, 17, 234, 236, 246, 253, 258, 268–69, 271, 278

Schoenberg, Arnold, 40
Schopenhauer, Arthur, 2, 9, 13, 15, 26, 38, 49, 51–52, 54, 60, 191
science, 5, 13, 31–35, 56–60, 63–69, 140–143, 188, 226, 272; applied, 59; experimental, 70–71; and feeling, 27; and Hegel, 57–58; physical, 26, 32, 92; and poetry, 42–46
self-consciousness, 67, 60–70, 77, 158, 243, 244
self-knowledge, 85, 108–9, 111, 142
self-realization, 108, 145, 147, 150, 157–58, 166, 168, 172–73, 176, 182, 184, 232
space, 50, 90–91, 97, 114–16, 118–20, 126, 139; interior, 191; of resistance, 264, 268
spirit, xiii, 29–30, 33, 39, 43, 53, 55–56, 58, 77, 126, 161, 166, 224, 260; abso-

lute, 13; French, 25; human, 33, 54; philosophic, 71; scientific, 57, 59
Stranger, The, 159, 198
suicide, 151, 163, 194
sympathy, 43, 146, 169–171, 173, 194, 200, 204, 217–221, 226, 254, 269

thought, 10, 18, 42, 44, 47, 54–59, 67, 77, 123, 128, 136, 193, 249, 259, 274
time, 15, 19, 50, 68, 97, 120–22, 126, 130, 139, 181, 245, 252
truth, 20–22, 26–27, 58, 124, 142, 177, 182, 241, 262–63, 265; absolute, 76, 186, 244–45; coherence theory of, 6, 128, 132, 200, 270; correspondence theory of, 132; idealism and, 59; instrumentalist theory of, 270

unhealthy, 14, 125–26, 134, 146–47, 151, 158–59, 193, 195, 198, 231
universal, meaning, 81, 128, 135, 142, 153, 168; progression, 145–47, 210; self, 20, 75, 79, 141, 150, 160, 162, 172–75, 177, 184, 240

Wittgenstein, Ludwig, 40

Žižek, Slavoj, 3, 10, 75, 146, 249, 258, 271–72, 278, 281

AMERICAN PHILOSOPHY

Douglas R. Anderson and Jude Jones, series editors

Kenneth Laine Ketner, ed., *Peirce and Contemporary Thought: Philosophical Inquiries.*

Max H. Fisch, ed., *Classic American Philosophers: Peirce, James, Royce, Santayana, Dewey, Whitehead, second edition.* Introduction by Nathan Houser.

John E. Smith, *Experience and God, second edition.*

Vincent G. Potter, *Peirce's Philosophical Perspectives.* Ed. by Vincent Colapietro.

Richard E. Hart and Douglas R. Anderson, eds., *Philosophy in Experience: American Philosophy in Transition.*

Vincent G. Potter, *Charles S. Peirce: On Norms and Ideals, second edition.* Introduction by Stanley M. Harrison.

Vincent M. Colapietro, ed., *Reason, Experience, and God: John E. Smith in Dialogue.* Introduction by Merold Westphal.

Robert J. O'Connell, S.J., *William James on the Courage to Believe, second edition.*

Elizabeth M. Kraus, *The Metaphysics of Experience: A Companion to Whitehead's "Process and Reality," second edition.* Introduction by Robert C. Neville.

Kenneth Westphal, ed., *Pragmatism, Reason, and Norms: A Realistic Assessment—Essays in Critical Appreciation of Frederick L. Will.*

Beth J. Singer, *Pragmatism, Rights, and Democracy.*

Eugene Fontinell, *Self, God, and Immorality: A Jamesian Investigation.*

Roger Ward, *Conversion in American Philosophy: Exploring the Practice of Transformation.*

Michael Epperson, *Quantum Mechanics and the Philosophy of Alfred North Whitehead.*

Kory Sorrell, *Representative Practices: Peirce, Pragmatism, and Feminist Epistemology.*

Naoko Saito, *The Gleam of Light: Moral Perfectionism and Education in Dewey and Emerson.*

Josiah Royce, *The Basic Writings of Josiah Royce.*

Douglas R. Anderson, *Philosophy Americana: Making Philosophy at Home in American Culture.*

James Campbell and Richard E. Hart, eds., *Experience as Philosophy: On the World of John J. McDermott.*

John J. McDermott, *The Drama of Possibility: Experience as Philosophy of Culture.* Edited by Douglas R. Anderson.

Larry A. Hickman, *Pragmatism as Post-Postmodernism: Lessons from John Dewey.*

Larry A. Hickman, Stefan Neubert, and Kersten Reich, eds., *John Dewey Between Pragmatism and Constructivism.*

Dwayne A. Tunstall, *Yes, But Not Quite: Encountering Josiah Royce's Ethico-Religious Insight.*

Josiah Royce, *Race Questions, Provincialism, and Other American Problems, Expanded Edition.* Edited by Scott L. Pratt and Shannon Sullivan.

Lara Trout, *The Politics of Survival: Peirce, Affectivity, and Social Criticism.*

John R. Shook and James A. Good, *John Dewey's Philosophy of Spirit, with the 1897 Lecture on Hegel.*

Gregory Fernando Pappas, ed., *Pragmatism in the Americas.*